THE AGE OF CHANCE

'This is a wonderful volume – smartly written, engaging and
filled with insights.'
Steven Seidman, *State University of New York*

From the Apophoreta of Imperial Rome to the ersatz grandeur of Las Vegas,
from ritual divination to weekly lottery fever, individuals have pitted
themselves against the chaotic forces of Fate. The Age of Reason promised
to bring such forces within our control, but as we look around us, it appears
that life has never been more uncertain: risk, speculation and flux are our
constant companions. We have entered the Age of Chance.

Characteristic of this age is the increasing popularity of gambling
throughout western society. Gerda Reith examines its enduring appeal,
exploring its complex relation to our underlying conceptions of the world,
and to the social and cultural backgrounds of those who fall under its spell.
Using a wide range of sources, she traces the origins of gambling in the
ancient world and follows its manifestation in games as diverse as the *patolli*
of the Aztecs and the Internet gambling of today. From an analysis of social
structure, she goes on to consider the subjective experiences and attitudes
of individual players, discovering some remarkable continuities: the same
deliberate seeking out of risk, a disregard for money and a variety of superstitious beliefs in luck and Destiny seem to typify gamblers throughout
history and across cultures.

This fascinating and extensive study, enlivened by interviews with
British and American gamblers, will be enthralling reading not just for
those interested in the cultural and social implications of gambling –
researchers in sociology, cultural studies and the history of ideas – but for
anyone interested in how we create meaning in an increasingly insecure
world.

Gerda Reith is Lecturer in Sociology at the University of Glasgow.

ROUTLEDGE STUDIES IN SOCIAL AND POLITICAL THOUGHT

THE AGE OF CHANCE

Gambling in western culture

Gerda Reith

London and New York

First published 1999
by Routledge
11 New Fetter Lane, London EC4P 4EE

Simultaneously published in the USA and Canada
by Routledge
29 West 35th Street, New York, NY 10001

First published in paperback 2002

Routledge is an imprint of the Taylor & Francis Group

© 1999, 2002 Gerda Reith

Typeset in Garamond by Keystroke, Jacaranda Lodge, Wolverhampton
Printed and bound in Great Britain by Biddles Ltd, Guildford and King's Lynn

British Library Cataloguing in Publication Data
A catalogue record for this book is available from the British Library

Library of Congress Cataloging in Publication Data
Reith, Gerda, 1969–
The age of chance : gambling in western culture / Gerda Reith.
p.   cm.
Includes bibliographical references and index.
1. Gambling–History. 2. Gambling–Social aspects. 3. Gambling.
I. Title.
HV6710.R45   1999
363.4'2–dc21   99-24303
CIP

ISBN 0–415–17997–1 (hbk)
ISBN 0–415–26309–3 (pbk)

FOR MY PARENTS,
MARGARET AND BILL REITH

Plate 1 The Dice Players, Georges de la Tour (1593–1652)
Source: Preston Hall Museum, Cleveland, UK/Bridgeman Art Library

Those iron hands of necessity which shake the dice-box of chance play their game for an infinite length of time: so that there *have* to be throws which exactly resemble purposiveness and rationality of every degree. *Perhaps* our acts of will and our purposes are nothing but just such throws.

Friedrich Nietzsche: *Daybreak*, Book II: 130

CONTENTS

CONTENTS

CONTENTS

ILLUSTRATIONS

PREFACE

Gambling, chance and the suspension of reality

Gambling has long played a significant part in the everyday life of people in western, and many other, societies. There is nothing unusual in wagering on any kind of uncertain outcome. Indeed, wherever and whenever outcomes are uncertain – that is everywhere and at all times – people place bets upon the future. The ubiquity of gambling, however, has roused little curiosity; its very familiarity, reinforced one suspects by an unacknowledged suspicion that it harbours something incomprehensible, seems to have resulted in a certain blindness to its intrinsic interest.

The great virtue of Gerda Reith's remarkable book is to redraw fundamental categories of experience so as to make gambling at once a central and obvious preoccupation of daily life without assimilating its difficulty and oddness to the imperious claims of modern rationalising tendencies. To put the matter simply: we cannot understand gambling on the basis of a 'rational expectation' on the part of the gambler. Gamblers lose; they lose repeatedly, so that any view of gambling which focuses directly on its outcomes confronts an essential contradiction. Either gamblers wager in the expectation of winning and this possible gain is the motive for playing, or they play *in order to lose*. They are either deluded or irrational. The first view has become conventional but, as an account of gambling behaviour, amounts to little more than an assertion that most people most of the time are both gullible and incapable of learning from their own (disappointing) experience. In this view the gambler is deceived by the prospect of an effortless win. And, as in the Enlightenment attack on religion, it is held that this deception is perpetrated on the naive masses by a sophisticated and powerful priestly class (casino owners, pools companies, lottery organisers and so on). Here two implausible and contradictory assumptions are combined; the gambler (i.e. almost everyone) is held to be both economically rational and culturally naive. The second view is favoured by Freud and a variety of his unorthodox followers. Here it is argued that gamblers (unconsciously) wish to punish themselves, thus relieving themselves of the guilt (inexplicable but ubiquitous) experienced as a general aspect of modern life. This approach, even if one accepts the general background of Freud's hermeneutics of human behaviour, offers little insight into the specific character of gambling as an activity.

Reith dismisses both the rationalist and irrationalist approaches as misleading and ahistorical. By the simple but compelling device of presenting a wealth of fascinating illustrative material drawn from pre-modern societies where the concept of 'economic rationality' has little or no meaning and, equally, where a variety of conscious and unconscious motives for all types of action must be painstakingly reconstructed, she exposes the arbitrary and hypothetical character of both perspectives. Reith also dismisses much current academic interest in gambling as a 'social problem', justifiably viewing this discourse as continuous with the long tradition of moralising opposition which almost all forms of gambling has aroused in western societies.

Nor does a sociological understanding of gambling have much in common with recent interest in 'the risk society'; which is best viewed as the recovery and extension of the theory of probability to situations of everyday life. In the mid-eighteenth century Thomas Bayes had already developed a fundamental approach to probability theory through a consideration of a variety of risks. By the time Pierre Simon Laplace came to summarise his own definitive treatment of the 'calculus of chances' in his classic work *A Philosophical Essay on Probabilities*, published in 1820, as a non-technical Preface to his more rigorous *Analytical Theory of Probabilities*, he took it as axiomatic that it arose and was applied in the context of 'the most important questions of life', which included the judgement of the testimony of witnesses in court proceedings, the composition of deliberative assemblies and the analysis of demographic trends which had been pioneered by John Graunt and William Petty (as well as a fascinating analysis of the probability of any letter being delivered to the wrong address in Paris).

Probability theory, though it emerged and developed simultaneously with new institutional responses (particularly insurance practices) to problems of uncertainty in everyday life, found its first and still paradigmatic elaboration in relation to games of chance. Cardano, Pascal, Fermat, de Moivre, Jakob and Daniel Bernouilli and Laplace established the new mathematical analysis of probability primarily through careful reflection on gambling. It was to its special world that they turned both to define fundamental problems and to illustrate their analytic results. The special status of gambling for the mathematical theory of probability is instructive. From the beginning of this development mathematicians recognised in games of chance a form of human activity *regulated* by chance and not simply (as all human activity) subject to uncertainty. The world of the gambler, therefore, was a world apart; a world that could not be grasped by analogy with either the reasons or passions which seemed adequate to an understanding of other common human pursuits in modern society. The peculiarity of gambling was grasped first, of course, by gamblers themselves who seem to have sensed the heightening of this difference with the emergence of modernity (universalism, scientific rationality, the rule of the market, the demands of the state).

Cardano, and later Pascal, were specifically asked by gamblers to solve the practical problem of how to divide the stakes in an interrupted game. One cannot help wondering what occasioned this repeated *aleator interruptus*. The general practice was to fix in advance the number of games to be played, at which point a winner could be declared. From the Renaissance onwards it seems, interruptions become sufficiently commonplace and aggravating as to prompt the search for a practical solution. As the young aristocrat is called away (one supposes 'on business'), the exemplary form of modern rationality which is developing in the 'outside world' is invited to the tables to sort out the consequences of its own imperious demands.

The tradition of mathematical rationalisation, of course, became vital to both scientific endeavour and the administration of the modern state, and Reith is able to draw on an impressive literature which has reconstructed its intellectual and social context. In this development probability theory, which began as a pure 'geometry of chance' (Pascal), became increasingly remote from the direct experience of the wager. It emerged, indeed, as the antithesis to the gambler's 'plunge' into the unknown.

The modern theory of games, that is to say, keeps the subversive experience of chance at a safe distance and conceals it behind the visible formalities of calculation. Particularly in its application in the physical sciences, probability theory was treated as a useful calculating device and method of approximation when dealing with natural processes of a level of complexity which rendered impractical reasoning and computation from first principles. Laplace authoritatively expresses the conviction that probability theory does nothing to undermine the scientists' foundational trust in the law of sufficient reason and the mechanical principles of efficient causality:

> All events, even those which on account of their insignificance do not seem to follow the great laws of nature, are a result of it just as necessarily as the revolutions of the sun. In ignorance of the ties which unite such events to the entire system of the universe, they have been made to depend upon final causes or upon hazard, according as they occur and are repeated with regularity, or appear without regard to order; but these imaginary causes have gradually receded with the widening bounds of knowledge and disappear entirely before sound philosophy, which sees in them only the expression of our ignorance of the true causes.
>
> (Laplace 1951, p. 1)

But the development of probability theory, particularly in the kinetic theory of gases, infected Nature with the virus of chance. While Laplace could remain confident that its application to natural philosophy was a kind of interim measure, for scientists during the second half of the nineteenth century (led by Clausius and Boltzmann) it became increasingly clear that at an elementary level the analogy of Nature with a game of chance was more precise than anyone had imagined; more precise than anyone had feared. The physicist of the twentieth century confronted a world of chance and, like any Renaissance gambler, was plunged into a strange and disturbing reality.

At the same time that probability theory struggled to conceal the shocking world of randomness, the social organisation of gambling developed its own rational forms. Reith charts the development from aristocratic gaming tables to Las Vegas casinos and the virtual gambling sites of the Internet with a wealth of insight and a rich variety of illustration. That Reith is able to illuminate this entire development and make so many suggestive comments indicates the poorly developed state of the most conventional forms of sociological research in this area. Nor is she content with supplementing this paucity of explanatory or interpretive material with a few well-chosen historical examples but, with admirable ambition, proposes a more comprehensive and meaningful model of its development. Gambling, which, of course, has ancient roots and a continuous tradition or traditions in pre-modern society, emerges in her analysis as a social form, so to speak, pre-adapted to the particular character of modernity. Gambling can be grasped sociologically as a form of exchange; indeed, as its purest form. It is simply the exchange of money itself; exchange liberated from the viscous medium of objects. In this process money gains the dignity of Being.

Contemporary gambling is thus emblematic of the most advanced tendencies of modernity. The dematerialisation of reality; the dissolution of all its forms into transitoriness and transitions, characterises every aspect of postmodern (un)reality. And with this dissolution has come a renewed intimacy with the world of chance. It is worth noting that precisely the same dissolution of the object occurred in the physical sciences. Probabilism could not in the end conceal the world of chance in which the objectivity and 'thing-like' facticity of matter was dissolved; 'force' dispersed throughout 'fields' replaced objects in motion as the underlying image of Nature. The pure and empty space of the Newtonian world (the container of objects) merged with bodies and itself became the carrier of the 'primary qualities' of reality. Science, as a result, abandons both efficient cause and sufficient reason and contents itself (as in Clausius' conception of entropy) with successive approximations to the most probable distribution of particles and energy states as the most compelling *explanation* of natural processes.

Chance infiltrates and suffuses modern life; not only as gambling and games of chance but, far more generally, as an 'orientation' to reality or, rather, as the fundamental category of reality to which we must orientate ourselves. Gambling becomes more widespread and loses its aura of dangerous unconventionality not because it has become assimilated to the rational practices of everyday life but, rather, because social life has become increasingly and openly randomised. This is not to claim that modern society is in a terminal state of disorder. There is nothing chaotic in chance; it is simply that the disconnectedness of events, the lack of relational qualities, is the ultimate guarantor (and more reliable foundation) of the order which appears 'magically' superimposed upon it. A reversal of perspective is involved here. Rather than see chance as a superficial curiosity – an arbitrary super-imposition on an 'underlying' coherence – coherence is a 'rationalisation' unrelated to (and therefore never in contradiction to) an underlying randomness.

The equivocal history of probability theory, and the sociohistorical development of gaming, though advancing well beyond the more popular reductive accounts of gambling, do not of themselves pose the most vital questions. Reith confronts a different, neglected and equally difficult problem in a remarkable way. What is the experience of chance? How is it constituted and represented? How is 'deep irrationality' acknowledged and made part of modern life? In this perspective gambling emerges as an institutionalised occasion of 'plunging' into the radically other world of chance. And, in this perspective, the anxious moment of wagering is altogether more essential than the outcome of the play. Winning or losing, indeed, is just one more unwanted interruption – the periodic normalising return to the world of rational self-control and 'waking' life – to the charmed experience of chance.

Reith's fundamental insight is that gambling is a mechanism for entering into and prolonging contact with the world of chance. But the social, ideological and mathematical discourses of gambling create a boundary which the gambler must cross and at which the everyday punter stops. Like the rich accretions of theological speculation, worship and institutional practice, gambling presents both a 'way' and an obstacle to union with the divine Goddess of Chance. The visible social fabric of gambling, that is to say, is not itself chance and, to a large extent, protects the world of chance from rationalisation as well as the world of predictable reason from the subversive randomness of chance.

Reith places herself within (rather than confronts) the gamblers' world in a decisive way and, necessarily in tentative formulations, seeks to describe the experience of chance. This is the most original and daring of her several bold departures from the conventional safety of orthodox research. Chance does not have a language of its own: how could it; the task appears doomed at the outset. Yet, by a process of analogy from phenomenological studies of the sacred, the extensive and insightful use of literary material and, above all, by the steadfast refusal to accept rationalising misdescriptions, she succeeds more completely than could be expected in revealing the true extent and inner richness of the world of chance.

Most people occasionally buy lottery tickets, place a bet on the Grand National and Derby, or join in the office sweep without even considering that they are gambling. And they would reject entirely the notion that they were, even momentarily, flirting with an alien experience that is potentially subversive of every settled notion and practical routine of life. Yet how often do they *also* circumscribe this behaviour with some magical ritual; always buy the lottery ticket from the same shop on the same day of the week, choose the same 'lucky' numbers and so on? Even a fleeting encounter with chance opens before us an abyss, not of moral ruin, addiction and irresponsible squandering of hard earned money, but of the real uncertainties of life and of our own existence. From the perspective of the normal, settled and rational world chance is fascinating and dreadful; in equal measure it attracts and repels, frightens and excites. But once across the boundary chance is endlessly and effortlessly absorbing; it is all there is.

The gambler awakens to a new reality and a new sense of selfhood: 'just as the play world is animated by a different set of rules from those which govern everyday life, so players within it are animated by a different set of motivations from those of their everyday routines in which they are free to experiment with new roles and temporarily adopt a new identity'. In a 'rhapsody of perception' (Cassirer 1953, p. 21), the normal perception of time and space is transformed:

> Time freezes, and gamblers become absorbed in a total orientation
> to the immediate Here and Now. In this state they become creatures
> of sensation; seeing, but not really aware of their surroundings;
> perceiving, but not truly cognisant of what is going on.
>
> (Reith, this volume, p. 132)

Repetition is the essence of play; it aims at nothing beyond itself. In the world of chance, time is a permanent transition, 'a *constant repetition of a fleeting present*' paradoxical from a rational position, uniting and dissolving the antinomies of waking thought.

Reith investigates the inner world of chance both through the reported experience of gamblers (happily many great writers were inveterate gamblers), and also in terms of a revival of ideas about the magical worldview. Concepts of 'participatory consciousness' and 'pre-logical mentality' arose primarily as descriptions of 'primitives', children and specific forms of mental illness; that is, as descriptive of an infantile and failed worldview. However, rather than view this in a now rightly rejected evolutionary or developmental perspective she demonstrates that it is, in fact, the appropriate way of orientating the subject within a world of pure chance; a world over which one has no control and in relation to which one is entirely dependent. But we all follow such rituals, and believe (however fleetingly) in the omnipotence of thought, of 'luck' and so on, not as a residual trace of a once dominating worldview, but as an acknowledgement of the continuing and ineradicable presence of the world of chance.

The paradox of the Age of Chance is that we think, at the very moment that contemporary society has become its creature, that Chance has finally succumbed to the forces of rationalisation; Gerda Reith tells us to think again.

Harvie Ferguson

ACKNOWLEDGEMENTS

The Age of Chance began many years ago, as a Ph.D. thesis, and I am grateful to many people who made the birth of the original idea as well as its development into book form possible.

I would like to thank the University of Glasgow for a generous award from the Robert and Agnes Fleck Scholarship which enabled me to attend a conference and conduct fieldwork in Las Vegas in June 1994, and also Robert Miles for supporting the proposal.

I also appreciated the assistance of the staff at the University Inter-Library Loans Department in tracking down lists of obscure items, as well as the interest of Ian Brown, Sue Fisher, Bridget Fowler, Faith Freestone, David Frisby, Mark Griffiths, David Harris, John Scanlan and James F. Smith for passing on many useful references. Thanks also to Geoff Woollen for 'the lost Balzac', to Richard Stalley for Aristotle and to Jan McMillen for commenting on an earlier version of the manuscript. Evelyn Crombie's deciphering of my barely legible scrawl and painstaking typing of the entire manuscript enabled me to finish the thesis – and so also the book – much sooner than otherwise would have been possible.

I am also grateful to all the gamblers who took the time to discuss their passion with me, and to my friends and family who listened when I in turn passed on my enthusiasm to them!

Finally, and most of all, my greatest debt is to Harvie Ferguson, whose intellectual stimulation, untiring enthusiasm and generous support made the process of research a pleasure.

INTRODUCTION

We are all gamblers. And, as long as chance and uncertainty persist as features of human existence, we will continue to be so. In the modern world however, as never before, chance has become an irreducible aspect of daily life: risk, speculation, indeterminism and flux are our constant companions in social, economic and personal affairs: we have entered the Age of Chance.

This of course is the broadest definition of gambling in which the activity is regarded as symbolic of mankind's struggle with uncertainty; a situation that we cannot – and might not even want to – escape or avoid, and in which the figure of the gambler can be seen as emblematic of the society in which s/he lives (and plays). There is a narrower, more precise definition however and it is ostensibly this with which this book is concerned. Briefly, in this more limited sense gambling can be defined as a ritual which is strictly demarcated from the everyday world around it and within which chance is deliberately courted as a mechanism which governs a redistribution of wealth among players as well as a commercial interest or 'house'.

Examination of this narrower definition however can shed light on the wider significance of gambling, for the latter can be seen as a microcosm in which more general issues about the role of uncertainty and chance in human life are played out in concentrated form. It has long been recognised that analysis of what may appear trivial or mundane can generate insights into fundamental aspects of social life. Drawing attention to the expression of the totality within the fragment, Sartre wrote that humans exist as totalities, not collections, and therefore reveal themselves in their most apparently insignificant and superficial behaviour. Citing Pascal, he explained how there exist certain activities such as sports 'which, while absurd if reduced to themselves, nevertheless contain meanings which transcend them' (Sartre 1957, p. 60). Gambling is one such activity.

One of the most striking features to emerge from a cursory glance at the phenomenon is its almost universal prevalence throughout history and across cultures: it unites peoples as diverse as the ancient Greeks and the North American Indians with the inhabitants of modern western societies. Despite its apparent insignificance as 'mere' games then, it can be said to constitute a

1

fundamental feature, in some form or another, of human life. The ubiquity of gambling does not imply a corresponding homogeneity of *form*, however, for significant variation exists between specific games played, the social groups who play them and the experiences they derive from their activities. These variables exist in a determined relation to social structures, social roles and cultural conditions.

It can be seen then that gambling is a complex phenomenon, although one which has often been oversimplified in the rhetorical response of much of the contemporary literature. In the late twentieth and early twenty-first centuries, a proliferation of academic monographs and specialised journals have given birth to the discipline of 'gambling studies'. The activity has suddenly become of interdisciplinary interest, researched in fields as diverse as psychology and history, sociology and mathematics, law and economics. This diversity of approach has at the same time fragmented the phenomenon: gambling is reflected from so many different perspectives that any broader image is lost in myriad narrow specialisms. It occupies a portion of many larger fields without establishing a paradigm of its own.

In order to pick through the many approaches that constitute the contemporary literature, it is useful to look first at their historical predecessors, and so outline their intellectual heritage. Out of this morass, two separate traditions gradually emerge, from which our modern perspectives can be traced. One 'tradition of licence' generally condones all forms of play as manifestations of the sublime element of human nature, while the other regards play in general and gambling in particular as inimical to a healthy society. Within a changing terminology of criticism, the latter has persistently regarded gambling as fundamentally problematic and condemned it as variously sinful, wasteful, criminal and pathological.

In the first and, from our perspective, least influential tradition originally propounded by Plato, all forms of play are viewed as noble, life-enhancing activities. Systematised in the *Laws* as part of his general theory of education, Plato regarded the natural instinct of children to 'leap and bound – and dance and frolic . . . with glee' (Plato 1934, p. 30) as a divine attribute which should be cultivated in adult forms of play. Play is fundamental, for man 'has been constructed as a toy for God, and this is the finest thing about him' (Plato 1934, p. 187). For Plato, the faculty of play is the highest attribute of humanity, and we have a duty to live by its precepts; to spend our lives 'making our *play* as perfect as possible'. This is the key to a happy, peaceful and above all, divine existence for, in Plato, the notion of play also has a *sacred* character (Plato 1934, p. 188).

The equation of play with the noblest virtues of humanity found renewed expression in German Romantic writers when, in the late eighteenth century, Schiller lamented the effects of commerce and rationalisation on creativity, and on the 'wholeness' of the human personality. However, at the same time he recognised the need for restrictions and rules: Rousseau's noble savage, free from all conventional constraint, was not for him. In modern life, *Spieltrieb* – the play impulse – satisfied these demands. As detached enjoyment free from purpose it represented the Kantian ideal, and it also embodied the individual's need for restraint without denying them freedom, thus realising the essential 'harmony' of mankind. In his *Fourteenth Letter*, Schiller described this *Spieltrieb*: 'as it abolishes all accident, it will also abolish compulsion, and place man, both morally and physically in freedom' (Schiller 1845, p. 105). Play is here the highest manifestation of humanity: in it the true nature of the individual can be realised and expressed. Schiller continues: 'in every condition of man it is play and only play that makes him complete, and unfolds at once his twofold nature' (Schiller 1845, p. 110). Ultimately man *'is only entirely a man when he plays'* (Schiller 1845, p. 111).

In the twentieth century, the continuing relevance of this perspective was stressed by Johan Huizinga with his ground-breaking *Homo Ludens* (1949), by Roger Caillois with *Man, Play and Games* (1962), and, to a lesser extent, in the sociology of Erving Goffman (1969).

For Huizinga, play is the basis of culture: civilisation does not come *from* play, rather 'it arises *in* and *as* play, and never leaves it' (Huizinga 1949, p. 173), for all forms of human expression – law, art, science, commerce, language and even war – are rooted in the 'primeval soil of play' (Huizinga 1949, p. 5). Huizinga's definition of play has been used as a working model, or at the very least, dutifully acknowledged as standard, by generations of subsequent writers, and in it we can clearly see the influence of the Platonic notion of sacred play, as well as the Romantic regard for its life-affirming tendencies outwith the sphere of material utility. However, despite his argument for the centrality of play in human culture, Huizinga is surprisingly dismissive of games of chance themselves, devoting less than two pages to their discussion and refusing to consider the applicability of his criteria of play to the specific instance of gambling. In two sentences, he dismisses them from his study: 'In themselves, gambling games are very curious subjects for cultural research, but for the development of culture as such we must call them unproductive. They are sterile, adding nothing to life or the mind' (Huizinga 1949, p. 48).

It is this omission that Caillois attempts to rectify. In a study that is perhaps as indebted to Schiller's comments on play as it is to Huizinga, Caillois includes gambling in a four-fold classification of games in general. This taxonomy rests on a formal definition of play as that which is materially unproductive, free and voluntary, uncertain, isolated in space and time, and bound by fixed rules (Caillois 1962, pp. 6–10). The four fundamental characteristics of play described by Caillois are *agon* (competition), *alea* (chance), *simulation* (mimicry), and *vertigo* (ilinx). Games of *ilinx* are based on the creation of physical vertigo or disorientation, while *mimicry* involves the players' escaping from themselves and becoming 'illusory characters'. *Agon* involves competitive games which presuppose training, skill and discipline

3

while in games of *alea*, work, skill and experience are negated and 'winning is the result of fate rather than triumphing over an adversary' (Caillois 1962, pp. 17–23). In conjunction with money, Caillois points out, these games include gambling games, and in fact, as we shall see later, traces of *all* of these characteristics can be found in gambling. Caillois posits a broad reciprocity between games and culture, writing that the favourite games of a society reflect, on the one hand, social traditions and attitudes, and at the same time, by 'educating and training the players in these very virtues or eccentricities . . . subtly confirm them in their habits or preferences' (Caillois 1962, p. 82).

Caillois argues that the evolution of these forms begins with the historical transition from 'Dionysian' societies based on the principles of *simulation* and *vertigo* to modern rational ones governed by *agon* and *alea*. The displacement of what he calls the world of the mask and ecstasy by the virtues of merit and democracy is testimony to the 'progress' of civilisation; a progress encapsulated in the games a culture plays. The games of the modern world are thus those governed by the principles of rational democracy – *agon* and *alea*. The social forms of Dionysian society do not disappear in modern times however, but continue to exist in the sphere of play. In rational society, the 'chaotic original' forces of *vertigo* and *simulation* are relegated to the realm of play where they function rather as do sports for Norbert Elias: as cathartic vehicles for the expression of sublimated desires and tensions.

The broad scope of Caillois' argument situates play at the centre of human culture, and, despite its obvious evolutionism, provides a formal definition of the principles and the importance of games of chance in modern society. It suffers however, as Downes *et al.* (1976) point out, from a failure to convey the *meanings* as distinct from the formal essences of different types of game. They state quite simply that: 'He analyses games in terms of their formal properties with great assurance, but we are left wondering why people really play them' (Downes *et al.* 1976, p. 14). For this, some investigation of the experience of gamblers themselves is required, and for illumination the authors turn to Goffman, whose long essay on risk taking – *Where the Action Is* – is an attempt to outline the experiential aspects of games of chance. Goffman sits (somewhat uneasily) within the tradition that recognises the centrality of play in human life: his unacknowledged debt to writers like Huizinga and Caillois is apparent in his description of the creation and realisation of character in risky – and especially gambling – situations. The 'action' of the title refers to 'activities that are consequential, problematic and undertaken for what is felt to be their own sake' (Goffman 1969, p. 136). In modern society, such activities are 'sharply curtailed' (rather like Caillois' *simulation* and *vertigo*), so that opportunities to display bravery, heroism and character have to be deliberately sought out in separate spheres, such as in games of chance. The 'maintenance of the self' in such situations displays evidence of character: courage, gameness, integrity, gallantry and composure emerge in stressful or risky occasions, and the individual becomes more fully human for them. As

Goffman puts it, 'These naked little spasms of the self occur at the end of the world, but there at the end is action and character' (Goffman 1969, p. 206).

In the second – and dominant – of the two traditions outlined above, gambling is perceived as essentially problematic; its deliberate courting of the chaotic forces of chance a threat to the moral order of society. Although the terms of the invective directed against it have changed, the persistence of the condemnation has continued more or less throughout history. While Plato was writing of man as 'God's plaything', Aristotle could see nothing but 'sordid greed' and 'meanness' in the pursuit of games, and particularly games of chance, comparing those who played them to pimps, despots and thieves (Aristotle, *Nichomachean Ethics* par.1122a, ll.1–7). Throughout the Middle Ages, prohibition of gambling on account of its unproductive nature and disorderly effects on the population was widespread, although games of chance were not specifically regarded as sinful. The Catholic Church never expressly forbade gambling *per se* and, despite its regulation of the activity, always allowed it at Christmas. The statutes of the Middle Ages were rather directed against a pastime that diverted efforts from activities more important to warfare – such as archery – and that dissipated the energies of labourers and the wealth of the aristocracy. It was not until the Reformation that a strong moral stance against gambling was adopted by the Church, and not until the emergence of the bourgeoisie that a group with a real antipathy towards the activity really appeared. Together, these groups fronted a massive assault on games of chance, the residue of which is still visible today. A stream of invective poured from the pulpits of the Reformed Church, damning gamblers as sinners for their idleness, greed, blasphemy and superstition. Games of chance forced God's intervention to 'decide the lot' on trivial matters, flouting the values of the Protestant by divorcing the creation of wealth from the efforts of labour, and reducing it instead to the vicissitudes of chance.

In the Enlightenment climate of moderation and reason, the idea of the sinful nature of play was replaced by an emphasis on its embodiment of irrationality. At the end of the seventeenth century and throughout the eighteenth, the mania associated with games of chance appeared as the epitome of irrationality, and, if the mark of humanity was reason, what was left of individuals once they voluntarily forfeit their rationality? In this formulation, gamblers were not exactly sinners, but nor were they altogether human either.

By the nineteenth century the essential irrationality of gamblers had become irrelevant so long as they possessed that other attribute of humanity – the ability to work. The industrialising west needed labour power; time became a commodity only slightly less precious than money, and gambling squandered them both. The problems of the organisation of labour were encapsulated in the figure of the (working-class) gambler – an individual who refused to acknowledge the importance of time, money or disciplined labour.

The imperative of the Protestant ethic now became institutionalised in laws forbidding games of chance along with other 'vices' such as alcoholism and prostitution: the gambler became a criminal.

Far from fading into obscurity as their era passed, such criticisms continue to be reflected in contemporary approaches to gambling. Despite its own unique response to what it perceives as 'the problem', a complex of historical continuities can be traced in what may be called the 'therapeutic' tradition of contemporary gambling literature. Conservative observers no longer seek to punish and outlaw what they regard as immoral, unreasonable or criminal behaviour. Instead, their more liberal descendants attempt to understand what is regarded as a manifestation of illness which, crucially, can be *cured*. Typical of the twentieth-century trend towards the medicalisation of deviance, the moralistic tone of previous centuries has been replaced by a clinical one: gambling is still problematic, but in a medical rather than an ethical sense. In the literature that is reviewed next, gambling is treated broadly as a pathology or defect; in psychology, as a sickness in the individual; in sociology, in the social order itself.

For the first half of the twentieth century, the framework for discussion was set by Freud's short essay on 'Dostoevsky and parricide' (1928), in which the gambler as a compulsive neurotic was born. Freud traced the descent of the gambling addiction from the 'primal addiction' to masturbation; the (rather tenuous) connection being the movement of the hands: 'the "vice" of masturbation is replaced by the mania for gambling; and the emphasis laid upon the passionate activity of the hands betrays this derivation' (Freud 1928, p. 241). Further, the guilt that was experienced afterwards was related to the Oedipus complex of the players' youth: the desire to kill the father and possess the mother. At this point, Freud referred specifically to Dostoevsky's ambivalent relations with his father and his subsequent 'mania' for gambling. The guilt the former felt for his hatred of his father was assuaged in gambling, where in exposing himself to fate he symbolically confronted his father, so that gambling became 'a symbolic means of self-punishment' (Freud 1928, p. 238).

This analysis initiated the description of gamblers in the psychoanalytic tradition as masochists, who, because of various unresolved conflicts in their past, were compelled to repeat an endless cycle of punishment. Bergler developed the theme of psychic masochism, describing the gambler as 'a neurotic with an unconscious wish to lose' (Bergler 1970, p. vii). Traces of the Puritan abhorrence of gambling are manifest in Bergler's research: his book is an exercise in moral contempt, an outburst of disapproval thinly disguised by medical imperatives. Gambling, he tells us, is a 'dangerous neurosis', and the gambler an 'objectively sick' individual, who, having failed to renounce the efficacy of the pleasure principle, lives in a 'fiction of omnipotence' (Bergler 1970, p. 16). Gambling activates the megalomania and grandiosity of childhood: thus gamblers are convinced they will win. However, their aggression towards the reality principle is paid for by feelings of guilt and from this is derived the need for self-punishment. Losing is such a punishment, and so, to maintain their psychic equilibrium, gamblers must play to win, but always lose. Continued by writers such as Greenson and Lindner, the psychoanalytic tradition persistently portrayed the gambler as an unbalanced, disturbed individual: 'an obsessional neurotic' plagued by 'an illness of the mind' (Lindner 1974, p. 237) and victim to 'the severely regressive character of the disease' of gambling (Greenson 1974, p. 214).

By the late 1970s cracks began to appear in the hegemony of the psychoanalytic approach and new perspectives became prominent. Despite changes in terminology, however, gamblers were still portrayed as sick individuals, with research becoming increasingly oriented towards 'therapeutic' models which abounded in programmes and policies that might 'cure' them. In 1980, compulsive gambling was formally accepted as a mental disorder by the American Psychiatric Association, and as a result was included in the third edition of the *Diagnostic and Statistical Manual of Mental Disorders* (DSM III) under the new title 'pathological gambling'. The move from 'compulsive' to 'pathological' shifted attention from the *activities* that the individual became compulsive about, to the physiological presence of a disease (Walker 1992, p. 172). In this climate, a range of theoretical perspectives flourished. Not all agreed with the label 'pathological', but the overwhelming majority considered the gambler as aberrant in some way, and sought to explain why anyone would voluntarily gamble to 'excess'; that notion of something to one side of a balanced ideal bequeathed to us from the Enlightenment. Of these, the sociocognitive model attempted to explain the perseverance of gambling behaviour in terms of the 'irrational cognitions' of the gambler. Such irrational cognitions include the 'illusion of control' (Langer 1975; Gadboury and Ladouceur 1988; Griffiths 1990, 1994, 1995), the 'belief in luck' (Li and Smith 1974; Oldman 1974; Wagenaar 1988), the 'biased evaluation of outcomes' (Gilovich 1983; Gilovich and Douglas 1986) and the notion of 'near misses' (Kahneman and Tversky 1982). These models present an image of the gambler as a hopelessly confused individual, bewildered in an environment of chance and prey to the vicissitudes of wildly 'irrational' impulses.

Arousal theories attempted a more 'scientific' explanation of gambling behaviour. Positing excitement as the motivation for continued play, they went on to attempt to measure it to support their claims. It has been suggested that such arousal may be automatic and/or cortical (Brown 1987), or opiod mediated (Pratt *et al.* 1982), and reversal theory's telic and paratelic states put forward to explain it (Anderson and Brown 1987). Ultimately, arousal theories are reducible to the search for a physiological dimension of addiction, and to this end, gamblers' brainwaves have been measured (and found wanting) in studies of EEG activation and hemispheric dysregulation (Carlton and Manowitzl 1987; Goldstein and Carlton 1988). The logical conclusion of this type of approach has culminated in the search for a 'gambling gene', and a sighting may already be imminent! Comings *et al.* (1994) have recently reported that variants on the DRD2 gene are found in certain addictions, including alcoholism and pathological gambling.

The medicalisation of human behaviour reaches its apogee in these types of model, with gamblers portrayed as automata, playing in a social vacuum, their activities determined purely by genetics and biological impulses.[1]

Despite – or perhaps *because* of – its unproductive nature, sociological accounts of gambling invariably attempt to endow it with some kind of utilitarian function. These accounts have never really recovered from Edward Devereaux's seminal study, *Gambling and the Social Structure* (1949), a functionalist, quasi-Durkheimian model of social dysfunction which rationalised gambling in terms of its latent social function. According to Devereaux, the tensions and conflicts in the capitalist economic system produce ambivalent feelings of anxiety and hostility, and these disrupt individual as well as social well-being (Devereaux 1949, p. 947). Certain activities that resolve or at least accommodate this disequilibrium are therefore vital in advanced society, and tend to become institutionalised. In this, they function as 'shock absorbers' or 'safety-valves' which either channel dangerous tensions into the service of the dominant system, or discharge them cathartically in a socially acceptable manner. Gambling is one such activity: 'a particularly convenient mechanism in which the psychological consequences of economic frustration, strain, conflict and ambivalence may be worked out without upsetting the social order' (Devereaux 1949, p. 955).

This theme of displacement and catharsis ran as a leitmotiv through the mainly American sociology of gambling of the 1950s, 1960s and 1970s with the addition of a 'deprivation' dimension in studies by Zola (1967), Herman (1967, 1976), Bloch (1951) and Newman (1972). Here, gambling emerged as a social safety-valve for frustrated (mainly working-class) citizens, providing a context in which the deprivations of the outside world could be compensated for by symbolic activity. For those denied access to socially legitimate modes of the pursuit of wealth, gambling provided an alternative economy, with its own set of rules and its own measures of success. It is in these terms that Newman described gambling as 'a structurally positive-functional component of the social system' (Newman 1972, p. 230). In all these studies, gambling serves as a compensation for a social deficit. In Zola, games of chance 'help deny [the] futility' of lives over which the working class have no control, and also act as a means of controlling their 'otherwise destructive frustrations' (Zola 1967, p. 31). According to Herman, horse betting 'fills a decision-making void' (Herman 1967, p. 102), while for Bloch it is 'an escape from routine and boredom' (Bloch 1951, p. 217). Functionalism and deprivation models are combined in Tec to form a kind of functional-deprivation hybrid. She writes that 'instead of turning against the original source of their deprivations and unfulfilled aspirations, bettors are relieved through gambling of some of their frustrations and hence are less likely to attack the existing class structure' (Tec 1967, p. 103).

In the idealised working-class communities where these compensatory games of chance go on, the surrounding society is generally portrayed as dysfunctional, oppressive and static. In these models, the only motivation for play can be frustration, the only reward release.

More recently, increased interest in gambling has given rise to a number of studies which could be described as more academically 'neutral' towards their subject. In Britain at least, specialised research into particular forms of gambling has flourished with, for example, Chinn (1991) and Clapson (1992) examining the historical development of horse-racing, and with Dixon (1991) and Munting (1996) sharing an interest in the historical regulation of gambling; the former in Britain, the latter in comparison with the United States. A more contemporary focus on the various social forms of horse-racing has been provided by Filby and Harvey (1988), Bruce and Johnson (1992; 1995; 1996), Saunders and Turner (1987) and Neal (1998); while Dixey (1987; 1996) and Freestone (1995) have examined the social and gendered nature of bingo. The dynamics of fruit machine playing – especially in relation to participation among the young – has been thoroughly examined by Fisher (1993; 1995; 1998) and Griffiths (1990; 1993; 1994; 1995). The most recent introduction to the British gambling scene, the National Lottery, as well as one of its oldest traditions, the casino, have yet to attract the widespread attention of academic researchers, our knowledge of these areas still being provided by specialist organisations such as OFLOT and market research companies. A more comparative, international perspective is to be found in McMillen's (1996) edited collection on *Gambling Cultures*, a valuable contribution to understanding a broad range of gambling behaviour, ranging from the globalisation of casinos to the existence of gambling in Cameroon and Senegal. Such research indicates the growing academic interest in gambling as a social phenomenon in its own right, an interest which is by now long overdue, but which nevertheless still tends to be coloured by the heritage of the two intellectual traditions discussed above.

Out of these two traditions has emerged the peculiarly ambivalent position of gambling at the start of the twenty-first century: on the one hand, condoned and encouraged by commercial interests and state authorities as a 'harmless flutter', on the other, denounced by treatment agencies and many academic researchers as a morally corrupt trade in human hope and credulity. In the academic study of gambling, the 'pathological' model still tends to dominate and so it is within the ideology of sickness and dysfunction that the terms of reference and parameters of discussion are set. In such a climate, we hear distinct echoes of puritanical and rational disapproval and, in the proselytising zeal of writers trying to 'cure' gamblers, we can still see the shadow of the Puritan damning them from the pulpit. However, the focus of this tradition tends to concentrate on a minority of 'addicted' gamblers[2] to the exclusion of all others. Such a narrow focus, intentionally or otherwise, gradually obscures the majority of the gambling population from view. With this loss of perspective, the problem area inevitably assumes massive proportions: there is no 'healthy' state with which to compare the 'diseased' one. This begs the question whether such 'pathological' researchers believe a normal gambling habit that is not a manifestation of addiction or a compensation for a deprived lifestyle exists at all. One gets the impression that for them, the only 'healthy' gambling state is one which is never played at all!

It is with the neglected majority that this book is concerned, and as such it is situated firmly in the former of our two traditions – 'the tradition of license' – in which Plato first condoned play as the best part of human nature. Assuming the fundamentally non-problematic nature of the activity,[3] it aims to provide an analysis of the nature and experience of gambling in western society; as something which is historically and culturally variable, and yet which nevertheless retains an essential character which transcends the specificity of individual games.

The book can be divided into two main parts. The first involves a cultural history of the development of various games of chance, examining the social, economic and intellectual climate in which they were played, as well as the social stratification of their players and the changing terminology of criticism that threatened to outlaw them throughout history. This chronological survey takes the reader through Chapters 1 and 2, and leads on to Chapter 3, where the diversity of the modern forms of gambling are reviewed. In the second part of the book the focus shifts from the variety of specific games of chance to what they have in common; from the social framework of gambling to the experiences and beliefs of individual gamblers.

In Chapter 1, the historical contingency of the notion of chance in modern thought is examined and its development from sacred to epistemological to ontological category traced. It is argued that after a lengthy period in which the operation of chance was denied and condemned as irreligious, in the seventeenth century a climate of increasing secularisation saw its gradual acceptance as a category in its own right and the emergence of the theory of probability to explain it. Now it was no longer understood with reference to notions of divine providence and the will of the gods but in the language of science – probability, odds and statistics. This was the beginning of a movement which culminated in the twentieth century, when ontological status was granted to chance as a constituent part of the universe. This development was coeval with wider socioeconomic changes which saw the emergence of a mercantile form of capitalism and culminated in a metaphysical state of 'ontological insecurity' in the twentieth century: the birth of the Age of Chance.

Chapter 2 goes on to examine the recreational pursuit of chance: the social history of various gambling forms as well as the groups who played them. These games existed in a dynamic relation with the ideas about chance reviewed in Chapter 1, with changes in one affecting and being affected by developments in the other. All of the basic forms of gambling – cards, dice and lots – originated in the ancient practice of divination, and as such were inseparable from religious ritual. Furthermore, the commercialisation of these games converged with the commercialisation of economic life and with the emergence of probability theory – the science that 'tamed' chance. The games themselves were not played in a vacuum: typical of their status as microcosms of society, their form and organisation reflected the values and inequalities of the culture that surrounded them. In other words, specific class alignments grew up around specific games, creating a stratified gambling network with, for example, lotteries patronised mainly by the poor and with private clubs and casinos the prerogative of the upper classes.

The gambling economy which emerged from these historical configurations is the subject of Chapter 3, where the economic and social constitution of each of the modern commercial 'gambling sites' is examined. Using a typology based on variables such as the degree of skill and chance present in a game, the element of player involvement, the length of time taken to complete a round or 'gamble', and the integration of the game with its surrounding environment, the form and experience of play unique to each of these sites is outlined and the diversity of contemporary gambling highlighted. The momentous changes brought about by the recent introduction of the National Lottery in Britain and the deregulation of the gambling industry are also examined here, and their impact on our gambling culture as well as society in general considered. It is argued that commercial forces are overturning centuries of condemnation, so that gambling is now beginning to shed its pariah status and to become incorporated into economic life as just another type of commodity.

Chapters 4 and 5 are concerned with what is common to the experience of gambling in all these sites: with a phenomenological analysis of what it is actually *like* to play at games of chance, and what the activity means to participants. Here play is presented as a 'thing-in-itself'; a self-contained social world, set against the world of utilitarian goals, with its own rules and conventions and within which the gambler's orientation to the everyday world is altered.

Chapter 4 looks at the experience of play itself: at the various psychological and affective states gamblers go through during the course of a game, as well as their perception of the fundamental categories of time, space and money. The implications of the deliberate seeking out of risk for the creation of self-identity and social status are also examined here. It is argued that together, these elements constitute the excitement of gambling – the 'thrill' of play. The essential nature of the gambling experience is described as the continued pursuit of this excitement – 'play-in-itself'- and not, as is often argued, the desire to win money for its own sake. Such play-in-itself is characterised as the repetition of an intense, fleeting 'thrill', and the simultaneous desire for order and meaning: both the deliberate seeking out of uncertainty and the need for the resolution of that uncertainty. This resolution forms the subject of Chapter 5, where the perception of causation and the creation of order and meaning in the world of play are examined. It is argued that gamblers' general rejection of the rules of probability and their adoption of various superstitious notions such as the belief in forces like 'luck' and 'fate' is not, as has often been claimed, evidence of 'irrationality' or ignorance but a system of belief which operates to overcome the uncertainty of the gambling situation. In this way, the 'gambling worldview' is found to be in fact magical and religious in nature; an order of knowledge which works to make sense of an environment of chance and, furthermore, to provide individuals with an efficacious basis for action while in it. It is here that the dynamic of gambling itself – the tension between uncertainty and order, chance and meaning – is to be found. Thus players' deliberate seeking out of the gambling environment is portrayed as a symbolic testing of their luck, whose implications reach far beyond the immediate game and into the wider uncertainty of life in an Age of Chance.

In this way then, *The Age of Chance* attempts to examine the phenomenon of gambling in both its historical and contemporary forms; in relation to social structure and to individual consciousness, and, from the analysis of its many separate fragments, attempts to arrive at a picture of it that is a 'totality not a collection' and which, in its essential form, reveals something fundamental about western society.

The five chapters of the book represent five different approaches to gambling, each one chosen for its ability to illuminate a particular facet of the activity. This eclecticism has been deliberately chosen as the means best suited to reflect the diverse nature of the object of study: the variety of gambling itself. It also means that, as well as contributing to the development of a linear argument, each chapter can also stand alone, in which case each one can either be read in numerical order, or, as they are also self-contained, randomly – in any order at all. The choice of whether to follow a pattern or plunge in at random rests with the reader. So, pick a chapter, any chapter. . . .

NOTE ON THE TEXT

Some of the material in this book was gathered from conversations with gamblers in various locations: bingo halls, race-tracks, fruit machine arcades, lottery queues and in casinos in Britain and Las Vegas. Wherever possible, these comments have been attributed to 'punters' in order to distinguish them from those that come from academic and literary sources, which have been attributed to 'gamblers' or 'players'.

1

THE IDEA OF CHANCE

THE AGE OF FAITH: THE ORIGINS OF CHANCE

In the twenty-first century, chance is understood as a constituent part of the world, codified in the rules of probability theory and, in the branches of quantum mechanics and chaos theory, an irreducible feature of modern science. However, this theoretical perspective is a recent development and represents the apogee of a long historical process that culminated in the separation of 'chance' or random phenomena from broadly religious notions of divine providence and fate.

Strikingly, in ancient, classical and 'primitive' thought, there was no such thing as chance! The random event was everywhere regarded as a sacred sign of the gods which, although meaningless in itself, could be interpreted to reveal a more profound message from the transcendent 'beyond'. In such worldviews, various forms of divination and fortune-telling were utilised as means of communicating with the realm of the sacred, and were also often inseparable from the recreational pursuit of games of chance.

In the seventeenth century, the separation of 'chance' from broadly religious beliefs finally began. During this period of mercantile capitalism, a system of enumeration and a secular appreciation of risk flourished, creating both new ways of looking at the world and of expressing such viewpoints. In a climate favourable to the scientific calculation of probability, chance came to indicate, not the favour of the gods, but an absence of knowledge. From being a *sacred*, it now became an *epistemological*, category. This transformation was intimately connected with gambling, the latter of which provided a practical focus for the resolution of probabilistic problems. However, as we shall see, it was a long time even after chance had emerged as a distinct secular category before it finally shed the last vestiges of its earlier religious meaning, and it was only when it was thoroughly secularised into a 'meaningless' determinism in the nineteenth century that a path was cleared for its emergence as a genuine part of the world. By the twenty-first century, chance has been stripped of its sacred and metaphysical attributes to become a secular tool of

13

scientific explanation, so that what were once regarded as divine laws came to be understood as statistical probabilities. For the first time, chance became radically autonomous; an ontological category in its own right.

This process can be regarded as a *secularisation* of chance, and it is this, as well as its implications for the removal of metaphysical meaning from the world, that are the subject of this chapter. In the process of drawing a broad picture of the intellectual climate in which the notion of chance existed and developed, this discussion lays the groundwork for an examination of its purely recreational pursuit in the form of gambling games, which is the subject of Chapter 2.

The origins of chance

The prevalence of chance in creation myths is indicative of its essential contingency, in an anthropomorphic universe, on the idea of the sacred; on notions of the will of the gods and of divine providence. In these myths, the world exists in a primal state of chaos, from the Greek χaos: 'the first state of the universe, a vast gulf or chasm, the nether abyss, empty space' (*The Oxford English Dictionary* 1989, vol. 3, p. 22). This is the state of 'primal nature', 'full of disorder' that is imagined by Plato in the *Statesman*. In it, God feared that 'all might be dissolved in the storm and disappear in an infinite chaos', whereupon he 'brought back the elements which had fallen into dissolution and disorder', so creating order and the world as we know it (Plato 1987a, pp. 588–589).

The image that continually reappears in these world-creating transformations is one of gambling. In Greek mythology, Poseidon, Zeus and Hades divided the world between them in a dice game; possession of the land of Norway was determined by a dicing match between two kings and backed by the hand of God, while the Ases of Scandinavian mythology, like the Hindu Siva, determined the fate of mankind by throwing dice (Huizinga 1949; Onians 1988; Ekeland 1993). In every case, order is conferred on chaos through the activity of gambling.

We see in these myths an image of chance as something intimately connected with the falling of dice or lots; an image which befits its derivation from the Latin *cadere*, to fall. The noun *cadentia* means 'the falling out or happening of events, the way in which things fall out; fortune; case' (*The Oxford English Dictionary* 1989, vol. 3, p. 10). The word 'chance' literally refers to that which falls to us; a sense which is still evident today when we speak of the *fall* of the cards or dice, or of good or bad fortune *befalling* an individual.

Chance and divination

From the symbiotic relation of chance to notions of fate and divine providence derives the efficacy of divination as a means of communicating with the transcendent 'beyond'. Regarded as meaningless *in itself*, in divination ritual, chance operates as a cypher for the expression of the will of the gods, and it is in this crucial relationship that the earliest conceptions of chance are to be understood. Because '*alea* signifies and reveals the favour of destiny' (Caillois 1962, p. 17), in divination, chance becomes a vehicle for sacred meaning. The word itself, from the Latin *divinatio*, clearly highlights the derivation of the activity from the divine. In divination the expressive function of the chance event was deliberately courted so that the gods might intercede and determine an outcome to a question put to them, which was then interpreted as a divine pronouncement. In this way, divination indicated the future course of events as well as the approval or disapproval of destiny with regard to human actions.

Divination was universal and pervasive, a wide range of techniques[1] being practised in societies as diverse as ancient China and Greece, medieval Europe, and among North American tribes. Its ubiquity was recognised by Cicero in his *De Divinatoire* when he wrote: 'I am aware of no people, however refined and learned or however savage and ignorant, which does not think that signs are given of future events, and that certain persons can recognise those signs and foretell events before they occur' (Cicero 1971, p. 223). The variety of natural phenomena which could be interpreted as divine signs was almost unlimited, ranging from the flight of birds, regarded by Euripidis as the 'messengers of the gods', to the formation of clouds, known by the Hindus as 'castles in the air'. Divination by an animal's liver was believed to be a particularly efficacious ritual by the ancient Babylonians, the Chinese analysed the cracks in turtle shells, while the Germans, who, Tacitus tells us, had 'the highest regard' for lots and omens, utilised strips of bark and even horses in their divination rituals (Tacitus 1982, p. 109). Dreams also played an important role in divination, for when the body relaxed in sleep, 'the reasoning portion of the soul was languid and inert' (Cicero 1971, p. 291), and so was open to communication with the world of the supernatural. Oneiromancy – the interpretation of dreams – thus found widespread acceptance as a means of divination.

In every type of divination, chance events were possessed of a sacred significance and nowhere was this more evident than in the practice of cleromancy – the drawing or casting of lots. As a mechanism for the articulation of the Divine Voice, the lot was the earliest and most basic application of the random event for divinatory purposes. A simple action, such as the tossing of sticks, arrows or animal bones, would be carried out by a suitably qualified individual – a priest or shaman – and a question addressed to a deity or fate. The formation of the falling objects would then be interpreted as the 'answer' of the god, for the disposal of the lot was *always* recognised as divine intervention.

Cleromancy was widespread throughout the ancient world and, despite the strident criticism that it would later direct at all blasphemous, 'pagan' practices as lot casting, Christianity was not initially opposed to the activity. References to it appear regularly throughout the Old Testament; for example, in Numbers 26:55 the allocation of the lands of Canaan among the Israelites is decided by lot: 'And the Lord spoke unto Moses saying . . . the land shall be divided by lot. . . . According to the lot shall the possession thereof be divided by many and few.'[2] Such a faith in lots indicated that to its practitioners, divination was never a resort to meaningless chance, but an appeal directed at transcendental powers, which, in the Judaeo-Christian tradition, happened to be God.

Divination played an important role in ancient society and was used primarily as a means of making – or at least consolidating – decisions. Before being undertaken, all enterprises of importance were referred to a diviner or prophet, who would establish whether or not they would succeed, and if so, which times were most propitious for such success. Van der Leeuw and Levy-Bruhl have drawn attention to the important (but often overlooked) point that in consulting the gods, enquirers frequently wanted to know not necessarily what would happen next, but whether or not what they *wanted* to happen would occur, repeating their questioning until they got the desired result (van der Leeuw 1967, p. 379; Levy-Bruhl 1966, p. 142).

Here we see an essentially practical, even irreverent, orientation towards the still very serious matter of man's relationship with destiny. It is an attitude recognised by Flaceliere (1965) in the 'genuine wisdom' and 'credulity' shown by the Greeks towards *their* divinatory practices. He points to the strand of scepticism which ridiculed the efficacy of divination and which existed within a society which, while considered to be the womb of enlightenment and reason, still had widespread recourse to such practices. Such ambiguity is typical of human life, for, while propitiating the gods on the one hand, individuals were under no obligation to take their advice, and in fact often used them as an excuse if a suggested course of action went wrong!

Social life is seldom demarcated into clear-cut areas, and it is often out of these ambiguous crevices that the most fertile insights can be found. Within the seriousness of divine ritual there was also room for some frivolity and equivocation, an attitude which provided a space into which other, less serious states of mind could grow. This was manifest in the intrusion of the play spirit into serious matters of ritual, for the rituals and the implements involved in divination were frequently identical to those utilised in gambling games (Tylor 1913; Caillois 1962; Levy-Bruhl 1966; David 1969; Halliday and Fuller 1974). In the process of divining the future, interested parties could entertain themselves by betting on the outcome of rituals – in a sense, attempting to pre-empt the will of the gods. Such a concurrence has frequently been utilised in evolutionary arguments as evidence for the development of one activity out of another. According to Tylor, 'primitive' gambling originated in the practice of divination (Tylor 1913, p. 78), while David holds that the wager, and hence gambling, grew out of the drawing of lots and the interrogation of oracles 'which have their roots deep in religious rituals' (David 1969, p. 7). However, far from presenting itself as evidence for evolutionary progression, it can be argued that the association supports the far more complex and subtle conflation of game and ritual which exists in the same instance as part of the irreverent attitude discussed above. It is not a case of one 'growing out' of the other, as the evolutionists have suggested, for the two were conjoined from the very start, each part of the same outlook. There existed a playful aspect to divination as well as a sacred aspect to gambling. The latter did not simply emerge, as a secularised version, out of the former, and in any case, the prophetic connotations of gambling have never been completely extinguished, either formally (for example, in the case of fortune-telling with cards), or in the mind of gamblers, whose beliefs will be studied in Chapter 5. The relationship of divination to gambling will be examined further in Chapter 2.

Chance, fate and necessity

Nowhere in ancient or primitive cosmology do we find systematic considera-tion of chance as a phenomenon in its own right. Instead, its occurrence was consistently conflated with notions of destiny and the will of the gods. Roberts *et al.* state categorically that 'explicit theories of chance do not appear in primitive cultures' (Roberts *et al.* 1959, p. 602), where the unexpected event instead has a meaningful place as part of an anthropomorphic universe of spirits and powers.

It is in classical Greek philosophy that we first find anything approxi-mating a consideration of chance, but here, as in primitive thought, the approach was never entirely divorced from religious ideas of the existence of the gods. From Socrates and Plato, through to the Stoics and Boethius, the existence of chance (*tyche*), luck and also timeliness (*kairos*) was consistently subsumed under more important questions of divine providence, determin-ism and the role of free will. An individual would be lucky because of fated circumstances: it would be the right time, the favourable moment, for an event to occur. This 'active' or 'dynamic' time – *kairos* – was predetermined, so that, far from denoting contingency, both the notions of luck and chance referred to the *fatedness* of human life, and revealed the intentions of the divine plan in their unfolding (Nussbaum 1986).

In the *Laws* Plato articulated the notion of God as the final *telos*, to which all so-called 'contingency' was subservient:

> One might be moved to say . . . that no law is ever made by a man, and that human history is all an affair of chance . . . and yet there is something else which may also be said with no less plausibility. . . .

That God is all, while chance and circumstance, under God, set the whole course of life for us.

(Plato 1969, p. 1300)

Greek philosophy resonates with the notions of fate and necessity, as Cicero puts it, 'applying forcibly to all things' (Cicero 1991, p. 91). The deterministic Greeks – and especially the Stoics – argued that the contents of the universe were united by 'universal cosmic sympathy', governed by fate and overseen by the all-knowing gods. Their belief in divine foreknowledge was thus an argument for universal determinism within which the existence of the gods was synonymous with the efficacy of divination (Flaceliere 1965; Sharples 1983). There was no room for chance within this worldview, for in a universe in which 'nothing happens that [is] not necessary' (Cicero 1991, p. 69) the very conception of it as an independent entity could have little real meaning.

In Aristotle however, we do find a specific consideration of chance as part of the doctrine of final causes. In a teleological system in which nature exhibits purposeful processes, chance for Aristotle was not an absence of causality, but rather an instance of coincidence – a 'coincidental cause'.[3] In the *Physics* he cites an example, whereby A wants to collect a debt from B and one day meets him unexpectedly at a market on the very day when B is collecting subscriptions (Aristotle 1990, p. 209). This is not chance, but merely a case of the coincidental intersection of two separate causes, which, as Sharples (1983) points out, is not incompatible with determinism.

As the link between ancient and medieval thought, Boethius attempted to resolve the problem of divine foreknowledge and human freedom. In his *On the Consolation of Philosophy*, we see an explication of the harmony of divine providence, as well as an explanation of chance in essentially Aristotelian terms. Once again, there is no room for chance, for all things are linked in a great cosmic design. Thus 'a certain ordering embraces all things so that what departs from its place in that order falls back into an order . . . so that in the kingdom of providence, nothing should be permitted to random chance' (Boethius 1991, p. 115). What appears as chance is only a manifestation of limited human understanding, for things only appear 'random and confused' when the principles governing their order are not known. It is only as an epistemological category, then, that chance can be said to exist, for if it is defined some other way, for example, as an outcome produced by random events, without cause, 'then chance does not exist at all' and in fact nor can *anything* exist: 'the world is, I judge, completely empty. For when God directs all things into an ordered pattern, what place at all can there be left for randomness?' (Boethius 1991, p. 125). Having said this, Boethius goes on to give his own Aristotelian example of the appearance of chance as coincidence. A man who digs to cultivate a field but finds gold is not subject to chance, but to 'unforeseen and unexpected coincidence', for there are *causes* of fortuitous gain which are not dependent on the intentions of the agent. Neither the man who buried the gold nor the one who tilled the field expected the gold to be found; its finding was simply an intersection of causes which were explicable in terms of pattern and design.

In all these philosophers we can see a strict determinism which encompasses notions of fate, divine providence, order and cause, and which resonates throughout the classical world, consistently obscuring, or at best marginalising, the study of chance as pure randomness. These issues were carried over into the Middle Ages, a period in which, despite the subsumption of philosophy to theology, the heritage of the classical thinkers excited 'fervent curiosity' and frequently 'deep respect' (Marenbon 1983, p. 3). The medieval concept of chance was derived from the Aristotelian notion of an absence of purpose or design, and was profoundly influenced by Boethius for whom chance as an absence of cause simply could not exist. However, monotheistic Christianity added elements of its own; most importantly a Church that railed against all forms of secular knowledge and saw evidence of the hand of God in every earthly phenomenon. In such a climate, the concept of the random event was rejected as pagan. Many Christians sought to explain 'chance' events on earth with reference to notions of fate, astrology or the will of God, hence the explanation of divine intervention behind miracles.[4] St Augustine anticipated the dominant medieval response to chance, explaining that it was the ignorance of man and not the nature of events themselves that caused the latter to appear to occur at random. Attacking Cicero's denial of determinism and hence of divine foreknowledge, Augustine argued that man's true endeavour was to submit himself to the Divine Will and not to question its workings by searching for the exceptional or unusual.

In medieval Christianity then, chance was insignificant in itself, being viewed instead as an epiphenomenon of a Divine order. The existence of such an all-powerful deity left little place for free will, and no place for chance; rather, every event was regarded as being divinely caused and the fate of every individual divinely predestined. In such a scheme, the entire universe was a harmonious, orderly manifestation of the will of God. Anselm's insistence on the consistency of God was thus a fundamental tenet of medieval thought. Order was everywhere, and it revealed that: 'The will of God is never irrational' (*Opera Omnia*, vol. 2, p. 59).

CHANCE AND DETERMINISM

Not having a field of study of its own, some of the most fertile analyses of the development of the notion of chance have come out of the study of probability, whose development, in Hacking's evocative phrase, engendered the 'taming of chance' (Hacking 1990). The creation of an 'empire of chance' (Gigerenzer *et al.* 1989) and the ambivalent Enlightenment attitude towards the 'shadows of chance' (Kavanagh 1993) have provided the subject matter for a series of studies on the place of the *aleatory* in human consciousness (Daston 1988). Backed by a profusion of vivid metaphors, these authors' interest in chance is thus mediated by their focus on its codification in probability theory.

An absent family of ideas

In the previous section we saw how the utilisation of chance in divinatory practice was widespread in ancient, primitive and classical societies, and how the history of gambling itself appears as a record of the recreational pursuit of the random. For Hacking, this ancient practical interest in chance was 'ubiquitous enough to be positively primeval' (Hacking 1975, p. 1), while David was aware that the proliferation of early references to gaming and divination was an indication that 'the random element . . . was pursued with assiduous fanaticism' (David 1969, p. 21). Interest in chance through gaming, religious ritual and the observations of everyday life was intense, and yet paradoxically, no corresponding analysis of it existed. The study and observation of randomness, frequency, betting and probability lagged well behind everyday involvement in the practicalities of such pursuits. The word 'probability' only appeared in its modern form implying a numerical idea of randomness in the seventeenth century, finding its way into print for the first time in 1661. Until the decade around the 1660s, such notions as the abstract quantification of chance were simply not found, and comprised what Hacking calls 'an absent family of ideas' (Hacking 1975).

In medieval Europe, there were clear reasons for this absence. Basically, medieval epistemology precluded the very consideration of randomness as a category in its own right. Chance was regarded as an epiphenomenon of the Divine Will, which in itself was nothing, and so could not be an object of serious study. The existence and manifestation of randomness was simply not an issue with which the medieval mind was engaged. Rather, what consideration of 'the random' did exist was formulated around the more immediate question of knowledge and opinion. Medieval natural philosophy did recognise the existence of events that happened 'by chance' – *ut in paucioribus* – but these were considered outside the range of true 'scientific' knowledge and could only be referred to as likelihoods, not certainties (James and Weisheipl 1982, p. 526). These twin axes of interest can be seen to constitute a medieval form of 'probability', not in its modern sense, but as a concern with the notions of *opinio* and *scientia*, from which the dualistic notion of probability that emerged in the seventeenth century can be traced. In scholastic doctrine, probability – *probibilitas* – stemmed from *opinio*, which referred to propositions resulting from reflection and argument. These could not be demonstrated and therefore were not considered as valid objects of knowledge or the focus of scholarly study. Furthermore, since truths about the world were not considered to be the proper subject of *opinio*, probability was not viewed as a realm in which real knowledge would be found.

An ancient family of ideas

The situation was very different in classical thought, however, and here the concern is more with an *ancient* rather than an *absent* family of ideas. Despite the essentially deterministic nature of the classical universe, strands of scepticism towards the primacy of fate and divine providence *had* existed in Greek thought. Although the practice of divination was generally held in high esteem, voices of dissent were frequently heard, most notably those of the cynical Epicureans, and Cicero. For Epicurus, it was not fate but chance that ruled the world. No design or providence was recognised in the universe, and everything that existed could be explained by the random motions of atoms in empty space (Epicurus 1990, p. 314). In Roman philosophy, Cicero rejected the view of chance as an aspect of divine providence, and wrote *On Fate, On Divination* and *On the Nature of the Gods* to deny the efficacy of divination and determinism, which he could not reconcile with his views of human freedom. In Book II of *De Divinatiore*, an understanding of what would later be known as the law of large numbers is evident:

> Nothing is so uncertain as the cast of dice, and yet there is no one who plays often who does not sometimes make a Venus-throw[5] and occasionally twice or thrice in succession. Then are we, like fools, to prefer to say that it happened by the direction of Venus rather than by chance?
>
> (Cicero 1971, p. 507)

In this practical, eminently secular understanding of the world, Cicero regarded lot casting firstly, as synonymous with games of chance, and secondly – and more cynically – as a deliberate encouragement of superstition.

Such scepticism about the divine function of the lot and the providential nature of chance was at its most scathing in Cicero, who gave voice to a strand of thought in the classical world that could imagine the outcome of a chance event to be an expression of something other than godly will. Together with a highly developed system of scientific logic and mathematics, this current amounted to the existence of what David calls an 'instinctive feeling for probability' (David 1969, p. 24).

Within the realm of mathematics and logic – the realm of certain knowledge – issues such as the enumeration of possibilities and causes were being tackled, and the suggestion that the likelihood of an event's occurrence was not merely a matter of subjective interpretation being discussed. David points to the first stirrings of combinatory theory in Xenocrates, who absorbed himself in the calculation of the number of syllables produced by rearranging the letters of the alphabet up to 1,002,000 million times (David 1969, p. 23)!

Thus alongside a strict, providential determinism we find in the classical world an understanding and codification of chance which could have led to the beginnings of a more mature theory of probability. In philosophy and mathematics, the Greeks demonstrated the ability to develop further from these promising beginnings. Yet such a development never happened; the precocious understanding of combinations and randomness did not lead to what we now know as modern probability.

Reasons for the absent family

We can see how the nature of medieval epistemology precluded the serious consideration of probabilistic ideas. As 'mere opinion', such a topic was not worthy of systematic academic pursuit. At the same time however, a tradition favourable to the recognition of randomness *did* exist in classical thought. Why then did it never develop to become anything more than an 'instinctive feeling' for probability?

The answer to this question has frequently focused on the relatively unsophisticated nature of Greek numerical systems (David 1969; Hacking 1975; Gigerenzer *et al.* 1989). Despite their mastery of logic and geometry, the Greeks had not made corresponding advances in arithmetical computations – especially the writing down of numbers. The symbolism that facilitates multiplication and addition is a prerequisite for the expression of a theory of probability, and the Greeks and Romans, whose notation, being rather cumbersome, did not lend itself to arithmetical operations, 'lacked a perspicuous notation for numerals' (Hacking 1975, p. 6). Furthermore, the manipulation of numbers as though they were objects was unknown in Pythagorean mathematics, for, in this tradition, numbers were regarded as bearers of magical and mysterious powers. Number was seen to express divine harmony and order and, thus mystified and hypostatised, was unable to simply represent the mundane, secular implications of individual quantities or occurrences. Until number could be released from Pythagorean mysticism, and until a workable notation for it existed, the arithmetical and algebraic level necessary for the full development of probability theory could not appear. Nor was scientific method conducive to the testing of chance that the calculation of probabilities relies on. In the classical world, a gap existed between the construction of theoretical hypotheses and the observation of empirical data, and, until this gap was closed during the Renaissance, the extensive, repeated testing and observation of large groups of numbers was impossible (David 1969, p. 23).

Among all this speculation, Kendell utters a word of warning: 'Mathematics', he says, 'never leads thought, but only expresses it' (Kendell 1970, p. 30). There are more fundamental reasons for the absence of probability theory than an insufficiently advanced number system. Rather, the absence of probability is to be found in an entire *worldview*: 'the very notion of chance itself, the idea of natural law, the possibility that a proposition may be true and false in fixed relative proportions . . . all comprise a cosmology in which there is no place for probabilistic thinking' (Kendell 1970, p. 30). In such fixed and hierarchical societies, events and individuals were all assured of their place, their function and their role in the world. This was not a matter of chance, but was determined by some providential power, and continued by the force of tradition. In such worldviews, there was simply no place for chance as an influential phenomenon, and therefore little point in devoting much energy to its study – even when to do so was not considered to be an impious act of human presumption. Any such study would have to be encouraged by an entirely different outlook; one in which social rigidity gave way to a degree of individual freedom and in which some self-determination was allowed alongside beliefs in determining, providential forces.

The Renaissance

Such a climate began to emerge in late fifteenth-century Italy, and in it, mathematicians like Fra Luca Pacioli and Geronimo Cardano raised some of the basic problems of the calculation of chances and began the first halting attempts to solve them (Kendell 1970).

The impetus behind these anticipations of probability theory was intimately related to the development of a system of mercantile capitalism. A new merchant class were emerging, whose dynamic, entrepreneurial ventures shook the static hierarchy of the medieval 'great chain of being'. This group were interested in matters of commerce: problems such as the distribution of goods in trade, the insurance of those goods and the likelihood of a journey being completed successfully. These were essentially numerical issues dealing with proportions, divisions and relative amounts: all problems intrinsic to probabilistic reasoning. Paciolis' *Summa de arithmetica, geometria, proportioni et proportionalita* (1494), famous as the origin of double entry bookkeeping, was a part of this commercial milieu, and was used by merchants in the calculations of profits and losses and the recording of commercial transactions (Hacking 1975, pp. 4–5).

The new commerce acted as an incentive to *statistical* development too. The trade and manufacture in fifteenth-century Italy became a subject for accountancy and mathematics as the need for numerical assessment paralleled the growth of commercial enterprise. The enumeration and quantification of the world in this period formed a kind of 'descriptive statistics' (Kendall 1970, p. 46), and went some way towards creating the arithmetical basis that was vital for the further growth of probability and which had been absent in its earlier, classical manifestation.

It was into this milieu that Geronimo Cardano's *Liber de Ludo Alea* (1550) appeared. This seminal work benefited from its author's vast knowledge of randomness, for Cardano was an avid gambler who used his experience of gaming in the calculation of dice throws. For the first time in the consideration of chance, the abstraction from empirical evidence to theoretical concept was made, and, also for the first time, the equal possibility of

23

throwing any number on a die on each subsequent throw, was stated: 'I am as able to throw 1, 3 or 5 as 2, 4 or 6. The wagers are therefore laid in accordance with this equality if the die is honest' (Cardano 1953, p. 193). Even now, Cardano's reputation is disputed between those who consider him to be a probabilist of unequivocal importance (e.g. Ore 1953; David 1969), and those who find his deficiencies typical of the intellectual limitations of the time (e.g. Hacking 1975; Gigerenzer *et al.* 1989). Gigerenzer *et al.* were concerned with the implications of Cardano's calculations, which 'mathematically obliged' him to assert that each face of the die should occur once every six throws. He resolved the problem with an appeal to luck; a phenomenon whose intervention disrupted the realisation of mathematical probabilities and reintroduced the ancient idea of supernatural guidance. Cardano thus relinquished his claim to the founding of the mathematical theory of probability, for classical probability could only emerge when appeals to factors such as luck were banished (Hacking 1975).

For us, however, the importance of Cardano as well as Pacioli derives simply from the fact that they were *aware* of the problems they attempted to solve. For Hacking, what is most striking about these early works 'is not that problems on chance [were] chiefly aimed at the new commerce, but that these books were quite unable to solve the problems. No-one could solve them until about 1660 and then everyone could' (Hacking 1975, p. 5). The solution to these problems would have to wait another century; time for an intellectual climate change in which the concepts of numbers, averages and signs as evidence would clear the way for probabilistic reasoning. The concept of the average – vital for the development of the notion of expectation – was developed by Pascal in the seventeenth century, and in it the solutions to Cardano's puzzles were eventually found.

THE AGE OF REASON: THE BIRTH OF PROBABILITY

The eventual emergence of probability theory in the mid-seventeenth century was an intellectual development long overdue, and represented the victory of *Scientia* – scientific understanding – over *Fortuna* – luck, fate or some other form of providential belief. However, once granted scientific status it developed rapidly and matured into an independent discipline over the course of the next two hundred years (Gigerenzer *et al.* 1989). In the course of its development from the 'doctrine of chances' to the science of calculations, the existence of chance became visible in more and more diverse epistemological fields, from philosophy and physics to biology and economics, until finally it became recognisable as the definitive feature of the modern age – the Age of Chance. It was the development of probability theory itself which made possible the birth of this age, for during its growth, chance began to emerge as a distinct entity *in itself*, separate from notions of fate and the gods. This separation was vital, for before probability could explain chance, chance had to exist as an independent phenomenon to *be* explained. Parallel to the emergence of probability, then, was the emergence of chance, which, between the mid-seventeenth and nineteenth centuries, became visible for the first time.

Pascal

The inexorable march towards the Age of Chance began, ironically enough, with a chance encounter. In Poisson's famous sentence: 'A problem about games of chance proposed to an austere Jansenist by a man of the world' (Hacking 1975, p. 37). The 'austere Jansenist' was Pascal, the 'man of the world' the Chevalier de Mere, a philosopher and gambler who wanted to know how much a stake in a game would be worth if the game were interrupted. The question created a surge of interest in proportions and chance and led to Huygen's *De Alea* and Pascal's correspondence with Fermat. The surrounding debate marked the birth of classical probability, a concept which was 'Janus faced' – the legacy of the medieval distinction between *scientia* and *opinio* – on the one hand, statistical, on the other, epistemological (Gigerenzer *et al*. 1989, p. 274). The former was concerned with stochastic processes, the latter with assessing degrees of belief, a duality of which Pascal was quite representative. In his 1654 essay on the arithmetical triangle, he introduced the notion of expectation into games of chance, and in so doing was able to solve problems which had baffled his predecessors for centuries. Cardano, Pacioli and other writers had thought the best way to divide the stakes of an interrupted game was to assume that the game played so far was representative or proportionate to what would happen next. In other words, they assumed that chance would behave in the future as it had in the past. Pascal however looked at the game in an entirely different way. He saw it as something like an unfinished story whose end was not determined by what had gone before. The past had no bearing on what would happen next, and so, crucially, the future of the game was not yet resolved by previous play. Any provisional division of the stakes, then, should be made in such a way that each player saw it as being in their interest to continue playing; with gains and losses treated as something which would alter during the course of the game, not simply as something which would repeat the pattern they had fallen into in previous play.

Pascal's interest in probability also took him in other directions; into consideration of subjective beliefs, and in this area, his essay on the belief in the existence of God in the *Pensées* is typical of the epistemological strand of probability. 'Pascal's wager' demonstrated that calculations about games of chance could be transferred to uncertain situations in general, and applied as a method of reasoning. The argument concerned the utility of the belief in God: either God exists or he does not – 'God is or he is not' – which way should we incline? Pascal argued that belief – the wager that 'God exists' – is a more rational course of action than disbelief – the wager that he does not. If God does not exist, neither belief nor disbelief will have any effect on us. However, if he does, wagering that he does not will bring damnation, whereas wagering that he *does* could bring salvation. Since damnation is the worst possible outcome and salvation the best, we should act as though we believe God does exist. Even if the chances of this are infinitesimally small, the payoff if he exists is infinitesimally great – far outstripping the potential reward if we opt for non-existence and he turns out not to exist after all.

Pascal's wager was an argument from expectation with an equal probability distribution, and its conclusion provided a strategy for rational behaviour. The existence of God was not, then, a matter of chance, but a question of reasonable belief, and the wager provided an outline for the action of rational man. For Pascal, the uncertainty faced by the doubter was like that faced by the gambler, and so he used the reasoning of the former as a template for the reasoning of the latter: 'Every gambler takes a certain risk for an uncertain gain, and yet he is taking a certain finite risk for an uncertain finite gain without sinning against reason' (Pascal 1987, p. 151). This type of reasoning was increasingly common by the mid-seventeenth century, and was indicative of the extent to which the intellectual climate was changing to accommodate the notion of uncertainty. The revival of sceptical philosophy undermined the ideal of certain knowledge, dominant in intellectual enquiry since Aristotle (Gigerenzer *et al*. 1989, p. 4). At the forefront of this revival was Descartes, whose attempt to eliminate doubt by disregarding all previously held certainties actually served to put it on a firmer footing by establishing it as a method of philosophical pursuit in its own right. In Descartes' rational scepticism, enquiry had to begin with *doubt* – how can I know anything? – to proceed to certainty (Descartes 1985).

These intellectual developments influenced, and were influenced by, a process of radical economic change, for in the seventeenth century Europe was entering a period of mercantile capitalism. This momentous period saw the emergence of an entrepreneurial, risk-taking milieu, the birth of modern science, of individualism, and of many of our contemporary institutions and ideas. In short, it gave us the birth of modern society itself.

The eminently *speculative* nature of this period of merchant capitalism branched out in two major directions, both of which encouraged the development of a numerical, probabilistic worldview. On the one hand, trading in stocks and shares created an international stockmarket in which companies and individuals alike competed with each other to amass vast fortunes through speculation in the new global economy. At the same time, the speculative mania extended in more conservative directions, in the creation of insurance and annuities (Hacking 1975, p. 4; see also Douglas 1992, p. 23). Originally intended for the assurances of marine risks, such insurance calculated the chances of a ship coming home against the chances of its being lost at sea. This practice had been around since the fourth millennium BC in what were known as 'bottomly contracts' – loans to ship owners, the repayment of which was contingent on the safe completion of the voyage – but in the seventeenth century, a form of marine insurance which dealt specifically in *risks* emerged, one which took account of the probability of losses and gains. This insurance was directly linked to the emergence of capitalism: to the expansion of long-distance trading and the spread of commercial innovations like bills of exchange and various credit mechanisms (*Encyclopedia Britannica* 1992, vol. 6, p. 336). From its first documented instance in the Lloyds company in 1613, marine insurance rapidly expanded into a multitude of smaller companies throughout the seventeenth century. Its objective also expanded, so that by the end of the century, marine risks had been left behind by ambitious companies organising a form of speculative insurance which could be purchased on anything, including lives.

It was also during this period of general socioeconomic upheaval that the meaning of *securitas* changed from the expression of a subjective state of freedom from care to an objective sense of *sureté*, later *securité*, in French (Luhmann 1993, p. 13). Luhmann writes: 'It is as if, in the face of an increasingly uncertain future, a secure basis for the making of decisions had to be found.' The idea that fate or providence would oversee the unfolding of events could no longer provide sufficient assurance to those whose goods might be at stake in trading situations. Individuals were beginning to feel the need to take matters into their own hands and to make practical, active efforts to ensure their security. This heralded the development of a rational orientation to action which formed itself around the newly recognised concepts of risk and insurance.

A dictionary of 1665 defined insurance specifically in terms of commercial risk: 'The Covenant of preventing Danger (commonly called Insurance) frequent among Merchants, added a Shadow of Law; whereby the Uncertainty of the Event is usually transferred to another with some certain Reward' (in *The Oxford English Dictionary* 1989, vol. 7, p. 1059). It is at this point that we also see the emergence of the notion of *risk*, in both its senses of 'danger, exposure to peril' and the more specific 'chance or hazard' of commercial loss in the case of insured property. Both these connotations appeared in the seventeenth century, from the Anglo-French *risqué*; the first instance of the term being cited in 1661 as '*Risqué* – peril, jeopardy, danger, hazard, chance' (in *The Oxford English Dictionary* 1989, vol. 13, p. 987). Slightly later the sense of risk as something linked with commercial exploits was made explicit. The 1728 edition of *Chambers* warns: 'There is a great Risk run in letting Goods go upon Credit to great Lords.' And later still, we find it linked (as it often is today) specifically with insurance against commercial loss. In 1750, it is described as 'A Contract or Agreement by which one or more Particulars . . . take on them the Risqué of the Value of the things insured' (in *The Oxford English Dictionary* 1989, vol. 13, p. 987).

In this new capitalising economy, as trade expanded into a system of international exchange, enumeration and accountancy became vital. The tentative, numerical development which had seen the beginnings of a form of Renaissance statistics continued with renewed vigour under the dynamic of nascent capitalist enterprise. The risking of money in speculative ventures encouraged the accurate calculation of many variables: for instance, the value of the goods invested, the quantities of time and space involved in their transportation, the amounts of money exchanged and any interest charged on the transactions. At the same time, the expansion of a money economy created a standardised, universal measure of value. Unlike the gold and land of the feudal economy, money existed as a 'universal equivalent', a convenient abstraction, in whose international language the most distant and disparate groups could communicate. This spirit of enumeration is apparent in the transition, during the seventeenth century, from the Renaissance concept of 'measure' in the sense of moderation and balance, to the modern concept of measurement as quantification; a move that is philologically visible in the German shift from *Maß* to *Messen* (Guttman 1978, p. 85).

Significantly for our study of probability, it was in this period of mercantilism that the widespread enumeration of society took place. The utilisation of number in rational accountancy is, for Max Weber, a precondition for the development of the spirit of capitalist enterprise, and it was in the seventeenth century that the need to quantify and compare individual events and phenomena according to a universal, numerical standard reached its apogee. This was a time when the mystical connotations of Pythagoreanism had been abandoned, and an image of number as the basis of all objective knowledge revived. Knowledge of number implied control over nature, for: 'A grasp of the numerical structure in things conferred on man new powers over his surroundings. In a way, it made him more like God' (Bertrand Russell, in Birren 1961, p. 11).

It was this enumeration of the world, along with the growth of a speculative, arithmetical *Weltanschauung* that created a climate in which events whose outcomes were uncertain could be observed and their natures calculated in terms of a scientific 'doctrine of chances'. The level of numeracy necessary for the 'arithmetical juggling' required by probability theory was thus attained in the developing mercantile markets of the seventeenth century.

The newly acquired calculative attitude extended over all avenues of life, and its symbiotic relation with games of chance was noted by one eighteenth-century commentator on English customs, who wrote: 'The probability of life and the return of ships, are the objects of their arithmetic. The same habit of calculating they extend to games, wagers, and everything in which there is any hazard' (Le Blanc, in Guttman 1978, p. 60).

At the same time, the intellectual changes outlined above were indicative of a milieu in which the study of a theory of chances could take place. The pursuit of the random was no longer considered an aberration, but had come into its own as a serious object of study. The birth of modernity, then, saw the recognition of chance as a distinct category. However, it was a qualified recognition, as we shall see in the next section.

'There is no such thing as chance'

> But there is no such thing as chance. Everything is either a test or a punishment, a reward or a precaution.
>
> (Voltaire 1990, p. 191)

Voltaire's *Zadig* expressed the eighteenth-century belief in meaning and purpose, reflecting the spirit of the Enlightenment and the direction of the thought of the early probabilists. After Pascal's wager and his correspondence with Fermat, a burst of interest and activity was initiated and, in the ensuing debate, several writers' excited responses to each others' discoveries marked out the parameters of the new discipline of probability. Between the mid-seventeenth and the end of the eighteenth century, the 'classical' European probabilists – Huygens, Bernoulli, Laplace, Montmort and de Moivre – turned their attention to gambling as the paradigmatic *aleatory* contract. In the analysis of popular games they found empirical examples of randomness in action, and from the conclusions they drew and applied to the world in general we can see the embodiment of the dominant Enlightenment attitude to chance. Just as in earlier times games of chance had functioned as a stage upon which the favours of the gods were enacted, in the seventeenth century gambling games once again acted as a stage upon which this time *scientific*, rather than sacred, dramas were played out. Probability theory, then, made its début on the stage of gambling games.

The early probabilists were imbued with deep religious conviction and unbounded optimism in the infinite potential of human abilities; an alliance that resulted in an epistemological determinism from which only a specifically subjectivist notion of probability could develop. For Gigerenzer *et al.*, this position 'maintained that all events were in principle predictable and that probabilities were therefore relative to our knowledge' (Gigerenzer *et al.* 1989, p. 11). Uncertainty, then, was fundamentally a state of *mind*, not a state of the *world*. Chance had emerged, but only as an epistemological category, as a deficit of human knowledge.

The belief in purposefulness dominated all Enlightenment thought; chance was banished as a sign of human ignorance which the rational individual had a duty to resolve, and in this we can see in the seventeenth century a recurrence of the classical concern with providential purpose and harmony. Representative of such a preoccupation was Spinoza, in whose determined universe the order of the world was subject to an abstract and all-pervasive God. In Proposition 29 of the *Ethics*, he expressed this determinism: 'Nothing in nature is contingent but all things are from the necessity of the divine nature determined to exist and to act in a definite way' (Spinoza 1990, p. 528). A similar providential order preoccupied Leibniz, who argued that: 'God does nothing which is not orderly . . . for everything is in conformity with respect to the universal order' (Leibniz 1990, p. 578).

Such ideas were central to the writing of the classical probabilists whose conception of a Cartesian 'prime mover' who fully determined nature meant that everything had a cause, however hidden. In this scheme of things, the concept of probability functioned as a kind of tool for human intellects too limited to penetrate the real nature of the Divine handiwork. This theme runs through the work of all the probabilists, in one form or another, from Huygens and Montmort to Bernoulli and de Moivre (Gigerenzer *et al.* 1989; see also Daston 1988).

In his *Essai D'Analyse* (1708) Montmort defined *le hasard* as an index of human ignorance, a manifestation of the workings of the Creator:

> Strictly speaking nothing depends on chance. When one studies nature one is soon convinced that its Author acts in a general and uniform way which bears the stamp of an infinite wisdom and prescience . . . all things are regulated according to certain laws of which usually the order is not known to us. . . . After this definition one can say that the life of man is a game where chance reigns.
>
> (Montmort, in Crombie 1994, pp. 1369–1370)

Bernoulli's *Ars Conjectandi* (1713) saw the articulation of an even stricter belief in efficient causes in a treatise whose principles would later be developed by Poisson as the 'law of large numbers'; a means for deriving certainty from repetition: 'If all events through all eternity could be repeated . . . we could go from probability to certainty . . . and we would be forced to assume amongst the most apparently fortuitous things a certain necessity or, so to say, FATE' (Bernoulli, in David 1969, p. 137).

The result of these early, deterministic studies was the swift removal of chance from the real world and its location firmly within the human mind. In the Age of Reason, everything had a cause, whether material or trans-cendental, and so chance had no place in the world. It was an irrational aberration which could be banished by the application of reason and the advance of knowledge. Chance thus had no real *being*, and existed only in an epistemological sense as a deficit, a lack of knowledge. The presence of 'so-called' chance was significant only insofar as it was a misunderstood sign of metaphysical meaning. Diligent observation of random phenomena would reveal its illusory nature, for in collections of disparate events, the classical probabilists saw patterns indicative of order and purpose. In his *Essay on Man*, Pope expressed the widespread acceptance of the belief in universal order during this time:

All Nature is but Art, unknown to thee;
All Chance, Direction which thou canst not see;
All Discord, Harmony not understood.
                    (Pope 1963, p. 50)

The ability to perceive such regularity in randomness was a recent development. Until the seventeenth century each event had been seen as an exceptional case; a perspective which had frustrated early attempts at probabilistic reasoning. Now the perception of patterns, aggregates and similar cases meant that writers like Pascal and de Moivre could compare events, and with the assimilation of such comparisons, grow to expect certain outcomes in certain situations. This intellectual development, new to the seventeenth century, would gradually gather momentum, reaching its apogee in the nineteenth-century's obsession with averages and regularities: the discipline of statistics.

Chance in Britain

In Britain, the approach to chance via mathematical quantification was taken from a different angle to that of the puzzles of *aleatory* games which so fascinated the rest of Europe. David declares that the English made no significant contribution to probability theory largely because a utilitarian view of mathematics and a lack of interest from Newton resulted in an orientation which saw little profit in discussing the falls of dice (David 1969, p. 125). However, Britons were not unaware of chance and their efforts to tabulate it took them in another direction, out of which the discipline of statistics emerged. At the same time that thinkers in Europe were finding order and regularity in games of chance, British writers such as Graunt, Petty and de Witt were discovering it in the more mundane realm of births, marriages and deaths. In his *Natural and Political Observations on the Bills of Mortality* (1662), John Graunt catalogued deaths, christenings, diseases and population counts of individual county boroughs, and through them discovered patterns and regularities within large groups of individuals. In this way, he introduced the first demographic study of Britain, and developed an early form of the discipline of statistics (Hacking 1975, pp. 106–107). The calculative outlook of Graunt, like that of the early probabilists, was rooted in commercial experience, for Graunt himself was described as a 'city tradesman' who became an 'opulent merchant' (Greenwood 1970, pp. 48–49). Despite their very different subject matter, the conclusions drawn from study on either side of the Channel supported that overriding seventeenth-century theme of order and coherence in the universe, evident in the ultimately meaningful nature of irregularity.

   This British development of statistics is important (and largely underrated) for its role as the direct precursor of the subject of probability theory after the dramatic 'epistemological shift' of the nineteenth century. As we shall see, this shift changed the subject and direction of probability theory and consequently revolutionised the understanding of chance.

Caveat: the paradox of probability

The development of probability has been described as 'the most important mutation in human thought since Aristotle' (Kavanagh 1993, p. 21), and was a crucial component in the creation of the Enlightenment's image of rational man, for by providing the conceptual framework for the measurement and evaluation of alternatives, it facilitated the ultimate rationality of action. It was part of the wider development of modernity: at the vanguard of an optimistic, modernising movement which saw the emergence of the bourgeoisie and their gradual ascendance over a declining feudal nobility, as well as the emergence of the individual increasingly freed from tradition and hierarchy (Kavanagh 1993, pp. 21–22).

However, although probability is described as the victorious 'tamer' of chance (Hacking 1990), in a sense it represents a hollow victory, for as Kavanagh points out, it did not tackle the *pure* form of chance but instead redefined the parameters of the debate into a form which could be made sense of by science.

Probability dealt with chance by abstracting reality to such an extent that it was no longer relevant to any specific moment or situation. In the law of large numbers it could safely make pronouncements as to what *should* happen in the long term, but never what *would* happen next. It could never tell us whether the result of tossing a coin would be heads or tails, or whether a roulette ball would land on black or red, but, as the number of tosses and spins were increased towards infinity, the law of large numbers would spring into action and predict that the outcome over the long run would be spread evenly – 50:50. In this way, probability could make general predictions about the long term, but had nothing at all to say about what was most crucial: the specific instance. As to what would actually happen next, it remained 'forever mute' (Kavanagh 1993, p. 15).

Probability theory dared not venture outside the large number and the extended period of time. The specific could only be considered at all as an *average*, as an instance of a more valid, generalised whole, a limitation which meant that probability 'tamed' chance only insofar as it excluded it from its models. As an abstraction, probability had internal logic and predictive power, but applied to the real world, it frustrated the real person with its inability to speak of *this* event at *this* moment (Kavanagh 1993, p. 17). These limitations were most evident in the field of the *aleatory* and in the figure of the gambler, the individual to whom the particular event, the specific moment, mattered most. Probability theory replaced the individual with the average, the unique with the general and the present with the long term. In this way it transformed chance into predictability, but only by changing its subject to such an extent that it was rendered unrecognisable to the gambler. The implications of this shortcoming will be further examined in the discussion of gambling beliefs in Chapter 5.

THE AGE OF CHANCE: CHANCE AND MODERNITY

In the nineteenth century, an 'epistemological shift' no less momentous than the birth of probability two centuries earlier radically altered human understanding of chance and resulted in the erosion of determinism. This process began with the 'mutation' of probability into the discipline of statistics.

The birth of the average

In the early part of the nineteenth century, the intellectual and social hegemony that had made the classical interpretation of probability possible dissolved. Contemporary observers watched the breakdown of a sense of cosmic order and social 'wholeness' and the replacement of stability and meaning with what was to become the distinctive feature of the modern age, what de Jong calls the state of 'ontological insecurity' (de Jong 1975, p. 14).

As a nineteenth-century philosopher poised on the brink of the twentieth, Nietzsche expressed this ontological insecurity in his celebration of a world devoid of God and meaning. His assault on rationalism was articulated by Zarathustra, who described the 'celestial cheerfulness that came over all things when I told them that no eternal will acts over them and through them' (Nietzsche 1969, p. 186). Nietzsche provided perhaps the most radical articulation of the nineteenth-century disaffection with rationality: 'In the great whirlpool of forces man stands with the conceit that this whirlpool is rational and has a rational aim; an error! The only rational thing we know is what little reason man has therefore' (Nietzsche 1968, p. 50).

With the end of the Age of Reason, the rational subject of probability theory vanished, changing its focus from *l'homme eclaire* to *l'homme moyen* — rational man to average man. Probabilists turned their attention from 'the rationality of the few to the irrationality of the many' (Gigerenzer *et al.* 1989, p. 36). The object of their analysis was mean values; its most important field of application, statistics.

For Hacking, the nineteenth century was characterised by an 'avalanche of numbers', which 'poured into' it in ever more diverse areas. This was an expression of industrial nation states' desire to classify, count and tabulate their subjects, and within it, the realm of statistics became ever more ambitious – from births and deaths it moved on to count diseases, suicides and deviance, and so formulate statistical laws of human behaviour (Hacking 1990, p. 2). These applications brought new objects of study into being, established new claims to authority and new standards of rationality. Gigerenzer *et al.* point out that it was 'part of the Pythagorean creed' to believe that with numbers came certainty, and so in the nineteenth century, the enumeration and tabulation of the world, while creating a space for chance, also tamed it by anchoring it to statistical laws (Gigerenzer *et al.* 1989, p. 270).

In 1835, Poisson proved an important limiting theorem – the law of large numbers – a mathematical demonstration that the indefinite repetition of events led to stable, mean values. It proved that the constant repetition of an event (such as the throw of a dice), while liable to fluctuation in the short term, tended to even out into patterns and regularity over the long term. Applied to the social world, the law explained how there could be statistical stability in social affairs: if individuals appeared to be too variable and inconstant to pin down, the law of large numbers advised they look to the aggregate instead – to society – 'for chance disappeared in large numbers' (Gigerenzer *et al.* 1989, p. 38).

For Kavanagh, the shifting orientation of probability theory into statistics created a new consciousness of the self, away from the Enlightenment ideal of a 'single rational consciousness confronting and mastering the uncertainties of the present' to a measuring of the self 'against a potentially infinite series of averages and means' (Kavanagh 1993, p. 23). The growth of concepts such as 'normal' and 'average' created an individual in no way privileged above any other whose self-knowledge came from comparison and valuation against others. Thus was *l'homme moyen*: average man, mass man, born.

The mutation of determinism

The regularities of statistics supported a strict brand of determinism at least for a time, providing evidence that history is subject to deterministic causality. They proved that the regular, lawlike course of social affairs is interrupted neither by the intervention of God nor by inexplicable individual acts of human free will. For Quetelet, statistics was the ultimate explanatory device. Its laws showed 'that order was universal, that irrationality had its reasons, that even crime was subject to law' (Gigerenzer *et al.* 1989, p. 41). A Laplacian-style determinism could prevail (and even find support) in this age of statistical reasoning and could continue to explain away unpredictability and chance in terms of relevant conditions. However, despite the apparent continuity of this influential idea, an important change had dramatically altered the meaning and implications of determinism. The theme of the classical probabilists was order and regularity – but it was a *meaningful* order and regularity; an expression of the will and intention of some higher being, usually God. But a 'profound mutation' (Kavanagh 1993) occurred in the course of the eighteenth and nineteenth centuries. What had been a great, divine Newtonian prime mover was now referred to as a more modest 'primitive cause' (Laplace 1830, p. 327). For Laplace and a plethora of statisticians, economists and criminologists, determinism no longer implied the existence of any kind of providential order or meaning.[6]

The most important facet of the nineteenth-century epistemological shift was this evacuation of meaning from determinism and the consequent development of the 'ontological insecurity' of the age. Once God's presence had retreated, and determinism was secularised, a hiatus appeared in which chance as a meaningful entity could flourish. For the first time, an opportunity existed for chance to appear, not as a figment of our ignorance which nevertheless signified higher meaning, but as a neutral phenomenon in its own right.

As a consequence of its loss of religious meaning, the parameters of determinism opened up to encompass contributions from all avenues of knowledge to such an extent that the notion of indeterminism itself was considered. The possibility that phenomena might not be subject to universal laws would lead to the most decisive conceptual event of twentieth-century physics – the discovery that the world was not deterministic. Precipitating this great event, the nineteenth-century debate around indeterminism, to use Hacking's phrase, 'cleared a space for chance' (Hacking 1990, p. 1).

Chance as explanation

Gigerenzer et al. describe the 'remarkable shift of perspective' that occurred when James Clerk Maxwell identified statistics with imperfect knowledge (Gigerenzer et al. 1989, p. 62). Until this time, it had always been associated with certainty: however, when Maxwell argued that most of our knowledge of the world was statistical, what he meant was that it was incomplete and liable to fluctuation and uncertainty.

Perhaps the most famous explication of the new status afforded to chance in the nineteenth century came from Darwin. In his mechanical account of the forms and patterns of nature, Darwin evoked chance to explain the origin of variation. In opposition to the then dominant 'use and disuse' theory propounded by Lamarck, Darwin stated that biological variation was a matter of chance, not adaptive necessity; of 'the natural selection of numerous, successive, slight, favourable variations . . . which seem to us in our ignorance to arise spontaneously' (Darwin 1888, vol. 2, p. 293). It was thus a matter of chance that an organism was born with a variation that promoted survival, although the evolutionary fate of that variation depended on whether it served survival needs; on what he called natural selection. In this way he argued that evolution progressed by a steady process of natural selection, with an organism constantly adapting to its environmnent. Their extremely complex nature, however, meant that the causes and nature of these adaptations 'we are forced generally to call mere chance' (Darwin 1857, p. 215). Such a radical utilisation of chance was not immediately accepted, and Darwin's formulations were widely criticised, especially by the scientist and philosopher John Hershal who decried notions like accidental variability as the 'law of higgeldy piggeldy' (in Gigerenzer *et al.* 1989, p. 152).

Darwin's fundamental insight made possible the notion of random mutation as a vital stochastic force, which is today widely accepted by evolutionary biologists such as Jacques Monod and Richard Dawkins. For Monod, the two properties characteristic of all living beings are invariance and teleonomy; in other words, chance and necessity (Monod 1971). The genetic transmission of information in the process of evolution is characterised by the reproduction of randomness; thus the principle behind the process of evolution itself is based on chance: 'chance *alone* is at the source of every innovation and all creation in the biosphere', and yet formed of necessity: 'Drawn from the realm of pure chance, the accident enters into that of necessity, of the most implacable certainties' (Monod 1971, p. 114). In biology, then, the world was no longer governed by a benevolent creator but by a blind watchmaker.

The philosopher and scientist C.S. Peirce anticipated the role which chance would come to play in the next hundred years and in this, Hacking sees not a man ahead of his time, but a man peculiarly *of* his time. Peirce's thought was the incarnation of indeterminism, for he believed in a universe of absolute and irreducible chance. In experimentation, he deliberately utilised chance to introduce a new level of control – a control that worked not by eliminating chance fluctuations but by adding more! For Hacking, Peirce's denial of the doctrine of necessity was 'oddly inevitable': '*He opened his eyes and chance poured in*' (Hacking 1990, p. 201). In this respect, although he was a scientist of the nineteenth century, Peirce was already living in a twentieth-century environment, in a world full of probabilities.

Here then is the scientific counterpart to Nietzsche who was already declaring the role of chance in the world through Zarathustra: 'I have found this happy certainty in all things: that they prefer to *dance* on the feet of chance' (Nietzsche 1969, p. 186). With this in mind, the only response available to the individual was the possibility of self-overcoming in the will to power. The chaos of life could be transmuted by an *overcoming* of life, and the way to do this was to 'live dangerously' – in effect, to plunge into chance. As demanded by Zarathustra: 'Live dangerously! Build your cities on the slopes of Vesuvius!' (Nietzsche 1969, p. 18).

The edge of chaos

By the twentieth century, the Age of Chance had arrived. The erosion of determinism over the previous hundred years meant that chance could emerge as an explanatory force in its own right. It was now *in*determinism that was the guiding principle of intellectual thought, and was especially evident in the field of physics.

The mechanistic Newtonian model of the world was fundamentally a model of *certainty*. Its basic categories of space, time and solid matter existed as properties with fixed identities which acted in definite, predictable ways. In principle, and given a certain amount of information, causal laws could predict any number of these properties. However, as quantum physics overtook the classical model, the inherent uncertainty of quantum reality replaced the familiar fixedness of the mechanistic world. The monumental discoveries of scientists such as Max Planck, Niels Bohr, Werner Heisenberg, Albert Einstein and Erwin Schrödinger at the beginning of the century meant that probability in physics became 'irreducible and uneliminable in principle, [and] so classical determinism was finally overthrown' (Gigerenzer *et al.* 1989, p. 175).

It was Planck who first coined the term 'quantum' by showing that energy is radiated in tiny, discrete quantum units rather than smoothly and continuously as classical physics had thought. A few years later Bohr demonstrated that electrons jump from one energy state to another in discontinuous 'quantum leaps'. These jumps were unpredictable and indeterminate; there were no causes or explanations for why an electron moved at a certain time in a certain way; it simply 'happened'.

Traditional notions of properties, measurements and the identity of things were blown apart by discoveries like 'contextualism', whereby quantum reality shifts its nature according to its surroundings. Zohar and Marshall liken the activity of electrons or protons to homonyms – words that look the same but have different senses depending on context. The actions of elementary particles also change, and are in 'constant creative dialogue' with the environment (Zohar and Marshall 1993, p. 21). The idea that light can be both a wave *and* a particle at the same time is one of the most revolutionary concepts of quantum physics. Far from the notion, in classical physics, that light must be permanently identified with one or the other, in the new physics, both properties complement each other and are necessary for a description of what light actually *is*. The fact that such duality cannot be measured was set out in 1927 in Heisenberg's Uncertainty Principle, a theorem which destroyed the bastion of classical physics by proving the impossibility of ascribing precise values to both position and momentum simultaneously. Measuring the position of, for example, light as a particle gives an indistinct reading of its momentum, while measuring its momentum as a wave gives a similarly indistinct reading of its position. Such measurements, Heisenberg showed, could only ever be *probable* (Gigerenzer *et al.* 1989, pp. 199–202).

The concrete either/or way of thinking in the classical mould was replaced by quantum physics' more fluid both/and dichotomy (Zohar and Marshall 1993, p. 20), an orientation demonstrated by Schrödinger's famous quantum cat. In this example, a cat is hidden in a box which also contains a device that will randomly feed it either poison or normal food. Using mechanistic logic we would expect the cat *either* to be dead (if fed poison) *or* alive (if not). But in quantum reality, so long as it is not observed the cat exists in superimposition – alive *and* dead at the same time. It is only when we open the box to see it that the cat's state must collapse into certainty.

Probabilistic thinking also influenced theories of atomic movement, with the discovery of Brownian motion in 1827 providing the earliest evidence for the random motion of molecules. Not only was atomic motion not guided by divine purpose, but as 'a movement totally devoid of memory' (Ekeland 1993, p. 160), it was not compelled by any form of purposefulness whatsoever, and so existed as an example of pure, secular indeterminism in action.

Within this framework, Einstein appears as a scientist of the classical mould, contributing reluctantly to the probabilistic revolution. The probabilistic implications of his work on radioactivity and non-locality posed problems for the Theory of Relativity, and he uneasily referred to chance in inverted commas, while arguing against non-locality as 'ghostly' and 'absurd' (Zohar and Marshall 1993, p. 35). His famous aphorism 'God does not play dice' is evocative of a Newtonian God winding up a clockwork universe; an image already anachronistically out of place in the stochastic world of the twentieth century.

By mid-century, further evidence of the non-continuous nature of reality was emerging in the form of chaos theory. The discovery that a modification of the initial conditions of a system could multiply at an exponential rate, resulting in a state out of all proportion to the magnitude of the starting condition, was labelled 'chaotic behaviour', and signalled a move towards the construction of non-linear systems (Waldrop 1992, p. 66). Because tiny perturbations could escalate until a system's future became utterly chaotic, prediction of that future would have to take such a vast amount of information into account that the calculation, in practice, would be impossible. The famous example of such unpredictability is of a butterfly flapping its wings and generating a change in starting conditions which, by the end of the year, have multiplied exponentially to trigger a hurricane in another part of the world. The game of roulette is a similar instance of how tiny changes of initial conditions, such as the angle of the ball or the speed of the wheel, can influence the final trajectory of a ball (Waldrop 1992, p. 287).

After their discovery in physical, chemical structures, chaotic systems were found to be inherent in larger structures, including economic and ecological systems, and are now widely applied to phenomena as diverse as stockmarket fluctuations and weather reports.

In the midst of all this complexity, we find the appearance of a fundamental – albeit incredibly complex – order. The laws of entropy and attraction provide stability, and lead to spectacular geometric constructions, such as the fractals sketched by the mathematician Beniot Mandelbrot. Predicting the outcomes of these processes can defeat even the most sophisticated computers but, as Zohar and Marshall point out, this is because they are limited, not because the processes themselves are truly indeterminate. Unlike quantum reality, where indeterminacy is an inherent feature of the world, chaotic systems are simply incredibly complex (Zohar and Marshall 1993, p. 25).[7]

The complexity of the order behind chaos theory, and the indeterminacy inherent in quantum theories of reality, means that traditional causation and linear systems are not applicable to modern physics. The unpredictability of phenomena (whether through complexity or inherent indeterminacy), far from being shortcomings of theoretical models, are now features of these models themselves. As a scientist at the vanguard of the formation of complexity theory describes it: 'the world has to adapt itself to a condition of perpetual novelty, at the edge of chaos' (in Waldrop 1992, p. 356).

The implications of all these intellectual discoveries were vast. With the removal of metaphysical meaning from the world, phenomena were no longer explained with reference to higher meaning, but by the chaotic movements of atoms in empty space. Now that there could be no recourse to certainty, only degrees of likelihood, the foundations of certain knowledge itself were shattered. In this way an era of ontological insecurity was ushered in, expressed by Willian James' comment on the meaningless of human existence, which he described as the 'aimless weather of the cosmic atoms' (James 1982, p. 491).

The irreducible indeterminism of the world is a fundamental tenet not only of modern physics but also of modern *thought*. It is a feature which has even come to be reflected in culture, in the atonal and random noise symphonies of composers like Arnold Schönberg and John Cage, and the apparently haphazard lines, or 'aleatory art', of modern painters like Jackson Pollock and Wassily Kandinsky.

By the start of the twenty-first century chance had emerged as an explanatory force in its own right. As an irreducible feature of the world, it is utilised in scientific understanding as well as cultural expression. In this transition from *epistemological* to *ontological* status, Chance has finally claimed the modern Age as its own.

Risk

As part of the erosion of determinism, the notion of risk has come to occupy a central position in the explanation of the social world. As distinct from its original seventeenth-century meaning of hazard or danger, and especially exposure to commercial danger, our modern usage of risk has come to express the probabilistic nature of reality. In the twenty-first century, the calculation of risk is an articulation of our probabilistic *Lebensgefühl*, and provides 'a theoretical base for decision-making' (Douglas 1992, p. 23). This concept is distinct from – albeit connected to – that of chance. Whereas the latter exists as a building block of the world, and a testimony to genuine stochasticity in life, the former is an expression of the calculation of possible outcomes based on the knowledge of the effect of chance on the world. While chance is neutral in this respect, risk retains its seventeenth-century connotations of danger and generally implies the possibility of loss. Furthermore, it is a loss that can be estimated. Risk, then, deals with knowledge. It represents an acknowledgement of the irreducible existence of chance in the world, and the formation of a new kind of enquiry based on this fact. This is an order of knowledge that does not aspire to absolute certainty, but one that deals instead with degrees of certainty; hence Knight's description of risk as 'determinate uncertainty' (Knight 1921, p. 46).

In the concept of risk then, we find a modern, probabilistic type of knowledge, whose main applications in the social sciences have been in the field from which it originally emerged – economics – and, more recently, in the sociological analysis of late modernity.

In the work of writers such as von Neumann and Morgenstern (1953), Knight (1921) and von Mises (1949), the role of risk as well as that of uncertainty and unpredictability is central to modern economic systems. Contrary to the classical economists' depiction of economic man as an individual acting rationally from perfect knowledge of certain conditions, in these systems, actors make decisions based on only *partial* knowledge. The uncertainty engendered by such ignorance is endemic in economic life, and: 'Once we admit the presence of ignorance in an economic world, we leave the comfortable confines of certainty and find ourselves in the wilderness of risk, or the swamp of uncertainty' (Tsukahara and Brumm 1976, p. 92).

That this uncertainty was a reflection of genuine stochasticity in the world had been recognised earlier when, at the end of the nineteenth century, the mathematician J. Bachelier proposed a model based on Brownian motion to explain the fluctuations of the stock exchange. His model did not rise to prominence until 1973, however, when Fischer Black and Myron Scholes demonstrated a 'formula' for the stockmarket based on stochastic calculus – 'the modern outgrowth of Brownian motion' (Ekeland 1993, p. 162). A similar application of mathematics to economic uncertainty later formed the subject of von Neumann and Morgenstern's seminal *Theory of Games and Economic Behaviour* (1953). Their insight was that, since in situations where an individual's course of action depends on what their colleagues or competitors are likely to do, absolute certainty concerning the future is impossible. Thus, since risk cannot be eliminated, the option with the highest probability of success is simply risk *minimisation*. The possible courses of action that arise from this resolution have since formed the basis of rational risk-minimising action in uncertainty.

The unpredictable and hence risky nature of action implied by such stochastic systems was regarded by some modern economists as a vital precondition for any kind of action at all. Thus for von Mises: 'If man knew the future, he wouldn't have to choose and would not act. He would be like an automaton, reacting to stimulus without any will of his own' (von Mises 1949, p. 105). This kind of view finds even more radical support in writers like Knight for whom the system of free enterprise itself arises as a reaction to risk, and for whom, according to some authors, consciousness itself would disappear in the absence of uncertainty (Arrow 1970, p. 1). Risk for Knight is objective, measurable uncertainty (as distinct from uncertainty *per se*, which is not measurable), and is *always* present in economic action, because ultimately the latter can only ever be guided by opinion: 'neither entire ignorance, nor complete and perfect information, but partial knowledge' (Knight 1921, p. 199). In Knight, we see a strand of radical doubt which is beginning to question just how much we can ever understand the world – and not just the economic world. According to Knight himself, this is not a questioning of the validity of logical processes, but a more profound query 'as to how far the world is intelligible at all' (Knight 1921, p. 209). 'Are we then to assume real indetermindness in the cosmos itself?' he asks uneasily, and, two pages of prevarication later, he is forced to answer in the affirmative (Knight 1921, pp. 220 and 222).

Elsewhere in the social sciences we find a number of authors attempting to construct a theory of risk as a paradigm for modern society.[8] According to Giddens, 'secular risk culture' is synonymous with modernity, since 'To live in the universe of high modernity is to live in an environment of chance and risk' (Giddens 1991, p. 109). This is not to say that pre-modern societies did not encounter risks, but only that our *perception* of them as such is distinctive; for today 'thinking in terms of risk and risk-assessment is a more or less ever-present exercise' (Giddens 1991, p. 124). In addition, and unlike in pre-industrial society, through the institutions of economic markets, labour power and investments, modern society can be said to be constituted by risks, rather than risk being incidental to them (Giddens 1991, pp. 117–118). Ulrich Beck regards risk as a definitive feature of modern life; the culmination of a lengthy historical process in which 'reflexive modernisation' has displaced industrial society and brought about the 'risk society' (Beck 1992).

Characteristic of this society is the increasing prevalence of the state of 'ontological insecurity' first experienced in the nineteenth century as the breakdown of a sense of order, of wholeness and meaning. By the early twenty-first century, such insecurity has grown into a 'radical doubt' about all forms of critical reason (Giddens 1991, p. 3). Symptomatic of this situation are works of postmodern depression by writers like Francis Fukuyama, who claims that since there is nothing left to know there will be no more progress, and we have thus reached the 'end of history' (Fukuyama 1992). The risk society, then, oversees the breakdown of certainty and the erosion of metaphysical meaning, for in the Age of Chance the pursuit of knowledge takes the form of the calculation of risks. As the universe of possibilities opens up, cultural pluralism overtakes cultural hegemony and certain knowledge fragments and dissolves into myriad subjective viewpoints. In a probabilistic world of risk, the idea of objective truth becomes anachronistic and every claim to 'knowledge' must be fought for. As Douglas puts it, 'Knowledge has to be defended at every point; the open society guarantees nothing' (Douglas 1992, p. 32). With the erosion of certainty in knowledge comes the perennial insecurity of modern life, described by Beck in tones redolent of Durkheimian anomie:

> People are set free from the certainties and modes of living of the industrial epoch. . . . The shocks unleashed by this constitute the other side of the risk society. The system of co-ordinates in which life and thinking are fastened in industrial modernity – the axes of gender, family and occupation, the belief in science and progress – begins to shake and a new twilight of opportunities and hazards comes into existence – the contours of the risk society.
>
> (Beck 1992, p. 15)

In this apocalyptic scenario, we are, he says, living 'on the volcano of civilisation'. With the co-ordinates of social meaning torn asunder, it is clear for Luhmann that 'there is no risk free behaviour. . . . There is no absolute safety or security' (Luhmann 1993, p. 28). Moreover, we must abandon the hope that greater knowledge will lead to greater security. Contrary to the optimistic Enlightenment belief that perfect knowledge would reveal the Divine and absolute order of the world, now quite the opposite is true – the more we know, the *less* certain we become. For the classical probabilists, the pursuit of knowledge was synonymous with the pursuit of certainty; the risk theorists of the modern age, however, have *uncertainty* as their subject.

For all these authors, the creation of risk is inherent in the capitalist system of production, and (with the exception perhaps of Giddens) the assumption that it has overtaken class as the dynamic of that system is implicit in their work. In fact, an actual antipathy to the notion of class is evident from their endless discussion of eco-politics and corresponding lack of debate about the kinds of politics that effect the differential distribution of risks in a stratified society. The kinds of risks the authors insist could affect *everyone* – nuclear holocaust, environmental disaster – have so far affected relatively few. Beck writes that 'In advanced modernity, the social production of wealth is systematically accompanied by the social production of *risks*' (Beck 1992, p. 19). Although he admits that risks adhere inversely to class, with wealth accumulating at the top and risks at the bottom of the social hierarchy, he insists that the 'globalisation of risks' affects everyone equally (Beck 1992, p. 35). Thus, unlike class positions, risk positions are universal and unspecific: 'In class positions, being determines consciousness, while in risk positions, conversely, consciousness (knowledge) determines being' (Beck 1992, p. 53). Luhmann makes a stronger statement of this view when he declares that technological and ecological risks have become the new object of sociology now that old 'prejudices' (presumably Marxism) are no longer of interest in our brave new postmodern world: 'Following the ebb of anticapitalist prejudice, it [sociology] now finds a new opportunity to fill its old role with new content, namely to warn society' (Luhmann 1993, p. 5). At the vanguard of this new sociology, Luhmann is in the interesting position of believing that 'in the real world there is no such thing as chance' (Luhmann 1993, p. 182). He should know better, for as well as the mass of evidence to the contrary, his own analysis of risk is based on the premise that chance exists as an irreducible part of the world.

However, despite their shortcomings, these works *are* in fact representative of the risk society: not because their imagined paradigm of postmodernity, in which risk has overtaken class as a dynamic of social action, bears any relation to reality, but because *it is now possible to conceive of such a model*. In this sense, they are more symptomatic of the risk society than they are its impartial observers. As Giddens has pointed out, it is not the case that risk is now paramount in social life: what is important is that the *perception* of these risks is now paramount. This perception should be seen as the product, not of a society that has suddenly become full of risks, but of a long historical process that gave ontological status to chance, and to us a probabilistic *Lebensgefühl*.

2

THE PURSUIT OF CHANCE

GAMBLING AND DIVINATION

Now that we have traced the intellectual development of the notion of chance, we can turn to its practical application in various gambling games. In doing this, it will be seen that various parallels and interconnections exist between the social forces that shaped the development of the concept of chance and its codification in probability theory, and those that shaped the development of gambling games themselves. It will be argued that the conflation of chance and determinism reviewed in Chapter 1 is matched by a corresponding conflation of early games of chance and divination. Their gradual historical separation (though never entirely completed) can be regarded as a process propelled by the same dynamic as that which saw the separation of chance from notions of divine providence and fate. It will also be argued that the various games and the people who played them are culturally specific and highly stratified along class lines. Chapter 3 will show that these configurations are continued in the gambling scene of today.

Sacred play

Most of our modern, commercial gambling games derive from the manipulation of cards or dice, both of which have their origin in the ancient casting of lots. In this they were inseparable from the practice of divination and the associated magical-religious beliefs about chance reviewed in Chapter 1. As we have seen, within these activities the boundary we generally expect to find separating 'secular' games from religious ritual simply did not exist. At these points in the social fabric the categories of sacred and profane blurred and ran into one another.[1] It was Plato who first pointed to this conjunction of play and ritual, suggesting the sacred nature of the former, when he said, 'man is made God's plaything, and that is the best part of him' (Plato 1934, p. 182). In this Platonic tradition, Huizinga identified the 'essential and original identity' of play and ritual, exemplified by games which frequently shared the same implements, the same formal structure and the same ceremonial preparation by the individuals involved:[2]

Just as there is no formal difference between play and ritual, so the consecrated spot cannot be formally distinguished from the play ground. The arena, the card table, the magic circle, the temple, the stage, the screen, the tennis court, the court of justice etc., are all in form and function play grounds; i.e. forbidden spots, isolated, hedged round, hallowed, within which special rules obtain. All are temporary worlds within the ordinary world, dedicated to the performance of an act apart.

(Huizinga 1949, p. 10)

This performance was usually dedicated to attempting to foretell the future, but the inclusion of a wager in gambling games shifted the emphasis in the latter, by giving the propitiate a voice and so a more active part in the proceedings. In a sense the wager was a kind of pact with fate or destiny: a token of the individual's involvement in the ritual, through which their opinions on the proceedings could be demonstrated. With the individual included in the ritual, the nature of the ceremony itself was changed from a straightforward case of divination to a more interactive activity. It was still a sacred encounter, but one in which the individual no longer passively awaited divine pronouncement, instead challenging destiny to reveal its intentions. Like the stake in modern games of chance, the wager in ritual brought together the propitiate and the propitiated. In the words of Baudrillard: 'The stake is a summons, the game a duel: chance is summoned to respond, obliged by the player's wager to declare itself either favourable or hostile.' In this way 'Chance is never neutral, the game transforms it into a player and agonistic figure' (Baudrillard 1990, p. 143).

Instances of the conjunction of sacred ritual with gambling games occur frequently in historical and anthropological literature, and can be found in each of the three main types of gambling activity: playing with dice, with cards, and in the casting of lots.

Dice

Dice are the oldest gaming instruments of human civilisation, occurring more or less ubiquitously throughout history in the ancient, 'primitive' and classical worlds. Archaeological excavations from prehistoric graves in North and South America, Africa and the Orient have uncovered primitive, four-sided gaming sticks from 6000 BC, while similar finds in the Egyptian tomb of Osiris date from 2000 BC (Sifakis 1990). These early civilisations gambled with dice made of many materials – plum and peach stones, pebbles and the knucklebones of cows and sheep, known as *astragali*. These *astragali* would come to rest when rolled and were used in this manner in both games of chance (where today dice still retain the slang term 'bones') and early divination ritual, especially in the casting of lots.

Some of the earliest dice games involved the tossing of bones or marked stones, with winning combinations deduced from the way they landed. In more complex games, like the Egyptian *tab* and the ancient Indian *chaturanga* (later chess), the throw of a die controlled the movement of counters on a marked playing surface, as in the backgammon of today (Scarne 1974, p. 37). Similarly, the dramatic Aztec games of *totoloque* and *patolli* used marked boards and counters, upon which golden dice were tossed in high stakes gambling games (von Hagen 1962, p. 64). In India, dice known as *coupon* were used as a means of divination in the practice of Ramala at the same time as they were used for gambling. The latter was recorded in the Indian epic, *The Mahabharata*, where Sakuni challenged Yudhisthiva to a contest, saying: 'the dice are my bows and arrows, the heart of the dice my string, the dicing rug my chariot!' The sacred significance of the game was apparent in Duryodhama's assertion that 'if we gamble, the heavenly gate will be nearer', and in the divine hall which was specially erected to contain the contest (*The Mahabharata* 1975, pp. 122, 123).

The Greeks and Romans frequently used *astragali* and *tesserae* (six-sided dice made of ivory, porcelain or marble) in both games and rituals. The Greek custom of *astragalomancy* utilised the *astralagus* for fortune-telling as well as for gambling, while the Romans used the same implements for casting lots, lottery draws and gaming alike. Inveterate gamblers, they enjoyed the quick results of dice games and chariot races which they saw as a demonstration of character. The reckless gambling of the Roman Empire was highlighted at the race-track, where the main attraction was the possibility of making rash bets – *audax sponsio* – on the spur of the moment, instead of those based on a sensible observation of the Racing Calendar. The Romans called their bets *pignus*, and regarded them as a mark of character (Harris 1972, p. 224). According to Steinmetz, Augustus 'gambled to excess', Claudius 'played like an imbecile' and Nero 'like a madman' (Steinmetz 1870, pp. 64, 65). Suetonius' remark that 'Claudius's reputation for stupidity was further enhanced by stories of his drunkenness and love of gambling' (Suetonius 1958, p. 185) is evidence of the low esteem with which gambling was officially held in the Roman Empire. Despite this, and despite the prohibition of the activity during the Saturnalia, the culture of the classical and pre-classical worlds was imbued with images of dicing. Excavations have revealed that makeshift gambling tables were frequently etched on porticos and basilicas, for any flat surface was regarded as a potential place to play and the appropriate markings quickly made. These tables would be used for simple throwing and guessing games such as 'odds and evens', as well as games like 'tabula' which were played for stakes of thousands of *sestertii* by moving counters and throwing dice. This favourite game of the later Roman Empire subsequently developed and spread westwards as backgammon (Sifakis 1990, p. 15). Its popularity was undisputed, and it is believed to have been played for Christ's garments at his execution: 'When the soldiers had crucified Jesus they took his garments . . . and said . . . "let us not tear it, but cast lots to see whose it shall be"' (John 19:23–24). In this three-dice game, all players lose their wagers if the player throwing the dice scores less than ten; more than ten and they win. Such a betting system bears some resemblance to the game of 'hazard', which was widespread throughout Europe from the Middle Ages, and by the nineteenth century had developed into the modern casino game of craps.

It is in Seneca that we find the most vivid portrayal of the Roman fascination with dicing, as well as its perceived link with the Divine. In *The Apocolocyntosis*, the gods' punishment for the dice-playing emperor Claudius was to force him to throw dice from a bottomless cup forever. In the description of such an exquisite torture, we see a reluctant admiration of so ingenious a punishment, symptomatic of a wider ambivalence towards dicing and its continued correspondence with divination in the classical world:

> When from the rattling cup he seeks to throw
> The die they trickle through the hole below
> And when he tries the recovered bones to roll –
> A gambler fooled by the eternal goal –
> Again they fool him; through his finger tips
> Each time each cunning die as cruelly slips
> A Sisphus' rocks, before they reach the crest
> Slip from his neck and roll back to their rest.
>   (Seneca 1986, pp. 232–233)

Although blood sports such as bear bating and cock-fighting involved heavy betting, from the advent of the Saxons, Danes and Romans in Europe, dice playing was the standard gambling game of the entire medieval period. It was widespread throughout society, and, although condemned by the Church, particularly popular among the clergy, as comments by clerics such as John of Salisbury (1100–1182) on 'the damnable art of dice-playing' among his colleagues testify (in Ashton 1898, p. 13).

Simple guessing games with dice were popular, as were variations on a 'hunt' game played with counters on a square or cross-shaped grid (Strayer 1982, p. 350). Representative of the agrarian society in which it was played, the game, known as *gwyddewyl* in Wales and *alquerque* in Spain, portrayed a kind of farmland battle. The aim was for the fifteen pieces – the geese – to corner the single piece – the fox – of the opponent, without the fox taking the geese, by jumping over them. A variation of the theme was known to the Vikings by the name of *hneftaff*, while a similar game combining dice throws and placing of men – like the 'tables' played by the Romans – was called *taefal* – a 'kind of backgammon' (Traill 1893, p. 313). The game of hazard (the forerunner of modern casino craps) was perhaps the most engrossing medieval dice game, especially favoured among soldiers. It involved a player throwing two dice, and the others betting on whether or not s/he would achieve certain numbers with them.

Dicing played an important role in the everyday life of the Middle Ages and was assiduously pursued by all classes of society. However, not everyone had the capital of players like Yudhisthiva in *The Mahabharata*, who staked a hundred thousand gold pieces, a thousand elephants, his slaves, his army and all his wealth in a single game. Finally he staked the liberty of his brothers, his wife and even himself (*The Mahabharata* 1975, pp. 128–137): a practice which, while unusual among the wealthy, was not uncommon among the poorer classes of society in an age when the vast majority of the population possessed little of value to stake in a game. While the wealthy could wager land and gold, the poor frequently had nothing to lose but their liberty. Describing the ancient German practice of 'vicious dicing', Tacitus records how slaves were frequently made from gambling sessions:

> They play at dice . . . making a serious business of it; and they are so reckless in their anxiety to win . . . that when everything else is gone they will stake their personal liberty on a last decisive throw. A loser willingly discharges his debt by becoming a slave . . . [and] allows himself to be bound and sold by the winner.
>
> (Tacitus 1982, p. 122)

Often their meagre stakes were virtually indistinguishable from these gamblers themselves, as with those who occasionally resorted to cutting off their fingers or their ears as wagers or as securities for gambling loans (Steinmetz 1870, p. 11)!

It is during the Middle Ages that we find, in innumerable bans and prohibitions, attempts to suppress the gambling activities of the working population. In what was an essentially pragmatic position, the Catholic Church recommended that individuals indulge themselves in moderate recreation just sufficient to improve their health, so fortifying them for the resumption of work. Field games, walks and serious conversation were regarded as fit for this purpose, while gambling games, having little to offer in the way of fresh air and exercise, and much to encourage idleness and usury, were generally disapproved of (Dunkley 1985, p. 37). Those activities condoned by the Church had the added advantage of maintaining a fit workforce, in an era whose violence made the existence of a reserve population who could quickly be rallied into an indigent army, extremely attractive. It was thus practical considerations which led to the encouragement of outdoor sports like archery, and the suppression of pastimes which might detract from them like gambling. Although gaming was ostensibly prohibited to protect the noble practice of archery 'to the terrible dread and fear of all strange nations' (Steinmetz 1870, p. 418), underlying the medieval statutes was also the fear (which would become increasingly pervasive) of the *disorderly* effects of such practices. To control the activities of soldiers, an edict was established 'for the regulation of the Christian army under the command of Richard I of England during the Crusade'. This regulation was stratified according to rank, with liberty to gamble declining with descent down the army hierarchy. Anyone below the rank of knight was forbidden to play dice for money. Knights and clergymen were allowed to play, but were not permitted to lose more than twenty shillings in a day, 'under a penalty of one hundred shillings to be paid to the archbishops in the army'. Monarchs could play as they wished 'but their attendants were restricted to the sum of twenty shillings and if they exceeded they were to be whipped naked throughout the army for three days'. Thus, a kind of 'sliding scale' of prohibition regulated the army, while, in succeeding statutes for the population at large, 'dicing [was] particularly and expressly forbidden' (in Ashton 1898, p. 13).[3]

Cards

In the same way that dice came into existence with religious ritual, cards appeared alongside the divinatory use of the arrow around the twelfth century. The etymology of the word belies this heritage; in Italy, cards are known as *naibs*, in Spain *naypes*, both of which are corruptions of the Arabic *nabi*, which means 'prophet' or 'predict' (Taylor 1865, p. 32). Casting rods and feathered sticks marked with four different symbols were used by the American Indians and also in the ancient Orient in rituals in which priests and other sacred figures interpreted the commands of the gods according to the direction in which the sticks fell. Contrary to Sifakis' assertion that the design of these throwing sticks was a gradual historical development, with decorative images and a general flattening of the sticks being added over the centuries (Sifakis 1990, p. vii), evidence from as early as 4000 BC shows that in fact such a design probably existed coeval with the most ancient sticks themselves. Ivory rods from Babylon and Egypt have been found bearing figures of father, mother and child that are similar in function to the tribal divisions of bear, tortoise and eagle marked on the sticks of the Alaskan and Haida Indians. The designs of these rods gave them specific values in divination practices as well as in games of chance, for as emblems of 'mystic power and authority' they were used in *both* types of ritual (van Rensselaer 1893, p. 42). The markings on these sticks represented social groups and individuals within them, and this 'enabled a man to ask queries of the gods in a most particular way' (Culin 1896, p. 181). To ask a question as a father, or a fighter, or a member of the Bear tribe, individuals would select an appropriate emblem to represent themselves, and interpret the meaning of the sticks surrounding it when it fell.

Our modern cards are descended from a similar design. Strips of oiled paper from twelfth-century Korea known as *Htou-Tjen*, or 'fighting arrows' (van Renssalaer 1912, p. 32), and originally used for fortune-telling, were modified by a Chinese design based on the organisation of paper money. A pack consisted of four sets – coins, strings, myriads and tens of myriads – the predecessors of our basic four-suit design. The recurrent four-fold division of these early cards is an aspect of the tendency to regard the world as an entity composed of four units, and, according to Cassirer, is a basic schema of religious thought. An east–west line represented the course of the sun and was bisected by a vertical north–south line, and so 'With the intersection of the *decumanus* and the cards, religious thinking created its first basic schema of co-ordinates' (Cassirer 1953, p. 100). It is this cosmic order that was represented by the decoration of divining arrows, and which the design of modern playing cards, with their distinction between four suits, continues in the present day.

The number and variation of the design of cards makes a pack a compact and ingenious system for play, with the maximum number of variables handled in a neat, economical manner. In this sense, cards are a more creative means of gambling than dice, with greater potential for manipulation and an enormous possible number of games. As a result of such complexity, they can be viewed as a symbolic system, with packs and games depicting an image of the society in which they are created and played.

In her beautifully illustrated *History of Playing Cards*, Catherine Hargrave examines the cards of Asia and Europe, building up a picture of these tablets as miniature pieces of artwork, the social and cultural life of their country of origin embodied in the exquisite detail of their design. They were, she writes, 'as individual and faithful a mirror of the taste and temperament and traditions of the people as other branches of their arts' (Hargrave 1966, p. 170). Early cards were crafted by hand on wood, copper and ivory as well as card and paper. The individual who wanted a set would commission a painter who would then design the pack according to the wishes of the purchaser; designs were usually images of purchasers themselves, their families or their hunting lands. The process of creating an entire set of cards by hand was painstakingly slow, but, with painters like Andrea Mantegna, Martin Schongauer and Botticelli employed at the task, the resulting set was a unique and fragile work of art.

In Plate 2, we can see this variation in card design. On the top left are ancient Chinese 'domino cards' used for fortune-telling as well as gambling; top right are Indian eight-suit cards; on the bottom left is a card painted for Charles VI of France in 1392; and bottom right are cards from the Japanese game *hana awase*, or 'flower game' (in Hargrave 1966).

The hand-crafting of cards made their cost prohibitive to all but the nobility, and, although popular demand encouraged their creation with stencils and wood blocks, the price of the resulting set put them out of reach of the majority of the population. It was not until the momentous invention of the printing press in the fifteenth century that cards came into mass everyday use and became widely disseminated throughout Europe (Sifakis 1990, p. 56). As well as increasing their number and availability, the printing

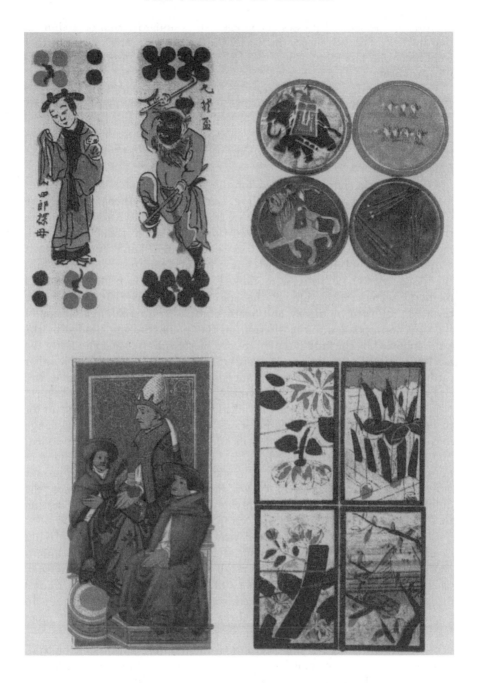

Plate 2: Ancient Chinese, Indian, French and Japanese playing cards
Source: Hargrave (1966)

of cards on mechanical presses encouraged the standardisation of design, so that by the end of the century the luscious images in Hargrave's visual history were becoming less idiosyncratic and less varied and beginning to look more like each other.

From their inception in the east, cards were introduced to Europe in the late thirteenth and early fourteenth centuries, probably first into Italy by explorers such as Marco Polo. These Italian cards, known as tarots, were highly decorative, and, as well as picture cards and numbers, had a third set, the *trionfi* which played an important role in the cards' fortune-telling function.[4]

Originally, the tarot were used for the amusement of children and for forms of divination like fortune-telling, but as their 'heathen' symbols were Christianised, they began to be used in games of chance. After the Chinese tradition of the four suits, the Venetians developed their own which represented the contemporary Italian social order. Long curved swords symbolised the nobility, cups the church, money the merchants and clubs the peasantry. These suits were ranked in a microcosm of hierarchical medieval society with cups at the apex, swords next (later these were reversed), followed by money, and finally clubs. The internal organisation of the suits corresponded to the divisions in the medieval army, headed by the king, followed by the knight (later replaced by the queen), valet and lastly the faceless foot soldiers – the number cards (Strayer 1982, p. 352). The number cards occasionally carried roman numerals, but most often their value was simply depicted by the individual symbols of their suit sign (known as pips, or peeps). These elaborate, highly involved patterns made it quite difficult for players to quickly see what number a card actually *was*. This would change in the nineteenth century, when identification numbers or indices were added, but until then, the design of early cards did not lend itself to the playing of number games. The joker carried on its status from the tarot. Having no suit or number it existed in a class of its own, and symbolised fate and chance; 'the unforeseen, the unexpected, uncertainty or uncontrollable fate and the destiny that presides over every walk of life' (van Rensselaer 1893, p. 55).

Over the following three hundred years the design of European playing cards was modified to reflect their social and political milieu. The idiosyncratic designs which proliferated as a result of the individual crafting of every pack created a corresponding diversity of suit designs. Sometimes figures from legend or myth were represented, sometimes contemporary heroes. In Germany, astronomical cards depicted the Copernican universe, while more terrestrial ones bore the images of national poets. Most common however were heraldic series – cards carrying portraits of the reigning families of the land. It was in this heraldic tradition that a new design emerged, replacing the Italian one with images more representative of the chivalric order it came from. *Coers* (hearts ♥) were the church, *carreaux* (arrowheads or diamonds ♦) the vassals, *trèfles* (clubs ♣) the husbandmen and *piques* (spades ♠) the knights.

The face cards showed the old European family system – father, mother and eldest son, rather than king, knight and valet. This new design served as a model for cards in the similarly courtly society of fifteenth-century England, where the first record of their recreational use was prohibitory. *The History of the Order of the Garter* (1278) discusses 'the Plays forbidden by the Clergy . . . which might be cards, chesse' (in Ashton 1898, p. 35), and in 1397 cards were sufficiently common to elicit a law forbidding them on work days (Strayer 1982, p. 352).[5]

As well as the cards themselves, the games played with them were representative of their social milieu. Games and cards existed in a dynamic relation with each other and with the social world in general. In the light of such reciprocity, cards became a microcosm of the society that played with them. Games were continually modified and altered, following the configurations of the world around them, with the result that those played in the fifteenth century, such as primero, pair, brelan and gleek, were very different from those of the seventeenth and nineteenth centuries.

The principle behind medieval card games was the acquisition of *combinations*, or murnivals and melds (Taylor 1865, p. 313). Certain cards have a prescribed value when grouped with others which they 'match', such as four of a kind – a 'murnival'. Examples of melds are a 'marriage' – a king and queen of the same suit, a 'flush' – three or more cards of the same suit, a 'sequence' – three or more cards in ranking order, and a 'pair' – two cards of the same rank. In games like primero, instead of each deal ranking as a separate event, play is continuous. In such an ongoing process, scoring follows the principle that cards not melded in significant groupings are penalties. In such games, it is assumed that all cards 'go together' with specific others in sequences, groups and combinations. Each card has a definite *place* in relation to a larger whole, and it is only in these configurations that their properties emerge and they are ascribed a value. Individual cards have no value, and are actively penalised in such a cohesive system. In these medieval games, individual properties such as number, suit and rank are less important than the overall picture given by the cards' place in relation to significant others. Such principles demonstrate a clear correspondence with the densely hierarchical society in which the games were played. Like the cards in their melds, the properties of people are predetermined by their position in social groups. Individual cards have no value because their 'nature' is only realised as part of a larger unit, and single cards thus carry a penalty. Similarly, the individual was treated with suspicion in medieval society for, in a world where everyone had a place in a fixed 'chain of being', character and lifestyle were to be found in conjunction with others. There was literally no place for solitude. This parallel between cards and society is particularly marked in the change of the rules of *triomphe* (later whist). The identity of the trump suit was originally determined by turning over a card, so that, consonant with a society of hereditary ranking in which both status and suit are fixed and outwith the control of the individual or player, the most important suit was chosen by chance. In the later development of auction whist, it is possible for players to bid for trumps with whichever suit they had the most of, or, if no one had the necessary cards, have no trumps at all. In the more mobile society of the nineteenth century, status is no longer fixed and determined by chance. The game is more competitive and individualistic and so any player with sufficiently strong cards and enough nerve to bid for them can chose trumps.

The gradual dissolution of the rigid medieval system between the seventeenth and eighteenth centuries meant that rank, suit and number started to become more important than place in games, and, by the nineteenth century, the rise of individualism saw a corresponding emphasis on the numerical values of single cards.

Throughout their history, the recreational and divinatory uses of cards (like that of dice) was often inseparable: all the while they were being played in games of chance, they were also being used to predict the future. The earliest work on cartomancy by Francesco Mariolini came from Venice in 1540, while in 1634 *Le Passtempts de la Fortune des Rez*, which explained the supernatural significance of various cards and their combinations, was popular. There was no shortage of such material in England either, where a multitude of divinatory series with explanatory leaflets such as *The Dreamers Oracle*, *Fortune-Telling by Cards* and *Napoleon's Book of Fate* proliferated between the sixteenth and nineteenth centuries.

At the same time that tracts on the mystical quasi-religious function of cards were being published, and cards themselves were being used for fortune-telling, another type of card-related literature was flourishing. By the seventeenth century, card games were so numerous and popular that a need to codify and record the rules developed, giving rise to a group of self-styled 'experts', who explained and formulated the rules and strategies of specific games. In a rational, scientific manner, such writers utilised the insights of probability theory and applied them to increasingly popular games of chance. In a time when books were still relatively scarce, 'rows upon rows of volumes' on gaming existed (Hargrave 1966, p. 205); scientific formulations on strategy sitting side by side with mystical directions for divinatory ritual. At times it may have appeared that the scientific had supplanted the religious worldview in the world of games, for, as von Renssalaer informs us: 'when any dispute arose, [Hoyle's] book was consulted and instead of the players saying "It is the wish (or the voice) of the gods" . . . it became customary to say "It is according to Hoyle"' (Hargrave 1966, p. 276).

Lots

We have already seen the ubiquity of lot casting in Chapter 1; a practice used to ascertain the preference of the gods, especially with regard to the appropriation of material goods. It is from this function that our modern lottery, and all games of chance whereby winning is simply dependent on the possession of the correct ticket, derives.

The word 'lot' is of Teutonic origin (Sullivan 1972, p. 4), and comes from *hleut* which designated a bean or pebble or some other token used to settle disputes. The term has similar meanings and sounds in other languages – in Anglo-Saxon, 'to cast lots' is *Hleut-au*, in Dutch it is *Lotten* and in Swedish *Lotta* (Ashton 1898, p. 222).

The origin of the lottery itself has been traced to the Roman Apophoreta, where gifts were given to guests upon leaving banquets (Sullivan 1972). Augustus Caesar was the first to sell lots to his guests, establishing a practice where he would 'auction tickets for prizes of most unequal value, and paintings with their faces turned to the wall, for which every guest present was expected to bid blindly, taking his chance like the rest' (Suetonius 1958, p. 93). Nero awarded prizes of villas and slaves to his revellers, while the eccentric Heliogabalus presented 'gifts' of dead dogs, flies and ostriches! An incipient form of lottery was practised by Caligula, who, at the Games, 'would scatter vouchers among the audience entitling them to all sorts of gifts', and Nero, who used lots to dispose of goods which he had stolen from shops (Suetonius 1958, pp. 158, 222). After the fall of Rome, feudal princes continued the tradition at banquets, finding the indiscriminate appropriation of tickets an ideal way of distributing gifts without exciting jealousy.

However, it was the advent of capitalism that really encouraged the development of large-scale lotteries. Sixteenth-century Venetian and Genoese merchants used the 'Lotto' as a means of disposing of their wares, selling tickets to their customers and holding draws to determine the winners in a practice which was soon found to return profits at least as large as from conventional methods of enterprise (Ashton 1898, p. 222). Lotteries were also used when an individual wanted to dispose of household goods or land – items which might be too expensive to find a single buyer.

Sifakis dates the first recorded European lottery to Burgundy in 1420, the proceeds from which were used for the fortification of the town (Sifakis 1990, p. 187), while Ashton finds it later in 1446 when the widow of the Flemish painter Jan van Eyck held a lottery in Bruges to raise funds for the poor (Ashton 1898, p. 222). The principality of Germany established a national lottery in 1521; Francis I began the French *loterie* in 1539, while Florence's first government lottery, *La Lotto de Firenze*, was held in 1528, with other city-states following suit. Such schemes raised vital funds for public projects, and in fact French fiscal policy depended almost entirely on its *loterie* during the period when its citizens refused to pay their taxes (Sullivan 1972, p. 4).[6]

The utility of these small-scale lotteries was obvious, and was soon grasped by the politicians and monarchs of the emergent European nation-states. From then on, the development of lotteries increased in rapid and uneasy symbiotic relation to the development of a capitalist system of production. On the one hand, as an alternative to unpopular taxation, the revenue-raising potential of a lottery offered obvious attractions to the leaders of new states; on the other, however, its 'pagan' ancestry in lot casting appeared sacrilegious to the defenders of the new religious order established by the Reformation, while defenders of the secular political order worried that its appeal to chance over the virtues of work was a disruptive (if not incendiary) force encouraging idleness and violence in the population. Such ambivalence can be seen in legislation which vacillates between outright condemnation and tacit encouragement of lottery schemes.

In Britain, the first public lottery was drawn in 1569. Participation was presented as a patriotic undertaking, for 'the Lotterie is erected by her majestie's order . . . towards the reparation of the havens and strength of the Realme, and towards such other publique good workes' (in Ashton 1898, p. 223). Revenue from this lottery and the ones following it did indeed benefit the realm, paying for the supply of water to London, the building of the first Westminster Bridge and the creation of public libraries. The interests of the realm abroad were also greatly advanced by the lottery: as British colonists struggled to create the New World, British subjects in the old helped to ameliorate economic hardship through participation in lotteries specifically designed to support the colonial venture. The colonies became the public work of the lottery *par excellence*: so much so that it can be said that the first American settlement of Jamestown was almost entirely funded by British gamblers playing the lottery. Buying a lot served to further the glory of the British Kingdom abroad and the appeal was taken up largely by the gentry. Having already invested in the Virginia Company, they played the lottery, not to increase their fortunes, 'but to enhance their status by following the example of great noblemen and government leaders already committed to financing overseas colonies' (Findlay 1986, p. 13). *These* 'gamblers' played to establish rank and status, less concerned with the possibility of profit than with the honour and dignity of the British Empire.

In 1694 £1 million was raised by lotteries; three years later it reached £1.5 million, and then, in 1699, at the height of their popularity, it was all over; an Act declaring: 'That all such Lotteries, and all other Lotteries, are common and publick nuisances, and that all grants, patents and licenses for such Lotteries, or any other Lotteries, are void and against the Law' (Ashton 1898, p. 227).

Ashton offers no explanation for this political volte-face, moving straight on to the reintroduction of the lottery in the reign of Queen Anne. It is in this Act of 1710 however, that a clue to the cessation of the lottery in the seventeenth century lies. In the new state lottery, 150,000 tickets were to be sold at £10 each, with prizes paid in annuities (Ashton 1898, p. 228). Such ticket prices would have put the lottery out of reach of all but the wealthiest sections of society and so effectively outlawed it for the poor. Private lotteries, with their unregulated minimum stakes, were next to go, proscribed by an

Act of 1721 which imposed a penalty of £500 for running them. These 'little goes' as they were known continued to run illegally despite the prohibition, and were patronised mainly by the poor who found them attractive for a number of reasons. Most obviously, they were easily accessible, simple to play and cheap, with the size of a possible prize far outweighing the paltry cost of a ticket. Furthermore, as Kavanagh (1993) and Dunkley (1985) point out, in a rigid social and economic system in which, despite its ideology of meritocracy, little genuine opportunity for advancement through effort or talent existed, sudden wealth through a lottery win appeared to the lower orders as a viable means – perhaps the *only* means – of material advancement. By the eighteenth century, the ideological basis for prevailing social divisions had been sufficiently weakened to encourage 'mobility aspirations' among the Third Estate (Dunkley 1985, p. 222). However, the material framework for realising these aspirations was not correspondingly advanced, and so a chasm between ambitions and the means of achieving them opened up. The lottery appeared to fill this gap, and sustained the dream – crushed in more conventional economic arenas – of social mobility. So, the poor played in the hope of relieving their living conditions by a spectacular win, spurning the bourgeois equation of hard work and modest wealth in favour of the possibility of instant riches. The legislation against lotteries can thus be seen as an attempt by the bourgeoisie to reimpose their values of hard work and material abstinence on the 'depraved poor'. The statutes also represented an attempt to maintain a social order whose stability was symbolically threatened by the lottery's creation of overnight wealth. As Kavanagh describes it: 'For the bourgeoisie, the spectacle of so rapid a social promotion amounted to a scandalous undermining of the whole equation of wealth and merit at the centre of their ever more triumphant ideology' (Kavanagh 1993, p. 60).

From the passing of the 1710 Act to 1824 no year passed without a state lottery (and, although officially prohibited, doubtless few years without various private, clandestine ones too). Although such lotteries provided a welcome source of government revenue, Ashton tells us that 'it began to dawn on the public that this legalised gambling was somewhat immoral' (Ashton 1898, p. 238). Just as likely, and now that the colonies no longer needed support from the motherland, it would have begun to dawn on the government that other sources of revenue, such as taxation, existed as a more viable alternative to lotteries. So by the nineteenth century, the lottery was no longer seen as synonymous with the honour of the nation, much less with Christian duty, and was regarded instead as a thinly veiled instance of gambling, the existence of which undermined the honest virtues of hard work and material abstinence.

In 1808 a government committee declared: 'the foundation of the lottery system is so radically vicious . . . that under no system of regulations . . . will it be possible for Parliament to adopt it as an efficacious source of revenue.'

The purpose of the lottery as provider of state revenue had come full circle; in 1819 a parliamentarian moved that the lottery 'manifestly weakening the habits of industry, must diminish the permanent sources of the public revenue' (Ashton 1898, p. 238). Inevitably, a final Act of 1823 made provision for its discontinuance, and the last British lottery was held in 1826. A satirical epitaph was inscribed on the hall of its last draw:

> In Memory of
> THE STATE OF LOTTERY,
> the last of a long line
> whose origin in England commenced
> in the year 1569
> which, after a serious of tedious complaints,
> *Expired*
> on the
> 18th day of October 1826
> During a period of 257 years, the family
> flourished under the powerful protection
> of the
> British Parliament;
> the Minister of the day continuing to
> give them his support for the improvement
> of the revenue
> As they increased it was found that their
> continuance corrupted the morals
> and encouraged a spirit
> of Speculation and Gambling among the lower
> classes of the people;
> thousands of whom fell victims to their
> insinuating and tempting allurements.
>
> (Ashton 1898, p. 238)

THE SEVENTEENTH-CENTURY EXPLOSION

In the seventeenth century, the phenomenon of gambling appeared suddenly to burst upon a startled society, which continued to reel from the shock of its almost epidemic proportions for the next hundred years. This was a manifestation of the general extravagance of the Baroque, an era that Huizinga described as characterised by the 'general tendency to *overdo* things'. It was, he wrote, an era that inspired 'visions of exaggeration, of something imposing, overawing, colossal, avowedly unreal'. Most importantly, it was an age immersed in play, for the 'Baroque, manifest[ed] the play element to an almost striking degree' (Huizinga 1949, p. 182).

If contemporary observers are to be believed, the nation was virtually turned upside-down, as 'that destructive fury, the spirit of play' (Neville 1909, p. 38) overtook the land, wreaking havoc, and leaving a trail of wrecked careers, lost fortunes, bankruptcies, suicide and madness in its wake. Writers and commentators watched this 'prophane, mad entertainment' (Pepys 1976, vol. 9, p. 4) sweep the nation with a peculiar combination of fearful, disapproving fascination. Gambling was a plague, a disease, a curse; but most importantly it was madness, the antithesis of an enlightened society's pursuit of reason. Cotton's definitive description of gambling in his *Compleat Gamester* (1674) articulates all these nuances of the ambivalent seventeenth-century response:

> Gaming is an enchanting *witchery* . . . an itching disease . . . a paralytical distemper which drives the gamester's countenance, always in extreams, always in a storm so that it threatens destruction to itself and others, and, as he is transported with joy when he wins, so, losing, is he tost upon the billous of a high swelling passion, til he hath lost sight both of sense and reason.
>
> (Cotton 1674, p. 1)

The unprecedented popularity of gambling in the seventeenth century has to be seen in the wider context of the growth of a mercantile society. Increased affluence allowed greater participation in games previously played only by the very rich, but more important were new notions of making money and the parallel between the dynamic of commercial development and that of games of chance. The growth of a money economy created a standardised, universal measure of value, and as such, its place in gambling was central. The universal equivalent in a capitalist economy became the universal wager in games of chance.

The expansion of international trade, the development of a money economy, the increase in enumeration and the concomitant rise of a numerical, probabilistic *Weltanschauung* was conducive not only to the theoretical examination of chance, but also to the practical enjoyment of the *aleatory*. Thus speculation and risk in economic life had their corollary in the speculation and risk involved in gambling games. The enumeration of the world, which we saw in Chapter 1, while encouraging the development of probability theory, also facilitated the calculations intrinsic to gambling games. A reciprocal relationship thus prevailed between games of chance and the development of probability theory in the seventeenth century, with the latter being disseminated among a wide lay audience keen to test its scientific application at the gaming tables. An article describing the dissolute existence of gamblers in *The London Spy* in 1704 inadvertently highlights this relation: 'they read no books, but cards, and *all their mathematics is to understand truly the odds of a bet*' (in Barnhart 1983, p. 27; my italics). As well as embodying the speculative, numerical spirit of the time, the activity of gambling was universalised by the involvement of money, a feature which made its eventual commercialisation in the nineteenth century a *fait accompli* of modern capitalism.

In the seventeenth and eighteenth centuries, the nature of the games played with cards had subtly altered. Out of the games of the Middle Ages, in which they were combined in melds to form significant groupings, cards broke free as bearers of number, suit and rank. Significantly, the joker, the representative of chance and destiny in the medieval pack, was all but banished from post-sixteenth-century games. The rational new society of the seventeenth and eighteenth centuries had no place for such an unpredictable 'wild card', and so devalued it to the status it holds now, as a mere replacement. In this period, games like bassette, ecarte, loo and nap emerged, based on *tricks*. A trick occurs when each player plays a card in turn and the best card – either the highest or the card of the 'trump' suit – wins all the cards played in a 'trick'. Often a trump suit may predominate and may be chosen by players on the strength of their hand (as in auction whist); otherwise suits have no order in the capture of tricks (Parlett 1979, p. 21). Unlike melds, in tricks cards have individual merit, and, far from being penalised, sole cards are now actively courted, for all tricks are won for their player on the strength of a good single card. This recognition of the value of individual cards in the games of the late seventeenth and eighteenth centuries can be seen as a reflection of the increasing individualisation of mercantile society. Released from the rigidity of the great chain of being, individuals were increasingly free to define themselves, not in relation to a fixed, traditional place, but according to the more fluid dynamic of a market economy. Just as one exceptional individual could rise above their station and enjoy commercial success in the wider world, so in the microcosm of games was one particularly good card empowered to break free from its dependence on others and determine the outcome of a game according to its individual value.

Out of that 'destructive fury' of the seventeenth century, three distinct but interrelated forms of gambling can be discerned, occurring as separate expressions of a single spirit. They are *gambling* in games of chance, *betting* between individuals, and *speculating* in economic ventures. These will be dealt with in reverse order.

Speculation

On 1 January 1695 the Bank of England was created, and from that time on 'we may date the methodical dealing in stocks and shares' (Ashton 1898, p. 243). On its authority, companies were formed and their stocks bought by hopeful adventurers, assisted by the expansion of a widespread system of credit. Speculation was rampant as new companies appeared every day, optimistically undertaking projects which had defeated science for centuries, such as the one for the creation of a wheel for perpetual motion and the company which aimed to transform quicksilver into a 'malleable fine metal' (Ashton 1898, p. 249). The field of economic speculation in which the new mercantile spirit was played out was part of a general entrepreneurial risk-taking milieu of which the playful urge to gamble was, to some, clearly a sinister branch. To the more conservative of the era, speculation was equated with gambling, and both were synonymous with chaos: it truly appeared as if the world had been turned upside-down. In the *Persian Letters* Montesquieu feared France to be at the mercy of 'upheavals which plunge rich men into destitution and swiftly raise the poor, as if on wings, to the heights of opulence'. The result of such an unholy unleashing of power was turmoil: 'The nobility is ruined! the State is in chaos! the classes are in confusion!' (Montesquieu 1977, p. 245).

The speculative energy of the time also extended, as we saw in Chapter 1, towards the creation of insurance and annuities. Likewise, the scientific measurement of time and space was encouraged by the risking of money on both gambling transactions and speculative investment. Ashton waxes indignant that a wager on a possible loss should be classed a lesser evil than one on a possible gain; that a certain class of gambler existed 'that is not considered harmless, but beneficial and even necessary' (Ashton 1898, p. 275). Rapidly expanding from its application to marine insurance, a form of speculative insurance had become a favourite form of gambling by the eighteenth century. This could be taken out on anything; lifespans were popular, and to help customers make up their minds who to 'back', daily quotations of the rates on the lives of eminent public people were issued by Garraways and Lloyds. In 1708 Taylor's Friendly Society advertised the insurance of the lives of adults and children with the logo 'longest liver takes all' (Traill 1893, p. 817)!

This period saw a dramatic transition in the locus of value that was founded in a shift in power in a capitalising economy. It was a transition in which the economic power of a declining feudal aristocracy, represented by gold, was overtaken by a mercantile bourgeoisie, whose wealth was rooted in money. The new foundation of wealth is eloquently articulated by Kavanagh, to whose excellent study of the period, *Enlightenment and the Shadows of Chance*, the following discussion is indebted: 'Money, no longer a lifeless moon only reflecting the true light of gold, was recognised as a demiurgic force thriving in its own movement' (1993, p. 87). It is such a 'demiurgic force' that Surly in Jonson's *Alchemist* refers to when he explicitly compares gambling with alchemy as two magical means of making money:

> Give me your honest trick yet at primero,
> Or gleek; and take your *latum sapientis* [sealing paste],
> Your *menstruum simplex* [solvent]: I'll have gold before you
> And with less danger of the quicksilver;
> Or the hot sulphur.
>
> (Jonson 1987, pp. 66–67)

Within this new order, the credit system and the value of stocks and shares were precariously linked to international political interests in the world economy. Its vicissitudes were reflected in the capricious nature of the stockjobber, described by Ashton in terms which made him virtually indistinguishable from Cotton's gamester: 'He rises and falls like the ebbing and flowing of the Sea; and his paths are as unsearchable as hers are. . . . He is ten times more changeable than the Weather' (Ashton 1898, p. 246). Montesquieu found it difficult to accept the unstable basis of the new wealth, satirising it in the mythical land of Bettica in the *Persian Letters*. Two mythological figures – the son of the god of wind and the 'blind god of chance' – sell air-filled balloons, saying:

> 'Citizens of Bettica, you think yourselves rich because you have silver and gold. Your delusion is pitiable. Take my advice: leave the land of worthless metal and enter the realms of imagination and I promise you such riches that you will be astonished.'
>
> (Montesquieu 1977, p. 256)

As Kavanagh points out, the legacy of the stock and credit companies of the seventeenth century was far more important than the success or failure of any single one of them, for they called into question a fundamental belief that the creation of economic wealth was somehow separate from the operation of pure chance (Kavanagh 1993, p. 85). Overnight, fortunes could be increased exponentially or lost altogether simply by making the right decision on the stockmarket, by buying the most buoyant shares or selling the least popular ones. Credit speculation shared the same spirit as pure gambling, and, when unleashed on the world, turned the seventeenth-century economy into 'an enormous casino, where all were obliged to risk their fortunes on the winning combination' (Kavanagh 1993, p. 86).

On another level, such speculation actually encouraged play at games of chance, for the dynamics of stock-trading had accustomed individuals to handling paper as a representative of wealth. This particular representation appeared less 'real' than gold however, and was used more extravagantly. In this frame of mind, it was but a short step to carry the cycle of profits and losses sustained in the economic realm over to the equally 'unreal', equally capricious fluctuations of wealth at the gaming tables (Dunkley 1985). This encouragement is reflected in the expansion of other forms of gambling during this era: betting between individuals and gambling on games of chance.

Betting

The explosion in the sheer amount of gambling in the seventeenth and eighteenth centuries was matched by a corresponding surge in the range of subjects on which one could bet; an activity which usually involved wagers between predominantly aristocratic individuals on uncertain events or matters of opinion. The 'curious mania for making eccentric wagers' (Neville 1909, p. 103) led *The Connoisseur* to declare in 1754 that 'there is nothing, however trivial or ridiculous, which is not capable of producing a bet' (in Hibbert 1987, p. 372). People lost no opportunity in placing wagers on the outcome of undecided events, turning the minutiae of daily life into tense gambling situations. Money was staked on marriages, births, deaths; even the colour of a horse. One of the more grotesque examples of such wagers is the (somewhat apocryphal) anecdote, attributed by Sifakis to Horace Walpole, in which a man collapsed in a gaming house. Bets were immediately placed on whether he was dead or alive, with those who had wagered that he was dead protesting that attempts to revive him would affect the fairness of the bet! Subsequently, he was left alone and died, much to the satisfaction of those who had bet on that outcome (in Sifakis 1990, p. 314; also Ashton 1898, p. 155).

When naturally occurring events were insufficient to sate the public appetite for betting artificial ones were constructed, over which considerable sums of money changed hands. In 1735, the Count de Buckeburg laid a large wager on his being able to ride a horse from London to Edinburgh backwards, while 'a young Irish gentleman' had £20,000 on his ability to walk to Constantinople and back in a year (Ashton 1898, pp. 163–171). Such 'matches against time' were common; the most famous being the wager of the Counte d'Artois to Marie Antoinette of 100,000 livres that he would erect a palace (the Bagatelle) in six weeks. In a feat almost as demanding, a journeyman won a bet by riding three times between Stilton and Shoreditch – 213 miles – in eleven hours thirty-four minutes, on fourteen different horses. A similar accomplishment won its executor £16,000 for covering fifty miles in two hours (Ashton 1898, p. 210).

In the twenty-first century, such betting appears fascinating in its quaint eccentricity and, in what appeared trivial and insignificant to observers at the time, we can see action which is highly symptomatic of the milieu in which it was performed. In bets like that between two nobles – five to one that King Charles would go to Scotland in 1641 (Stone 1967, p. 568) – we can see the development of a probabilistic awareness of the world. The decidedly arithmetical nature of seventeenth- and eighteenth-century wagers demonstrates a new-found tendency to break down the world into discrete, quantifiable units. Concomitant with the development of mercantile society, and paralleling the rise of a 'doctrine of chances', betting behaviour in the seventeenth and eighteenth centuries demonstrates the emergence of a probabilistic *Lebensgefühl*, in which worldly phenomena are perceived as numerical entities. This enumeration of the world reaches its apogee in the quantification of the categories of time and space to a degree of precision that would have been unthinkable in agrarian society. Not so much the undertaking itself, but the *description* of the eleven-hour, thirty-four-minute, 213-mile journey seen earlier, is only conceivable in a modern society which requires and values the accurate measurement of time and distance. In bets like that of 'the young man who undertook for a considerable sum' to pull a pound weight on a mile-long string towards himself in two-and-a-half hours, and the £500 bet that a man could travel from London to Dover and back before another made a million dots on a sheet of paper (Ashton 1898, p. 230), we see the numerical reduction of the world to the language of an arithmetical equation: 'take x quantity y distance in z time.'

The eagerness with which so many people attached money to opinion in matters of uncertainty was demonstrative of another seventeenth-century trend. In commercial society the measure of value was no longer found in the utilitarian function of an item, instead being derived from its motion in exchange. Money, the 'universal equivalent', embodied the potential of all such exchange and was thus the ultimate representative of value. This peculiarity of money could be displaced so that as well as being a *measure*, it could also be seen as an *attributer* of value. The ultimate association of an article, event or even opinion (however trivial or worthless in itself) with money could, as if by magic, bestow on the former the value of the latter. This transference of the value of money to various arbitrary phenomena was concomitant with the measurement of value in monetary terms and embodied a new measure of legitimacy in mercantile society, a move away from chivalric codes of honour. As Neville put it: 'As a means of settling disputes the wager was stated to have supplanted the sword, all differences of opinion being adjusted by betting' (Neville 1909, p. 38).[7]

In the seventeenth and eighteenth centuries, the craze for betting on anything was a means of applying money – and hence value – to opinions which, in an age of dramatic economic, political and religious upheaval had become unstable. This insecurity was particularly acute among the old feudal order who, almost daily, witnessed the erosion of their authority by an ascendant bourgeoisie. It is thus no coincidence that it is among this group that we see the most extravagant and reckless bets. Their betting frenzy is evidence of an insecure class attempting to validate their opinions and to re-establish their authority by ranging themselves behind the new measure of value. By proffering money as representative of their opinion, they made the latter tangible by expressing it in the new language of commercial exchange.

The aristocratic response to money at this time was, however, ambivalent. While some declared the value of their opinions in it, other groups demonstrated patrician disdain by squandering it in huge amounts in games of chance. This attitude will be examined next.

Gambling

Beginning in the mid-seventeenth century and continuing throughout the eighteenth, a gradual demarcation of the gambling world into private and public leisure spheres began, of which the latter developed into a stratified network of commercial gaming houses. During this period, and backed by various legislature, leisure was becoming increasingly class bound in its submission to the economic imperatives of capitalist development. Nowhere were these developments more apparent than in the social arena of gambling.

The private sphere

Private gambling was carried on in aristocratic court circles: the homes of the nobility, exclusive upper-class haunts like Newmarket and Windsor and 'watering places' like Bath and Spa. Tucked away in private social spaces, court gambling led the fashion in games and constituted an exclusive network of privilege with its own rituals and rationale of play. The high-stakes play of the court of Louis XIV – the 'Sun King' – established the form for aristocratic games throughout Europe, and so extravagant and intense was the gambling there that Versailles itself became known as *ce tripot* – the gambling den. By centring aristocratic life on the court, the King removed from the aristocracy the chance of proving themselves competitively, and so reduced them to idleness and impotence. As a result, gambling became a kind of compensatory ritual, and an integral part of the life of the *ancien régime*. It was especially popular with women who, long excluded from independent economic and political activity, found in such rituals a sphere of influence in their role as the arbiters of taste and leaders of fashion in the latest games.

The fever of gambling activity led to a situation in which the ability to play the most fashionable games was a prerequisite of entering polite society. With this in mind, many parents hired 'gaming masters' to instruct their children in the arts of various games, causing Montesquieu to lament the degree to which gambling had become a measure of social status: 'Being a gambler gives a man position in society; it is a title which takes the place of birth, wealth and probity. It promotes anyone who bears it into the best society without further examination' (Montesquieu 1977, p. 119).

At court, the sheer scale of these 'gambling orgies' and the spectacular 'leviathan' bets of the aristocracy rendered their gambling both very *private* through its exclusivity, and also extremely *conspicuous* through its prodigality, making it a baroque form of 'conspicuous consumption'. The size and frequency of court wagers quickly passed into popular folklore. A Lady Couper refused to sit down at one game when she saw that no one was playing with less than £200 a hand (Traill 1893, p. 191), while in France, a Madame de Montespan lost four million livres in a single evening at cards (Kavanagh 1993, p. 32). A welter of gloomy prognostications accompanied such flamboyant acts, with conservative journals like *The Connoisseur* muttering, 'we shall soon see the time when an allowance for bet money will be stipulated in the marriage articles' (in Ashton 1898, p. 157). For Walpole the crisis was even more serious; such excessive play was 'worthy of the decline of our empire' (Hibbert 1987, p. 313).

These dire misgivings were, however, unfounded. The excesses of aristocratic play, watched with such foreboding by many bourgeois commentators, was indicative not of the establishment of a new social order, but of the frenzied death-rattle of an old one. At court, gambling was more than a simple recreation, and, as an important symbolic activity through which the nobility could demonstrate their detachment from money (Kavanagh 1993, p. 38), it was in fact actively *expected* from courtiers. For centuries the existence and status of the nobility had been rooted in the unquestioned authority of tradition, heredity and honour, but in the seventeenth century a momentous divide appeared, interrupting the seamless lineage of history and undermining the very foundations of aristocratic life. A new social group had begun to emerge whose authority and status were predicated entirely on the anonymous force of money, already ubiquitous throughout society. Everything was reducible to this universal equivalent, and therefore anything could be bought, even, to the general chagrin of the aristocracy, a noble title. Thus a rift appeared in the aristocratic order with the traditional nobility on one side and the 'new' nobility on the other. The two groups represented antithetical worldviews; while the Old Guard linked prestige with land and lineage, the ennobled bourgeoisie saw value as synonymous with individual wealth, an equation which earned them the contempt of their more ancient peers (Kavanagh 1993, pp. 49–51).

Games of chance, and the notions of tradition, honour and duty that surrounded them, became the focus for this conflict. Gambling debts were not legally binding and so the gambling contract depended entirely on the word of the parties involved. Thus to pay one's gambling debts demonstrated honour and integrity, and so gambling became an arena in which to demonstrate status and gain prestige. Knowing how to lose was an important test of character, and showed one's indifference towards money. For the nobility, such gambling was a 'metaphoric substitution' for an old way of life, and by playing, aristocrats showed their allegiance to the old order of tradition and demonstrated their contempt for the modern values of pecuniary gain (Kavanagh 1993, p. 42). These grand rituals, then, can be seen to constitute a form of what Veblen was later to call 'conspicuous consumption'; the large-scale, non-utilitarian consumption of wealth and goods, regarded by those who engaged in it as a mark of human dignity (Veblen 1925, pp. 68–102). Aristocrats did not gamble to win, but rather to project a self-image of honour. In the way that the upper classes participated in the Virginia lottery scheme, status, not financial gain, was the motivation of *these* gamblers. In fact, financial interest was reprehensible to this group, as is apparent in one noble's warning to her grandson that 'to playe for gayne more than recreation illegitimates all good meetings' (in Stone 1967, p. 569). Aristocratic play of the late seventeenth and early eighteenth century can thus be see, as a desperate attempt by the old feudal order to reaffirm their rapidly declining position in a world where 'the sway of money was already irresistible' (Kavanagh 1993, p. 51).

The aristocracy's nonchalance while handling large sums of money demonstrated their indifference to it, as well as to the values of a society in which they were becoming increasingly marginalised. Kavanagh draws our attention to Mauss' essay on *The Gift* which provides an insight into the motivations behind these flamboyant rituals. In it, Mauss describes the 'gift' economies of archaic systems of exchange, where the function of the exchange of goods and services is not to increase personal wealth, but to establish the giver's merit in a hierarchy of prestige and honour. In this, Mauss explicitly identifies gambling as a form of *potlach* and means of gaining prestige, along with war, hunting and wrestling.[8] As in court etiquette, these exchanges are *expected* of participants, for in spite of appearing 'voluntary, disinterested and spontaneous', they are actually 'obligatory and interested' (Mauss 1954, p. 1). Such behaviour can be seen as a form of the ceremony of the potlach of the North American Indians. Here, a group displays its superiority by presenting another with magnificent gifts, which the recipient is obliged to return in ever greater magnitude. The large-scale destruction of a tribe's own goods also features in the potlach, and serves to demonstrate the destroyers' indifference to material possessions and their noble distance from economic utility. In these societies prestige is valued over economic wealth, and the system of potlach is a means of converting one into the other. In this way, a peculiar kind of commerce is instigated, 'but it is an aristocratic type of commerce characterised by etiquette and generosity; moreover, when it is carried out . . . for immediate gain, it is viewed with the greatest disdain' (Mauss 1954, p. 36).

The gamblers of the *ancien régime* can be seen to be engaged in such potlach-style behaviour – activities in which the heroic dissipation of whole estates, jewels and money displayed to the world the magnanimity and status of the nobility.

While they were engaging in this conspicuous consumption however, another type of economic behaviour was being practised within their ranks. The figure of Dangeau – eventually the Marquis de Dangeau – epitomised the struggle for ascendancy within the aristocracy. When gambling at court, Dangeau was hugely successful in a manner that was anathema to the aristocratic style of play. He played to win and he based his play on rational calculation, thus bringing the bourgeois value of financial accumulation to the gaming table (Kavanagh 1993, p. 53). To an aristocratic observer, the difference in style was startling, as Madame de Sevigne recorded:

'I saw Dangeau play! – what fools we all are compared to him – he minds nothing but his business, and wins when everyone else loses: he neglects nothing, takes advantage of everything, is never absent; in a word *his skill defies fortune*, and accordingly 200,000 francs in ten days, 10,000 crowns in a fortnight, all go to his receipt book.'

(In Steinmetz 1870, p. 90; my italics)

The image of the player in aristocratic gambling was always of an individualised unit, while gambling itself was 'the personalised and individual conflict between each specific person and his opponents' (Kavanagh 1993, p. 64). Dangeau was well aware of anonymous mathematical probabilities and of the notion of the average, and in this he represented the end of the old feudal order. As an individual who made use of the new tool of probability theory, he anticipated 'the coming universal victory of the scientific man, the average man, the economic man' (Kavanagh 1993, p. 64). On the other hand, the insouciance of the aristocratic gambler was the incarnation of Nietzsche's allegorical dice thrower, a romantic figure who already appeared anachronistic in a world steadily submitting to the imperative of capitalist organisation. In their patrician rejection of economic necessity and the needs of the workaday world, aristocratic gamblers exemplified the Platonic tradition of play as a non-utilitarian activity in which the display of human values – in this case, the virtues of honour and nobility – were paramount.

Ironically, it is in the figure of the aristocratic player, not the bourgeois Dangeau, that we recognise the character of the twenty-first century gambler. Although Dangeau represented the vanguard of the new intellectual paradigm out of which probability theory would develop, future generations of gamblers did not go on to copy his style or utilise the insights presented by the doctrine of chances. Apparently oblivious to the rational calculation of odds, modern gamblers tend not to play according to any kind of objectively judicious rules. Unlike Dangeau, they do not play 'sensibly' or conservatively, and above all, they do not (normally) play to *win*. The play itself, and the demonstration of character and nerve in the course of the game, are the motivations of the modern gambler, and these will be considered in Chapter 4.

Commercial gambling

In the conflict within the aristocracy, we see in microcosm a glimpse of the shape of things to come. The values of the ennobled bourgeoisie were already a dominant social force, visible in the gambling arena in the development of a socially stratified network of commercial gaming houses, which mirrored the commercialisation and stratification of the world outside. From the luxurious rooms of private clubs to the 'hells' tucked away in taverns, gambling was for the first time being carried on in a commercial environment which, by the early nineteenth century, would have profoundly altered the nature of play and the very style of the games themselves.

Clubs

At the top of the gaming hierarchy were the private clubs such as Whites, Almacks and Crockfords which, with their strict membership and dress codes, were reserved for the exclusive use of the upper classes – gentry, dandies and society men. The licensing of public gaming houses belonged by patent to the royal Groom Porter, and was not given out without careful consideration of the social position of the applicant; courtiers and peers were the most common recipients. The play here was a private affair, and therefore, like that of the nobility, not subject to the law.

Legally at least, gambling was not the sole focus of these places, although in reality, their abundant supply of free food, wine, music and dancing only provided the smallest of distractions to their real purpose, which revolved around the gaming tables. Opened in 1698, Whites attracted the wealthiest nobles of the day and, while offering popular games like hazard and bassette, also oversaw private bets between individual members on subjects ranging from politicians' longevity to the likelihood of contracting venereal disease! 'Leviathan' bets still went on – whole estates could be lost and careers ruined in gambling orgies that went on all night. By the nineteenth century, Crockfords was recognised as the most exclusive and popular club of its time, offering a variety of games to nobles who, two centuries earlier, would have been playing their high-stakes hands in private gambles at court.

'Hells'

While the upper classes played in luxurious surroundings, the middle and lower orders experienced a very different world of gambling. What was tolerated as legitimate entertainment for the rich was considered unsuitable for the rest of society, and so attempts were made to restrict and control the playing of games of chance among the poor. Such attempts had been enshrined in legislation since 1397 when cards were outlawed on work days. A further statute of Henry VIII confined *all* gambling to Christmas when, assuming the lower orders would be celebrating anyway, its disruptive effects would be minimal. This Act stated that:

> no manner of artificer . . . apprentice, labourer, or any serving man, shall from the said feast of the Nativity of St John Baptist, play at the tables, tennis, dice, cards . . . or any unlawful game, under the pain of *xxs* to be forfeit for any time.
>
> (In Ashton 1898, p. 60)

In the eighteenth century, a flurry of legislation removed gambling even further from the reach of the poor by imposing taxes on gaming instruments: sixpence on a pack of cards and five shillings on a pair of dice. Jonathan Swift observed the desired result in his *Journal*, writing that 'Cards are very dear, which spoils small gamesters' (Swift, in Traill 1893, p. 817). This was followed by another statute which outlawed specific games and, while penalising the owners of public gaming houses, excused the play of the rich: 'The games forbidden are Ace of Hearts, Faro, Bassett and Hazard, *except in Royal Palaces*' (in Ashton 1898, p. 59; my italics).

These later prohibitions should be seen within the general eighteenth-century condemnation of excess, which had special resonance for the activities of the lower orders. In the rational society of the Enlightenment, the threat of disorder – *desodré* – posed by gamblers was regarded as particularly acute from gamblers of the lower classes. As well as disrupting the health of the individual player, gambling was feared to disrupt the well-being of the social order, encouraging the indiscriminate mingling of the classes and under-mining the orderly social values of thrift and family loyalty. The effects of gambling on poor families were regarded as especially ruinous, for such families, reduced to destitution by the reckless play of their breadwinners, would be unable to pay their taxes and so become a burden on the state. The familial cohesion of the lower orders was thus regarded as a pressing moral problem in the eighteenth century, and one in which the activity of gambling had a particularly negative role.

It was in this climate that concerted efforts to restrict working-class gaming were made, resulting in the increasing stratification of the gambling economy. In this period, the vast amount of privately owned land and the declining availability of public space made leisure increasingly class bound. The outcome of such a spatial segregation was a shrinking of public space which pushed the poor into ever smaller and less visible areas (Cunningham 1980). Excluded from clubs, and with cards and dice kept artificially expensive, they were forced to gamble in illegal taverns and in lotteries. With their cheap, easily available tickets, the latter were immediately accessible to all but the most impoverished, and offered the hope of unimaginable riches for a minimal stake. Meanwhile, in unlicensed alehouses and coffee shops, cards and dice were played with 'enthusiasm and vigour' throughout the land (Mitchell and Leys 1950, p. 305). In their small, dimly lit interiors stakes were low, and anyone could play with only a minimal bet. Not being clubs, these bawdy houses or 'hells' were illegal and liable to be raided at any time and their owners imprisoned. The need for concealment was pressing, and so these clandestine houses often had four or five doors separating them from the outside world. Grilles, secret passages and watchdogs made the gaming room deep in the interior inaccessible to all but the initiated. The contrast with the plush opulence of the clubs is stark, as Cotton's unsavoury depiction of an eighteenth-century hell testifies:

The day being shut in you may properly compare this place to these Countries which lye far to the North, where it is as clear at midnight as at midday. . . . This is the time when ravenous beasts usually seek their prey.

(Cotton 1674, p. 6)

The 'ravenous beasts' to which Cotton is referring were the professional cheats and robbers who made up the criminal underworld of the gambling scene. Unobserved and unregulated by the law, these illegal taverns were home to a hierarchy of card sharps – 'takers-up', 'versers' and 'robbers' – practised in the various techniques by which an honest player – a 'cousin' – could be relieved of his money. The clandestine goings-on in these hells frequently made the operation of chance a mere secondary consideration in the outcome of a game.

Stratification and commercialisation

By the eighteenth century, a clear social stratification, with clubs at one pole and hells and lotteries at the other, had emerged. A world of difference distinguished the conspicuous, leviathan bets of the aristocracy from the modest, clandestine play of the poor, for generally the classes played different games and had different motivations for playing them. Although the lower classes *did* play cards, and the wealthy *did* participate in lotteries, by the end of the eighteenth century a broad class allegiance to specific forms of play had emerged, with the gambling of the upper classes characterised by high-stakes card play at court and in private clubs, and that of the lower classes made up of a majority of gamblers who pinned their hopes on the lottery. While the conspicuous dissipation of wealth by the aristocracy demonstrated the latter's indifference to money, the engagement of the poor in the lottery was a contract whose sole aim was the pursuit of wealth. For a minimal stake they hoped to reap great riches, and aspire to a social mobility that was denied them through more conventional economic means. So, as the rich proved their status through their losses at cards, the poor hoped to improve *theirs* by winning the lottery. This stratification left an indelible mark on the physiognomy of play, traces of which are still evident in the gambling economy of today, as we will see in Chapter 3. For the moment however, we should note that even while it was at its height, this stratification was being challenged by the increasingly powerful force of commercialisation, which would bring in its wake the equally powerful trend towards the democratisation of gambling.

A complex division of labour which saw the employment of croupiers, waiters and directors developed within the public gaming houses and clubs of the eighteenth century as the economic imperative of capitalism extended to the practice and organisation of gambling. The indiscriminate flux of individuals wagering and collecting money, as well as those actively involved in running games of chance, gave way at this time to an ordered collection of employees, each with a specific function. Such a recognisably modern organisation mirrored the changing nature of play itself. Since clubs and hells were run as businesses, gambling was organised in such a way that the house itself might profit from the money wagered between individual bettors. This applied to all ranks of the public gaming hierarchy, and contributed to the standardisation of the activity. Although the games themselves appeared to be the same as their privately played counterparts, their nature had subtly altered. Instead of players' losses being the gains of their direct opponent(s), they now became incorporated into commercial enterprise and partially absorbed as the gains of the faceless house – the ubiquitous opponent in *every* game. By interposing an anonymous opponent between real flesh and blood gamblers, this commercial reorganisation of play to some extent depersonalised high-stakes gambling contests, removing the element of face-to-face confrontation that was so important in the creation of prestige among the upper classes. The introduction of percentages and house edges took away something of the excess, and so expurgated the whole notion of the heroic 'noble exchange' from gambling in clubs. At the other end of the scale, they also took away some of the cheating from the hells. Since it denied them the opportunity to intervene and take their percentage, it was not in gaming houses' interests to allow cheating. Efforts were therefore made to eliminate all 'irregular' practices, with rules tightened up and harsher penalties inflicted on cheats. In these ways the introduction of commercial interests began to regulate the experience of gambling, 'evening out' its extremes in a process that would gradually make it more homogeneous across the classes.

'The sport of kings'

In horse-racing, we see the encapsulation of the forces of commercialisation and democratisation that were gaining influence in the wider society, and being bitterly resisted at every turn by the patrician legislation of a steadily declining aristocracy.

In the seventeenth century, consistent with a tradition stretching back to the Assyrian kings of 1500 BC and the Roman Emperors of the first millennium, horse-racing was the privilege of the very wealthy. The cost of upkeep confined horse ownership to the upper classes, a group whose over-riding concern was the maintenance of the privilege of racing and betting on the animals as their exclusive right. In twelfth-century Britain, the elitist nature of the sport seemed to promise the indefinite continuation of the situation, for racing tended to be a private affair between gentlemen who rode their own horses on their own grounds. Under the Royal Patronage of Charles II – 'the father of the British Turf' – post-Restoration racing was gradually systematised, with rules of play laid down and professional jockeys installed.

During this period of patronage, racing appeared more than ever as 'the sport of kings', with successive monarchs Charles II, James II and Queen Anne building homes by Newmarket racetrack and entering horses to race in their own names.[9]

However, events which were dramatically to change the face of racing, turning it from an elite pastime to a mass spectator sport, were already underway by the eighteenth century. The role of popular broadsheets was crucial – by the 1750s London papers were carrying advertisements of major meetings and news of results to a wide public (Chinn 1991; Clapson 1992). Such a dissemination of information meant that, for the first time, it was no longer only owners and their friends who were privy to information on the time and location of races. As a result, huge crowds began to gather at races, stimulating the demand for more and larger courses. When Tattershalls came into existence in the 1770s, betting finally became formalised according to the rules of probability. No longer carried out face to face, it was now organised by anonymous bookmakers according to set odds. Just like card and dice games, racing was regulated by the science of probability; a regulation which took it out of the hands of individual upper-class patrons and placed it in the public domain of commercial interests. The proliferation of racetracks, encouraged by the spectator appeal of the sport, stimulated racing for small stakes, so that by 1722, over 112 towns and cities were holding small races. Horrified by the erosion of the exclusivity of 'their' ancient game, the aristocracy resisted the trend, and a tide of defensive legislation surrounded the proliferation. Thus, because 'the Great Number of Horse Races for Small Plates, Prizes or Sums of Money, have contributed very much to the Encouragement of Idleness, to the Impoverishment of the meaner Sort of the Subjects of the Kingdom', an Act of 1740 insisted that every race have an entrance fee and a £50 prize, effectively excluding the 'meaner sort' from participating (in Cunningham 1980, p. 19). The very integrity of racing came to depend on its separation from the lower classes. In 1674 this was made explicit, when a tailor was punished for racing his horse against a planter's, 'it being contrary to Law for a Labourer to make a race, being a sport only for Gentlemen'. The planter was also punished by an hour in the stocks for the crime of arranging the race in the first place (Findlay 1986, p. 22)!

But it was all too late. The inexorable march of capitalism was dragging racing, along with cards and dice, out of the private recesses of the upper classes and into the public domain, and no amount of retrograde legislation could stop it. By the end of the nineteenth century, the democratic *coup* would be complete.

THE NINETEENTH CENTURY: PLAYING WITH NUMBERS

In the nineteenth century, various changes occurred which dramatically changed the face of gambling. The commercialisation of games of chance during the Industrial Revolution converged with the commercialisation of economic life and with the denouement of probability theory – the science that had 'tamed' chance. As the calculation of odds became more fully understood, the nature of the games played changed so that they became more amenable to commercial organisation, more homogeneous and, ultimately, more 'sellable'. It is in this period that the recognisably modern forms of the casino, the public racetrack and the mechanised slot-machine first appeared. In place of the huge sums wagered by the individuals of the seventeenth-century aristocracy came more democratic games for many players organised around modest stakes which allowed for prolonged rather than excessive play. These conventions are still visible in the gambling behaviour of today, and are discussed further in Chapters 3 and 4.

The casino

In the industrial discipline of the nineteenth century, the separation of the spheres of leisure and work, which had been ongoing for the previous two hundred years, was finally consolidated. Such a development was particularly evident in the gambling arena which at this time was disengaged from its surrounding social life and organised into distinct, highly commercial spheres. The casino was perhaps most representative of the trend; it emerged in the second half of the century as a collection of public rooms devoted exclusively to gambling, away from its earlier formulation as a dancing saloon and summer-house (McMillen 1996).

In this period, the fashionable watering places of the aristocracy continued to be popular gaming centres and were supplemented by the development of a series of resorts throughout Europe, in which gaming houses – now casinos – were the central attraction. This development of what Turner and Ash (1975) describe as a decadent and extravagant 'Pleasure Periphery' in the French Riviera included Nice, Cannes and Monte Carlo, or, as the French called them, 'the World, the Flesh and the Devil'. Baden Baden, Bad Homberg and Wiesbaden were small localities whose deliberate expansion turned them from health spas into gambling resorts (a process which would be perfected in the twentieth century in the creation of Las Vegas).[10] Although generally exclusive, the commercialism of at least some of these resorts bore witness to some degree of democratisation. In Bad Homberg and Wiesbaden the great mass of visitors were of the middle and lower-middle classes, causing Steinmetz to note with disapproval that 'the general run of guests is by no means remarkable for birth, wealth or respectability' (Steinmetz 1870, p. 213).

By the end of the nineteenth century then, dramatic changes had trans-formed the nature of commercial games of chance, overseeing the formulation and codification of what we now recognise as modern casino games. Just as the economic imperatives of emergent capitalism were reflected in the growth of commercial gaming houses, so the games themselves came to reflect the social logic of a capitalist system. It is these changes we shall turn to next.

Cards

In cards, traditional games that revolved around various kinds of patterns and sequences, such as the gaining of suits, trumps and tricks or the making of combinations like flushes and marriages in melds, were being supplanted by a new form of game. This new style of play was based on the arithmetical values of the cards in their properties as individual numerals, and forms the basis of all modern casino card games.

Such a shift was made possible by an experiment of the Woolley Card Company. In 1884, in keeping with the statistical spirit of the times, they printed a numerical value at diagonally opposite corners of each card in what was known as an *indice* (Hargrave 1966, p. 189). As numbers 'poured into' the nineteenth century, so they poured on to packs of cards. With this seemingly trivial development, the face of cards was literally changed forever. The value of these new cards was depicted by a bold unequivocal number, no longer rep-resented by an image, which was necessarily more ambiguous. The authority of the number was not open to interpretation; it was a fact. Not only was it instantly more striking, in the new style of games, but the number on these cards was also more *important* than all the other information they contained. In games based on the speedy calculation of number, it was vital that each card be immediately recognisable to the player. A simple digit in each corner met this requirement in a way that a more vague pictorial depiction never could. Given the commercial environment of the new games, it was not only important that players should quickly recognise their cards, but equally, that other players should *not*. Until now, the backs of cards had been either plain or decorated with a single one-way design. This meant that they could easily be marked, or, in the case of decorated cards, arranged with some backs upside-down, for example, to distinguish high cards from low ones, face cards or suits (Sifakis 1990, p. 57). The possibilities for cheating with such packs were unlimited; even a player with a poor memory could not fail to recognise specific cards from their backs after a while. In the nineteenth century this golden age of cheating was ended when companies began experimenting with uniform back designs so that, by the end of the century, simple two-way designs had rendered cards indistinguishable. These twin developments made cards at once both unique *and* standardised. As instances of 'the same kind of thing' they were indistinguishable, yet within this general category each one was recog-nisably the bearer of a specific value. Similarly, in the wider society, *l'homme moyen* was characterised by his representativeness of all others of his kind. At the same time, these characteristics came out in individual properties which displayed as much statistical variation in their particular sample as, say, the individual cards in their particular pack. In the nineteenth century then, both *l'homme moyen* and the new-style cards came to be represented as individual variations on a single, standard theme. By streamlining them, the numbering and standardisation of cards was integral to the development of new styles of play, loosely termed banking games, which evolved into casino games.

In the game of *vingt-et-un* (which later grew into pontoon, and then the casino game of blackjack), and *chemin de fer* (baccarat), suits and court cards were irrelevant, numerical values paramount. From their regal status as the most important cards in the pack (many bearing the image of their owner), in baccarat, picture cards were dethroned and given no value at all. A similar fate befell court cards in blackjack which were also democratised and given a single numerical value – ten. Consonant with the statistical spirit of the times, cards in these games, like all the others in the pack, were only important through their representation of number. Both games were basically arithmetical exercises whose principle was to assemble cards whose value did not exceed a specified number: twenty-one in blackjack, nine in baccarat.

With their emphasis on calculation and the irrelevance of any distinctions other than numerical ones, we can see in these games the mirror of the commercial, statistical interests of an increasingly capitalist society.

It was not only in card games that the dynamic relation between games and society was apparent. The early probabilists used games of chance to develop their theorems, and their discoveries in turn affected the games they experimented with. As probability became more fully understood, the games it was applied to became more complex, so that games and theory developed by feeding off each other in an ever more complex dialectic of theoretical and practical application.

Roulette

The game of E–O (even–odd) was popular during the eighteenth century in fashionable resorts like Bath and consisted of a wheel with forty cups alternately marked E for even and O for odd. A ball was released as the wheel rotated and players wagered whether it would fall into an E or O pocket. Pascal experimented with a similar ball and wheel device, but did not, as is sometimes claimed, 'invent' roulette. The game as we know it today was actually developed in the nineteenth century when the French addition of thirty-six numbers and colours to the wheel revolutionised the simplicity of the original game (Sifakis 1990, p. 256). The impact of the addition was enormous, greatly increasing the variety of betting available from one to ten, with different odds on each. Players could still bet odd or even, but now any single number or combination of numbers as well. The addition of numbers made roulette a far more exciting and complex game than its rather staid predecessor, and, with the inclusion of a zero (two in America), also made it a very commercial one, for when the ball landed in this pocket all bets were won by the house.

Dice

Advances in the study of probability, aided by commercial developments, also transformed the ancient game of hazard into a faster, more streamlined version known as craps. Hazard had been played in the same way for centuries, with players betting that they would eventually throw a certain number with two dice, throwing until they did and then continuing to throw until the original number or 'point' came up again. However, since the odds of certain numbers coming up before others varies, a competent player would require a basic understanding of probability to play well. Such an understanding of averages and odds in relation to dice simply did not exist until the seventeenth century, with the result that most bettors did not comprehend all the ways various combinations could be achieved with two dice. For hundreds of years 'A hustler could indeed have made a fortune' (Sifakis 1990, p. 147)!

In France, hazard was known as krabs (after the English word for a throw of two or three), later corrupted to creps or craps. When introduced into America by French colonists, a modified version grew in popularity among black slaves in New Orleans and took its name from French craps (Scarne 1974, p. 39). In the nineteenth century, the incorporation of ever-increasing knowledge about odds and percentages reformulated the rules of hazard into what we now know as the modern game of craps. Dozens of types of bets now became available to the player, with many more variations of each type.

With its multitude of betting strategies and combinations of odds, the appeal of craps as a lucrative commercial game was obvious. To entice it into the casino, further modifications were made, which changed its structure yet again. A small charge was made by the house whenever the thrower made two or more passes. This was known as a take-off game. Next, the house took the opposition against the thrower, so that *all* players now had to bet the dice to win against the house. A simple table layout bearing the six and eight, the field, win and come bets, was drawn up to play on, exactly half of the table layout today. The house now took its cut 'not as a direct charge, but indirectly and less noticeably by offering short odds so that it gained a percentage' (Scarne 1974, p. 41). A further development offered players the opportunity to bet the dice to *lose*, as well as to win. In effect, every bet could now be either for or against the dice or the house. Betting opportunities were doubled, and the craps table reflected the change, changing its shape from a semi-circle to a full oval, with one half a mirror image of the other. The game of craps at times appeared as the archetypal game of probability theory, with its complex permutations of odds, pay-offs and house percentages, a working (or rather *playing*) example of a theoretical construction.

Gaming machines

One of the most significant developments of the nineteenth century was the introduction of gaming machines. The Industrial Revolution had laid the foundations for automatic gambling when a London bookseller created a vending machine in order to sell proscribed literature, although the introduction and proliferation of coin-operated machines did not appear on a mass scale until the last quarter of the nineteenth century. During this period of technological innovation, the automation of the leisure sphere was complemented by that of the workplace, so that the development of what Costa (1988) called 'automatic pleasures' was symptomatic of the automation of the wider world of the late nineteenth century.

Being born into a secular, industrial age, the ancient image of divinatory drama which ran as a leitmotif through most older, established types of gambling would not be expected to feature in this young form. However, slot-machines did manage to maintain the link of all gambling with the sacred, for the automated machines from which the early gaming machines drew their inspiration were originally used for fortune-telling. In the white heat of the technological revolution, the art of divination was not made redundant, it was simply mechanised.

The earliest gaming machines invited individuals to discover their future by means of a spinning pointer, a card dispenser or some kind of animated figure (Costa 1988, p. 21). Their patents stated that they could be used either as divinatory devices or as games of chance, although in an attempt to limit their appeal, both forms of amusement were only allowed to return tokens such as cigarettes and chewing-gum and not cash, as prizes. The design of many of these first machines was simply an automatic adaptation of already existing games – hence the popularity of images of cards and horses, as well as of pieces of fruit, from which the term 'fruit machine' is derived.

The first automatic three-reel machine, or 'one-arm bandit' – the prototype of our modern gambling machines – appeared in San Francisco in 1905 when Charles Fey developed a device in which a handle was pulled to spin three wheels and, if a winning combination was made, a stream of nickels poured out into a tray below (Sifakis 1990). The one-armed bandit (which Fey patriotically named the Liberty Bell) was developed in a rush of pioneering individualism typical of the Gold Rush state of that time. Throughout the nineteenth century risk-hungry Californians, whom Findlay (1986) called 'people of chance', were possessed of a dynamic, innovative spirit which culminated in their westward advance across Nevada and the subsequent creation of Las Vegas. It is no wonder then that in an era of technological advance, it was these 'people of chance' who gave slot-machines their final configuration and so created the most modern form of gambling device.

Horses

The numerical preoccupation of the nineteenth century, along with technological innovation, was to dramatically change the face of horse-race betting. The role of newspapers became steadily more important in this process, along with newly established journals such as *Sporting Life* (1863) and *Sporting Chronicle* (1871), disseminating tips, news and forecasts to a hungry audience. For the second time in history,[11] print encouraged – and was encouraged by – gambling. This plethora of sporting journals fed the voracious public appetite for information, and was crammed full of facts and statistics about horses, races, jockeys and odds. Aided by the electronic telegraph system, which meant the press could quickly publish results and starting odds, and the establishment of a credit network, the 1880s saw the development of large-scale organised betting (McKibbon 1979; Chinn 1991; Clapson 1992; Munting 1996). In a move which the aristocracy would have fought bitterly against, railways helped to make horse-racing a national spectator sport by sponsoring races and linking towns (and therefore fee-paying punters) to courses.

These nineteenth-century developments revolutionised racing. Now thoroughly democratised, its status was reversed from being the prerogative of a rich elite to being a massive working-class entertainment. Under the sway of commercial developments, spectacular, individual upper-class bets disappeared and popular betting between a mass of punters – both on and off the track – took over. Such bets were subject to strict odds: the chances of a horse winning a race were calculated by taking many variables into account, and expressed in a numerical equation. Pay-offs were equally subject to strict calculation, based on the amount of the original stake and the odds on the particular horse. No longer a simple 'gentlemen's agreement' for a set amount, betting became a complex contract between bettors and central race organisers, relayed through a number of betting shops. The physiognomy of betting also changed: from being private and limited it became public and widespread. Its role in providing a source of excitement as well as hope of financial gain at a time when poverty made alternative forms of economic advance, such as saving, unrealistic, meant the popularity of betting was assured (Chinn 1991; Clapson 1992). This broad place in working-class culture was reflected in an increasing dissemination of bookmakers, runners and their agents on street corners, in the backs of shops and throughout private homes. The first betting house opened in Britain in 1847: three years later over 400 existed, and almost immediately, an 'epidemic of gambling was declared to have attacked even the poorest class' (Neville 1909, p. 99). Needless to say, a wave of legislation – the Street Betting Acts of 1853, 1874 and 1892 – swiftly appeared, designed to eradicate all forms of popular, working-class betting.[12] Again, it was too late. The popular tide of betting simply went underground, largely unaffected by the 'suppression', until betting shops were reinstated in 1961.

The new style of play

The highly numerical nature of all these forms of gambling was consonant with the statistical milieu of the nineteenth century, and was particularly suited to the imperatives of commercial organisation. These developments were to change the experience of play forever. In gaming halls and public houses, people played all day and all night at games like craps and roulette, which had been refined and organised in such a way as to include a 'space' for a 'player' who always won – the house, or dealer. Commercialisation encouraged dealers to rely increasingly 'upon the more predictable and more secure profits provided by odds fixed inflexibly in their favour' (Findlay 1986, p. 91). Realising the impossibility of winning the games they operated, these commercial interests – 'the house' – made a brilliant move whereupon winning was assured. Rather than participate in a game, they removed themselves from it altogether and allied themselves with the very law that told them they had to lose. By placing themselves actually *within* the probability equation, they could simply sit back and await the profits which would inevitably result from favourable odds once the law of large numbers was given enough time to come into effect. Backed by the indomitable authority of probability, the house could not possibly lose. On the other hand, the alliance of both odds *and* house edge meant that individual gamblers could not possibly win. They found themselves competing against an invisible opponent with a permanent place at every table and unlimited resources. What is more, they were forced to play against the house, for this element of competition had been built into the commercial games and was now inherent in their structure. Gamblers no longer played against each other but against the house, whose invisible impersonal force mirrored the imperatives of economic behaviour, the 'invisible hand' of market forces.

Commercialisation also changed the social composition of play by encouraging less wealthy players. As wagers became smaller, participation dramatically increased. Hiding behind the iron laws of probability, gambling entrepreneurs made profits, not by increasing the stakes of games, but by increasing the volume of players. They might not make 'leviathan' wagers, but these more modest players could be relied on to place a regular flow of smaller bets, so guaranteeing the profits of the house.

As its nature was transformed through commercialisation, the experience of gambling itself underwent a change. Participation, not winning *per se*, became paramount and, as Findlay points out, this changed the meaning of gambling itself: 'Players still hoped to win . . . but they looked upon betting more as a commodity for sale . . . as an experience worth purchasing with losing wagers' (Findlay 1986, p. 92). In a capitalist economy, gambling had finally succumbed to commodification. But this was no ordinary commodity, for it had a unique experiential component. Players continued to gamble, but as much for the thrills and excitement of the game itself as for financial rewards. Fast games and moderate stakes became valued for prolonging participation and therefore maximising excitement. Now that their main motivation was participation, gamblers played simply to *play*, for: 'Next to the pleasure of winning is the pleasure of losing, only stagnation is unendurable' (Bankcroft, in Findlay 1986, p. 94).

Out of this process of commercialisation emerged a distinctive type of gambling which, despite distinct differences, also shared common elements with the gambling of the seventeenth-century aristocrat. Crucially, for both, money served only as a measure of play, unimportant in itself. The high stakes of the aristocracy showed their indifference to money and as such, the aristocrat played to *participate*, never to win. The low stakes of the nineteenth-century gambler at first seem far removed from the leviathan bets of the aristocrat, but they served a similar purpose: to lengthen participation. Again, money was only a *means* of play, and the indifference of these latter gamblers to it stemmed from their participation in play itself. These orientations are also to be found in modern gamblers, and will be examined further in Chapter 4.

The commercialisation of gambling was to gather speed over the following hundred years, overseeing its gradual development into a widespread, popular and – just as importantly – legal form of consumption. In this process centuries of condemnation which had persistently attempted to eliminate games of chance from social life – and especially the social life of the poor – were finally overturned. Before going on to look at the victory of commercialism in Chapter 3, we shall first briefly review the nature of the criticisms it vanquished.

POSTSCRIPT: THE VORTEX OF VICE

Various forms of suppression and condemnation ran alongside the long history of gambling, a persistent and largely ineffectual distraction to the serious frivolity of play. From the Roman prohibition of gaming during the Saturnalia to the medieval bans for the 'protection of archery', the practice of gambling was accompanied by a succession of specific legislative prohibitions and enforced by individual rulers. The criticism was generally constructed in terms of the threat that the chaos of chance, deliberately courted in gambling, posed to the order of society, with various eras expressing this fear in different terms. In the Reformation it was regarded as the embodiment of sin, in the Enlightenment it epitomised irrationality; the Industrial Revolution of the nineteenth century legislated against its disruptive nature, so defining it as a crime, while today its negative effects have been medicalised, and excessive gambling viewed as 'pathological' or a sign of illness.

In the sixteenth century, just as gambling reached unprecedented popularity, attempts to forbid it suddenly became more draconian, and previously disparate criticisms were focused into a coherent and intensely vitriolic assault. The fulminations of a new Protestant bourgeoisie against the 'Satanic vice' of gambling made the relatively perfunctory criticisms of feudal monarchs appear quite lenient. What had been tolerated by the Catholic Church was not by the Reformed one.

By the seventeenth century, the condemnation of gambling was virtually a shibboleth of the Protestant bourgeoisie. A stream of invective poured from the pulpits of the Reformed Church, damning gamblers for their idleness, greed, blasphemy and superstition. Games of chance displayed a blatant disregard for the values of the Protestant by divorcing the creation of wealth from the efforts of labour, and reducing it instead to the vicissitudes of chance. Hard work in a calling, glorification of God through earthly activity and an ascetic disregard for material gain were shamelessly flouted by the actions of the gambler and thus existed as a blasphemous assault on the divine order. Although Christianity had always recognised the virtues of work, with the Protestant emphasis on worldly activity, its value was 'mightily increased' (Weber 1990, p. 83). Especially for Calvinists, diligent labour in a calling became defined as a virtuous activity, which would result in gradual, predictable, and, more importantly, *virtuous* rewards, whereas idleness and the squandering of precious time were regarded as the epitome of vice. The activities of gamblers represented the antithesis of these virtuous pursuits. Their reaction to wealth was one of *immediacy* and *extremity*. Instead of the slow accumulation of money, appropriated for the future through saving and investment, gamblers' financial transactions were located firmly in the present, where their economic standing could soar to immense riches or plummet to penury, out of all proportion to physical effort. Such fluctuations were seen to disrupt the ideal of a meritocratic social balance, and, in the new moral-economic climate, gambling represented unearned, therefore immoral and illegitimate wealth. It was this orientation that prompted the Puritan John Northbrooke's outburst in his *Treatise against Dicing, Dancing, Plays and Interludes* (1577) against '*turpe lucrum*, filthie gaine' which, because it was 'gotten in a trice over the thumbe, without any trafficke or loan' was simply regarded as theft,[13] and would be counted against its winners 'at the last daye of judgment if they repent it not' (Northebrooke 1843, p. 125).

It was the waste of time and money inherent in gambling that preoccupied the Protestant bourgeoisie during the period when, for the bourgeois, the systematic use of both were necessary for capitalist expansion, and for the Protestant, both were appropriated by God. The rational management of time and money was a prerequisite of the labour discipline which, in the early years of capitalist development, was pursued mainly by the bourgeoisie. Thus the aristocracy were attacked primarily for their profligacy; their gambling for its wastage of *money*, while the poor were attacked for their laziness; their gambling for its wastage of *time*. Both committed a further sin by deliberately invoking the hand of God for the resolution of a trivial matter, to 'decide the lot': a blasphemous profanation of the Divine Will. Robert Burns' (1786) later description of playing cards as 'the devil's picture beuks' indicates the continued association of the former with supernatural, and specifically diabolical, forces.[14] In this climate, gambling was the apotheosis of sin, and the gambler was defined primarily as a sinner.

In the Enlightenment climate of moderation and reason, the idea of the sinful nature of play was replaced by an emphasis on its embodiment of irrationality. The loss of reason which the Enlightenment saw inherent in gambling was anathema to its ideal of rational progress, and was a particularly abhorrent form of madness. Gamblers made a decision which no reasonable human was supposed to be able to make – they *intentionally* gave up their most precious faculty, their mark of humanity, for nothing more tangible than the vicissitudes of chance. Such a rejection of reason was contrary to the very nature of civilisation itself which was based, if anything, on the minimisation of chance and uncertainty. Writing in this Enlightenment tradition, Montesquieu stated that God forbade anything which disturbed reason, and, since they produced 'anxiety and frenzy', he especially denounced games of chance (Montesquieu 1977, p. 120).

It was not that the Enlightenment condemned gambling *per se*, but rather that it feared the disequilibrium that could be brought about by *excessive* gambling, an attitude which should be seen in the context of broader eighteenth-century ideas about rational recreation. The valuation of productive work, associated with the Protestant ethic, was also an important Enlightenment ideology, condoned by moralists and enshrined in the legislation of the period. However, the need for 'reasonable' rest and recreation was also recognised, and the balance between this and productive work admired as rational and godly (Dunkley 1985, p. 64). As legitimate recreation, games were not bad in themselves, but the danger lay in their being pursued to excess. When this happened, the reason of the individual was overcome by extremes of emotion and, worse, the social order was disrupted. In removing the principles of moderation and balance on which the individual and society rested, the entire edifice of ordered society was threatened by chaos. Thus gamblers tended to be criticised for their possession of extreme characteristics – of idleness or excess, profligacy or greed, caprice or persistence – traits which always stood to one side of the balanced, moderate bourgeois ideal. As such, the figure of the gambler was generally perceived as a member of the aristocratic or labouring classes. Jean Dusaulx in *De la passion du jeu* (1779) described the physiognomy of the gambler who succumbed to passion in this way, existing as 'an empty space within the triumphant discourse of reason' (Dusaulx, in Kavanagh 1993, p. 36). In this state, the gambler was the incarnation of that primordial chaos, χαος, which, as 'an abyss or empty space', characterised 'the first state of the universe' we saw in Chapter 1.

Plate 3 represents two images of the 'vice' of gambling. The top picture, a caricature by Thomas Renton from 1790 entitled *The Dangers of Dice*

Plate 3: *The Dangers of Dice Addiction*, Thomas Renton (above); and *Lawyers and Soldiers are the Devil's Playfellows* (right)
Source: Arnold (1993)

Addiction, outlines the havoc wrought by that 'destructive fury, the spirit of play' on seventeenth-century reason, while the caption of the lower picture, *Lawyers and Soldiers are the Devil's Playfellows*, suggests the specifically sinful nature of the activity (in Arnold 1993).

The horror of the gambler's rejection of reason continued to run as a leitmotif through the nineteenth century. However, by this time the essential irrationality of gamblers had become less important than their ability to work. The industrialising west needed labour power; time became a commodity only slightly less precious than money, and gambling squandered them both. The problems of the organisation of labour were encapsulated in the figure of the (working-class) gambler – an individual who refused to acknowledge the importance of time,[15] money or disciplined labour.[16] This figure also represented the forces of urban disruption: the perceived menace of 'the masses' out of control, roaming the cities and indulging in various immoral and illegal activities, threatening the orderly balance established by the bourgeoisie. At a time of economic and political upheaval, when British productivity was being overtaken by Germany and the USA and British soldiers were being defeated in the Boer War, gambling became a convenient scapegoat. It was blamed for declining industrial production, military failure, and general social unrest: in short, for no less than the decline of the Empire (Dixon 1991). It was in this climate that various philanthropists and moral reformers launched an ideological attack on all forms of working-class gambling. In 1890, a coalition of Nonconformist Protestant Churches formed the National Anti-Gambling League (NAGL), whose stated aim was:

> Nothing less than the reformation of England as regards the particular vice against which our efforts are aimed. . . . There is humiliation in the thought that the chosen Anglo Saxon race, foremost in the civilisation and government of the world, is first also in the great sin of Gambling.
> (Bulletin of NAGL 1893, vol. 1, no. 7, p. 1)

It was an apocalyptic vision, conceived virtually as a crusade which would halt economic decline and defend civilisation. Now, the imperative of the Protestant ethic became institutionalised in laws forbidding games of chance along with other 'vices' such as alcoholism, drug use and prostitution. Caught up in a tide of patrician legislation, the gambler, and anyone else who promoted the activity, became a criminal. The Gaming Act of 1845 removed gamblers from the protection of the law by making gambling transactions unenforceable, while the Street Betting Acts of 1853, 1874 and 1906, and the Betting and Loans (Infants) Act of 1892 actively penalised them and all those associated with them. These laws attempted to prohibit working-class gambling by outlawing betting in public places – broadly defined as anywhere individuals might congregate to play at games of chance.

Advertising or promotion of such games was also prohibited, and gamblers, agents and bookmakers fined for participating. Later, the definition of 'place' was made even wider to include any equipment (such as desks and even the boxes which bookmakers stood on) necessary for gambling transactions. None of these prohibitions applied to the betting of the upper classes: members of clubs were excluded from its strictures, as were any individuals who were able to gamble without 'resorting' to public premises (Dixon 1991, p. 39).

In these statutes, we can see the bourgeoisie struggling with the problem of labour discipline and the wider fear of irrational disorder. To this end, attempts were made to sweep examples of roaming irrationality out of sight and (at least until a decision in 1892 reversed it), gamblers were frequently convicted under the terms of the Vagrancy Act. If found gambling in the street, individuals were to be 'committed to gaol as rogues and vagabonds' and sentenced to corporal punishment and hard labour. Such confinement was the remedy for the 'common and intolerable nuisance' of young boys and men 'sprawling about the pavement . . . and playing . . . at games of chance' (Steinmetz 1870, p. 427). Imprisonment confined gamblers to a secure space where, out of public sight, they could no longer exist as an affront to the rational industrial society around them, and where they would learn the value of hard work and self-discipline.

The nineteenth century also laid the groundwork for the twentieth century's medicalisation of the 'pathology' of gambling. Metaphorical treatments of gambling as a 'disease', a 'virus' or a 'leprosy' which attacked the healthy individual were taken almost literally and applied to its 'contagion' of the social body – and especially the social body of the lower classes (Dixon 1991, p. 60). By the beginning of the era, it was believed by certain members of the British Medical Association that gambling was explained by the nervous tension of *fin-de-siècle* Britain and psychologists began to concern themselves with the possibility of the hereditary effects of the 'disease' (Brenner and Brenner 1990, p. 141).[17] It is in this era of social Darwinism that we can see the genesis of the medical psychology of the twentieth century, including the origin of the contemporary search for a gambling 'gene'. Such perspectives were voiced in the hysterical polemic of reformers like Anthony Comstock, who wrote that gambling was a trap set by Satan which swept morals 'with the fury of a tornado' into the 'vortex of vice'. Comstock could barely articulate his loathing, which poured out in a stream of rhetoric: 'That human beings can sink so low seems almost incomprehensible. . . . These are caricatures of true men. They are forms hollowed out by this cursed traffic until there is nothing but form left' (Comstock 1961, pp. 58, 83). This image of gamblers as individuals somehow 'hollowed out' and devoid of humanity should be familiar by now: we have encountered it already as the primordial abyss – χαος – and again in the Enlightenment's description of the gambler as an empty space within the discourse of reason.

In this, it was the articulation of the perceived threat posed to civilisation by its opposite – chaos – of which the gambler was the prime representative.

However, various forces were pressing on this critical tradition, and would gradually, over the next hundred years, erode centuries of condemnation. By the twentieth century, gambling would find itself in the peculiarly ambivalent position of being, on the one hand, condemned and regulated, and on the other, tolerated and even encouraged. As the century progressed, the latter position came increasingly to dominate the former, and it is to the resulting situation that we now turn.

3

PLAYGROUNDS – A MAP OF THE MODERN GAMBLING SITES

Outrage against the 'vortex of vice' could not halt the growing popularity and legitimation of gambling forever. The inexorable march of commercialisation, begun in the nineteenth century, gathered speed over the following hundred years, where, aided by various social and political factors, it turned gambling into a major form of consumption.

The relationship between these factors, and their impact on the position of gambling, is complex, amounting to nothing less than a social history of Britain in the twentieth century, and it is beyond the purposes of this discussion to go into them in great detail here. The interested reader should refer to David Dixon's excellent *From Prohibition to Regulation* (1991), in which the period of change is subjected to meticulous analysis. However, a summary will suffice at this point.

In the early decades of the twentieth century, the NAGL went into decline, becoming increasingly associated with religious forces in a society which was becoming progressively secular. Although anti-gambling arguments had caught a certain 'mood' at the turn of the century, they appeared less relevant and immediate after the traumas and social upheavals of the First World War. Despite being hastened by financial problems, the reasons for the end of the NAGL were really quite mundane: it simply withered away 'because its frame of reference and its values were no longer valid in English life in the twentieth century' (Shirman 1988, p. 248, in Dixon 1991, p. 300).

Into this growing liberalisation of social values came a consumer boom which, although temporarily halted by the advent of the Second World War, continued throughout the middle of the century, and which encouraged the expansion of commercial betting opportunities. Higher wages meant that the population – and especially the working classes – were more able to afford leisure activities, which in turn duly increased to meet the demand. Cinemas were popular, as was dog racing and football pools, run by companies like Littlewoods and Vernons. In this postwar period of full employment and relative prosperity, arguments about the deleterious economic effects of gambling – so beloved by its earlier critics – lost much of their impact.

Added to all this was the Treasury's ongoing interest in the financial potential of gambling. If it was impractical to outlaw it altogether, then better to permit it: ensure it was organised honestly, and also to make some budgetary gains from the revenue generated by taxing it. In this climate, the 1961 Betting and Gaming Act legalised betting offices, moving gambling off the streets and into private, commercially run premises. Organised by legitimate businesses and answerable to the state, they maintained public order and ensured that gambling was kept out of sight – but still, crucially, allowed it to go on. Severe restrictions were imposed on shops to ensure that they did not stimulate demand by enticing customers in, with the result that many ended up looking more like 'undertaker's premises' than places of entertainment (in Dixon 1991). The principle of 'unstimulated demand' and punter protection was continued in the 1968 Gaming Act and applied to all other forms of commercial gambling. The paternalistic tone of the Act was designed to limit what was still generally regarded as a morally dubious activity and so stipulated that gambling facilities could not *encourage* the public to gamble in any way, but could only 'satisfy existing demand'. Strict rules thus forbade advertising of any kind and the 'proliferation' of facilities that exceeded demand. This led to a peculiar situation whereby members had to wait forty-eight hours after joining a casino before they could enter it; casinos and bingo halls were not listed in the telephone book, and could not advertise for staff (this counted as 'promotion') and betting shops were required to use one-way glass in their windows to conceal themselves from the world outside.

In a climate of increasing toleration, which was nevertheless still accompanied by a wary regulation, we can see a gradual dismantling of the anti-gambling laws of the previous century and their replacement with a set of rules designed to 'protect' gamblers from themselves – without, however, preventing them from playing. It was a liberal, regulatory strategy based on commercial and political expediency as much as that of the previous century had been based on moral condemnation and patrician legislation. This is what Dixon described as the move from prohibition to regulation, and it meant that, for much of the twentieth century, the status of gambling remained ambivalent. However, current trends appear to indicate that this is beginning to change.

MODERN GAMBLING

In the early twenty-first century the stratified gambling network which emerged in the seventeenth century has been consolidated and institution-alised through a process that has culminated in the commodification of chance. The global expansion of the industry, accelerated by the influence of tech-nology and the impact of sophisticated communication systems, its increasing popularity as a mass leisure activity and its incorporation into state fiscal policy looks set to change centuries of condemnation, bringing gambling into the fold of 'legitimate' business enterprise.

Much has been written on the capitalist embrace of gambling,[1] with the similarities between the two frequently being expressed in the common use of the term 'gambler' to describe both economic entrepreneurs and recreational players, and in phrases referring to economic life such as 'casino capitalism' and 'global casino'. The notion of 'risk' is increasingly invoked to delineate the contours of our post-industrial, 'postmodern' society (Giddens 1991; Beck 1992) and, with the latter's reorganisation and restructuring of labour markets, risk is also increasingly called in to explain the social and personal insecurity engendered by such shifts. In the world of high finance, futures and shares trading, the absence of the creation of any tangible product and the reliance on correctly predicting future changes in the market have brought economic systems under the sway of an increasingly extreme form of speculative enterprise, leading some to conclude that 'the western financial system is rapidly coming to resemble nothing as much as a vast casino' (Strange 1986, p. 1). Thus it is in the language of games that a currency dealer advises companies on how to play the markets: 'It's gambling,' he states: 'Problems arise when people don't see it as a gamble and try to dress it up with macro-economic wisdom. It's a gut feel. Dollar's up. Sterling's down. Let's trade' (Bellini 1993, p. 57).

This speculative economic trend often goes unremarked until unforeseen events result in huge losses. Then, like any gambler who starts to lose and is labelled 'compulsive', the economy is declared sick, unstable and in imminent danger of collapse. Commentators suddenly become aware of the correspondence between gambling and economic speculation and, much like those in the seventeenth and eighteenth centuries, draw back in horror at the recognition. Since the speculative boom of the seventeenth century and the disastrous bursting of the South Sea Bubble, the economic history of the west has been littered with such gambling losing runs, including the Wall Street Crash of 1929, Black Wednesday in 1987 and most recently, the collapse of Barings Bank due to the over-ambitious bets of trader Nick Leeson.

Despite its failed bets, the capitalist economic system seems to be both driven by the risking of money on uncertain future events and limitlessly able to cope when the risk fails. For these reasons it always appears slightly disingenuous of commentators to feign surprise when the gambling–speculation equation is highlighted by a spectacular loss. When Strange writes that our old image of bankers as 'staid and sober men' has been displaced by one that is altogether more entrepreneurial, and that something 'radical and serious has happened to the international financial system to make it so much like a gambling hall' (Strange 1986, p. 2), we are forced to point out that surely by now it is apparent that this kind of speculative risk is part of the very nature of capitalism itself. Those stereotypes of Weberian rationality described by the author occupied only a fleeting moment of economic history, for the dynamic of capitalist expansion has, since the seventeenth century, been lodged in the casino.

It is appropriate that in this era of heightened sensitivity to indeterminism in economics, Borges should write his tale of hypostatised Chance, 'The lottery of Babylon'. In the mythical society of Babylon, the lottery has swallowed up all other institutions, subsuming the laws of justice and economics to the rule of chance, so that the narrator says: 'I come from a dizzy land where the lottery is the basis of reality' (Borges 1985, p. 55). The sacred draws which are held every sixty days determine the course of a citizen's life for that period, and since the lottery has permeated every social institution, individuals could find themselves imprisoned or fined with an unlucky ticket and promoted or rewarded with a lucky one.[2] In such a scheme, the edifice of society has been turned on its head so that social consequences are arbitrarily divorced from their actions, and it is no longer economic reason but chance itself that determines the infrastructure of society. The land of Babylon then 'is nothing less than an infinite game of chance' (Borges 1985, p. 61). In this, it is not unlike Montesquieu's 'Bettica', an imaginary land created to satirise what he considered to be the illusory basis of the speculative wealth on which it was based. Montesquieu's 'blind god of chance' who oversaw the selling of air-filled balloons to the citizens of Bettica performed a similar allegorical function to Borges' lottery society in which a hypostatised chance threw the lives of its citizenry into confusion and disarray. Both fables can be seen to express a similar disquiet with chaotic economic conditions: one eighteenth century, the other twentieth, and both descriptive of our present situation of 'casino capitalism'. It is not surprising that such an economic system as this should so willingly embrace the pure form of its own dynamic – the arena of games of chance.

The salient point which emerges from all this is that, after a lengthy historical suppression, gambling, while still retaining some moral ambiguity, has shed its pariah status and become fully incorporated into western capitalist economies as just another type of commercial enterprise. The ability of market economies to embrace almost any kind of activity has resulted in games of chance, for the first time, being encouraged, developed and organised according to the homogenising dynamic of entrepreneurialism. Such is the embrace of what Balzac acutely described as 'an essentially taxable passion' (Balzac 1977, p. 21). The embrace is global in its reach: the rapid spread of commercial gambling practices and new technologies has seen the proliferation of gambling throughout Europe, the Americas, Australasia, Africa, the former east European communist bloc and the developing countries of South East Asia. The development of mass tourism and leisure industries and the spread of international financial markets have led to the incorporation of gambling into the world economy, and to the movement of gamblers across increasingly fluid national boundaries (McMillen 1996).

Having achieved ontological status, chance has been commodified as the ultimate twenty-first century product, sold by business and purchased by the consumer – the gambler. An excerpt from the *Circus Circus* Casino's 1989 annual report illustrates this new status, explaining that, like any shop: '[The casino] is an entertainment merchant. It's just that we happen to merchandise playtime to our customers rather than goods' (in Spanier 1992, p. 101). Gambling is now a major form of consumption and a mainstream leisure activity. In Britain alone, the gambling industry has an estimated annual turnover of £27,000 million, with punters staking an average of £75 million a day (OFLOT 1998).

Along with its institutionalisation and commercialisation, the democratising trend begun in the nineteenth century has led to a certain degree of *homogenisation* of gambling behaviour. The previous stratification of the gambling economy, with horses and high-stakes casino play the prerogative of the aristocracy and lotteries patronised mainly by the poor, is gradually breaking down, the middle classes – traditionally opposed to all forms of gambling – becoming incorporated into the map. As the organisation of this gambling economy comes increasingly under the sway of commercial interests, casinos and racecourses are becoming less exclusive while bingo halls and bookmakers are 'upgrading' their image to attract more affluent customers. These changes are leading to the homogenisation of once disparate areas of gambling activity and to the inclusion of all classes into their fold. At the same time, however, it must be emphasised that these sweeping changes do not signify the breakdown of social distinctions altogether for, since games can only reflect the society in which they are played, as long as social divisions remain in the world outside, so will they remain in the world of play.

The historical stratification of gambling which we saw in Chapter 2 has been continued in the organisation of the modern forms. For example, the working classes are still over-represented in the lottery, the middle and upper classes in the casino. Exceptions do occur however, as in the case of horse-racing which, with the advent of the popular press and the rise of rail travel, broadened its basis of participation to become a mass spectator sport. Even here, though, new fault lines have appeared, with a preponderance of middle-class gamblers actually *at* the race-track and working-class gamblers removed from the action at the bookmakers. New forms of gambling, such as bingo and Internet betting, have also made their mark in contemporary gambling life, while the young have been affected by recent additions to our modern gambling culture, such as scratch cards and the National Lottery.

Just as, throughout its historical development, gambling represented the social milieu in which it existed, so contemporary gambling represents *its* period and in this way can be said to exist as a microcosm of modernity. The apogee of this process of incorporation is the differentiation of the gambling economy into distinctive gambling sites, or 'playgrounds', each bound by its own rules and governed by its own dynamic. Many types of commercial game now exist, attracting a wide range of players, each with their own social affili-ations, motivations and experiences of play. It is the purpose of this chapter to outline the diversity of modern gambling by drawing a map – a typology – of its major areas or 'sites', and to distinguish the nature and experience of play in each.

THE MAP: A TYPOLOGY OF GAMBLING

The major commercial gambling sites of the twenty-first century are the lottery and its derivative, the bingo hall, the slot-machine arcade, on- and off-track betting, the casino and the Internet. A typology of gambling can be drawn up by delineating the categories of skill and chance, the rate of play of a game, the player's relation to the game, the spatial organisation and social integration of the site, and the socioeconomic constitution of the players themselves. These categories can be regarded as a set of co-ordinates upon which the gambling map is based, and are intended neither to be exhaustive nor mutually exclusive.

Skill and chance

Two broad forms of gambling exist: games of skill and games of chance. The practical orientation of the player to the game is different in each, for the former imply the possibility of (at least some) mastery over the game while the latter imply submission to the blind laws of chance.

The structures of belief underlying these two forms rest on different foundations, for while knowledge and training tend to be associated with games of skill, superstitions and magical beliefs surround games of chance. In fact, the greater the degree of chance in a game, the greater the degree of the gambler's superstition (Devereaux 1949; Caillois 1962; Brown 1994). The mystical orientation that results from exposure to *alea* will be examined in Chapter 5.

Although the existence of chance is pervasive, games of skill such as horse-race betting and poker facilitate the exercise of varying degrees of ability on the part of the player. Choice in the placement of one's wager can be informed by the rational application of relevant knowledge; by research and analysis of previous outcomes. Various skills can be applied to different games; for instance, numeracy and psychological insight are vital for the poker player, while the synthetic, probabilistic analysis of many variables are prerequisites of the successful handicapper. Through the exercise of these types of skill, gamblers can demonstrate a variety of abilities which extend beyond the immediate game being played. Qualities such as determination, courage and gameness can earn the respect of peers, and thus enhance reputation and status. This type of gambling has been described as work (Herman 1967;

Rosecrance 1988), but we can call it *betting* in order to distinguish it from involvement in games of chance which will be referred to as *playing*.

The orientation involved in betting can be distinguished from that of games of pure chance, whereby winning numbers or combinations are generated at random. For Caillois, such *aleatory* games include 'all games that are based on a decision independent of the player, an outcome over which he has no control and in which winning is the result of fate rather than triumphing over an adversary' (Caillois 1962, p. 17). Here, outcomes are determined by the laws of probability, where the past is irrelevant for future results, and so it is impossible to enhance one's chances of winning through knowledge or skill. Prediction is impossible and skill irrelevant. Gamblers may be involved, but their actions are not influential in play; all they can do is to offer themselves up to chance, and wait and see what happens. Such games are the antithesis of betting games, and exist as 'constant external reproaches to those who would try to manipulate the cards, dice or chips as they would operate a lathe or balance a set of accounts' (Cohen and Taylor 1978, p. 105).

Part of the 'unique appeal' of games of chance is their absolute *democracy*. Just as it abolishes the efficacy of skill, so chance abolishes inherited or acquired differences, as well as those based on merit, patience, hard work or education. The undeserving millionaire is just as likely to win the lottery as the deserving poor. As Gogol put it: 'Play is no respecter of persons. . . . All men are equal at cards' (Gogol 1926, p. 220). This merciless egalitarianism was illustrated when the *petit-bourgeois* Trina won the lottery in Frank Norris' *McTeague*: '"Why should I win?"' she asks, '"Eh, why shouldn't you?" cried her mother. In fact, why shouldn't she? . . . after all, it was not a question of effort of merit on her part' (Norris 1985, p. 110). The undiscriminating favour of destiny was not met with such equanimity by the ragman, Zerkov, however, for the converse of its democracy can be seen as the unjust caprice of chance: '"$5000. For what? For nothing, for simply buying a ticket; and I have worked so hard for it, so hard, so hard . . . fought for it, starved for it, am dying every day"' (Norris 1985, p. 126).

It should be pointed out here that the analytical distinction between games of chance and games of skill is somewhat artificial. As noted earlier, *all* games, even those most amenable to the skilful prediction of the player, contain an element of chance. The distinction outlined above is therefore not an *absolute* separation, for even in games like poker, a winner depends on not being dealt appalling cards while opponents are dealt favourable ones, and all the skill involved in handicapping is rendered obsolete if at the last minute it rains or a horse becomes ill. No amount of skill can ever eliminate uncertainty and confer absolute control, for chance is an ontological feature of the world; its influence is pervasive and the outcome of a gamble is always a contingent event.

Rate of play

The rate of play of a game includes 'the number of complete gambling transactions which take place in any given unit of time' (Devereaux 1949, p. 44). The length of time that elapses between the placing of a wager on an uncertain event and the resolution of that event constitutes the duration of the gamble or risk, while the intensity of the risk is affected by whether or not the event is settled instantly or gradually. For example, in roulette the outcome is decided as soon as the ball comes to rest in its cup. Before that happens, the result is completely unknown – it is completely undecided and then suddenly it is final. On the other hand, in poker the structure of the situation changes with every hand and gamblers must therefore reassess their position in each round. The risk experienced in such games, while still intense, is more drawn out, subject to a succession of peaks and troughs, rather than one sudden, decisive outcome.[3]

The shorter the rate of play, the more tense and immediate the game, for the gambler will be present, and probably involved, as each round unfolds. This feature has been found to be associated with an increased propensity of problem gambling (Griffiths 1990, 1993). In other words, some games are structurally more likely to encourage repeated play than others. For example, the rate of play in scratch cards (which is defined by the time it takes to purchase the card and rub off its windows) is extremely fast, and the tension high; characteristics which lend themselves to the repeated purchase of further cards more or less immediately.

Player relation to game

A player's relation to a game and to other players is complex. Whether they participate directly or are removed from the action depends on the separation of the event from the betting on it. In a sense, all gambling 'events' (with the exception, perhaps, of horse-racing) are artificially created situations which would never be instigated but for the fact that people bet on them. Events like lotteries are set up for the sole purpose of generating an uncertain situation on which to wager money. What is important here is whether or not such events directly engage the gambler, and in this sense, the player's relation to a game can take one of three forms: (1) physical participation, (2) observation at close proximity, or (3) distance. Goffman's (1963) distinction between focused and unfocused interaction can be introduced here to illuminate the form of inter-personal relations in gambling. Whereas in cases of the former, individuals extend deliberate communication to each other, in the latter, communication occurs merely by virtue of their being in the same situation (Goffman 1963, p. 83). All forms of gambling can thus be seen to be instances of unfocused interaction.

In casino games like blackjack, craps and baccarat, and in slot-machine play, gamblers are physically involved and are betting on a situation which is at least superficially derived from their own actions. Their sheer physical presence is necessary for such games to occur for they must manipulate cards, throw dice and activate buttons on slot-machines for play to continue. Despite the interactive nature of such games, and despite any sociable aspects they may have, the presence of other players is nevertheless extrinsic to the gambling experience itself, for it is not they, but the house or the machine that gamblers play against.

Games where the relation is one of distance are non-interactive. The player is not physically involved, and need not even be present at all, as is the case with lotteries and races. Here the player's relation to the game is distant and mediated by technology: telephones, cables and fax machines can all be employed to place a bet on an event which may be occurring thousands of miles away. Technology thus expands the 'reach' of gamblers so that they can expand and project their 'gambling body' into a thing of huge proportions over vast distances in such a way that their *actual* bodies need not be present in any single specific space. Bookmaking was probably the first form of gambling to be transformed by technology in this way, with telephones and runners removing the need for face-to-face contact between bookmakers and bettors. Today, the development of technologies such as the Internet take this trend even further, with games being played on-line in sites such as *Virtual Vegas* and *The Cyber Casino* in a global gambling economy.

Observation at close proximity is a peculiar relationship in which the gambler is neither physically involved nor physically distant from the game. Pari-mutual wagering is the sole example of this 'in between' state. Unlike fixed odds, in pari-mutual betting, gamblers wager among themselves with the result that the odds on horses change before the race as an expression of the changing confidence and opinions of the bettors involved. Changes are reflected on the tote board which records shifts in odds as well as wagers and so registers the collective betting opinion 'in a manner analogous to the stock market ticker tape' (Abt *et al.* 1985, p. 86). Pari-mutual betting is thus a competition among bettors. Although these bettors are not directly involved in the gambling event – the race – their non-physical presence – their *opinions* – are necessary for the event to be defined as a gambling one. Their presence does not affect the nature or outcome of the gambling event, although it does affect the odds placed on it, i.e. the value of successful bets.

Spatial organisation and social integration

The spatial organisation of a gambling site refers to the concentration or diffusion of the gambling environment. Concentrated sites are areas of intense, localised activity like the casino and race-track, while diffuse 'sites' are disseminated over a wide area, as in the case of the lottery, and especially in Internet gambling.

Such spatial organisation is related to the social separation or incorporation of sites into the larger social fabric, with concentrated sites tending to exist outwith the local environment in their own separate spheres and diffuse ones tending to be incorporated into the routine of daily life.

Spatial organisation affects the players' relation to a game. Upon entering a concentrated site, they are likely to be physically immersed, if not actually involved in play, whereas a diffuse site *has* no tangible 'site' to enter and hence gamblers do not participate in the means of play themselves. Diffuse sites provide many intermediary points of contact where gamblers may interact with the larger game going on elsewhere. Such sites as lottery vendors exist like spokes in a wheel, reaching deep into the social fabric from a central hub – the lottery draw. These 'spokes' radiate outwards to the most everyday locations such as shops and kiosks and are thus incorporated into their local surroundings, while concentrated sites that have no such outlets are demographically separated in their own exclusive spheres. The casino is an example of such a site – self-contained, enclosed, separate from its surroundings – while the lottery, with its seamless integration into the local neighbourhood, is an instance of a diffuse one.

Player profile

The gambling sites host a variety of social groups, each with their own motivations for playing and with their own relations to chance. The socio-economic constitution of players varies between individual games, creating an affinity between the structure of a game and the characteristics of the individuals who engage in it. Given this, player profile will be examined separately in each site, and will only be summarised here. Briefly, the lottery has a broad demographic appeal, although relative play is highest among the poorest groups in society. Casino patrons tend to be mainly middle class, as are regular race-track goers. However, the betting shop is patronised mainly by working-class men, bingo by working-class women, while slot-machines are the game of choice of young people. To date, no research has been conducted into the profile of individuals who gamble on the Internet.

THE SITES: PLAYGROUNDS

Every gambling site forms its own separate world, each with its own distinctive ambiance. Each one has the character of what Goffman calls 'social occasions': events which are bounded in space and time and which are possessed of 'a distinctive ethos' (Goffman 1963, p. 10). Utilising the formal characteristics of games set out in the typology above, the remainder of this chapter will begin to outline the nature and experience of gambling unique to each site, as well as describing the material conditions upon which such experiences are built. This analysis will be continued in the final chapters, where the focus will shift from what is distinctive to what is *common* to the experience of gambling across all the sites.

The lottery

Although lottery-type games like football pools have been run in Britain for years, the creation of a state lottery in 1994 institutionalised the form, creating almost overnight the foremost type of national gambling and effectively sweeping away competition from companies like Littlewoods and Vernons. It is estimated that 33 million people play the lottery each week – 58 per cent of the population – spending an average of £2.08 on tickets (OFLOT 1998).

After 168 years of prohibition, the British state lottery was reinstated to resume its original function of state fund-raising and the creation of private profit. In an era in which the government is unwilling to levy unpopular taxes for services it is reluctant to fund at all, the lottery's role as state fund-raiser again comes to the fore. Once again arguments against the 'immorality' of games of chance go unheeded as the vested interests of capital see in such games the opportunity for pecuniary gain. Just as sixteenth-century British lotteries funded the growth of a nascent state – bridges, libraries, and its exploits abroad – so the present day one finances the recreation of a declining one – opera houses, sports fields and the exploits of its organisers closer to home. The proceeds from stake money are divided between players, organisers and government, with 50 per cent going to winners, 5 per cent to retailers, 5 per cent to lottery organisers Camelot, 12 per cent to the treasury and 28 per cent for 'good causes' such as arts funding and charities.

At the start of the new millennium the embrace of lotteries by state fiscal policy is more apparent than ever, with lotteries worldwide running un-ashamedly as capitalist ventures, distributing revenue for both public works and private profit. Far from the lottery taking over other social institutions as in Borges' tale of chance, western economies have proved themselves quite able not only to incorporate it into their structure, but also to use the lottery for their own ends.

The launch of the lottery in November 1994 signalled, in the words of one market analyst, 'the biggest event in Britain's economic life since decimalisation' (*Guardian*, 21 March 1995, p. 22). Spending £5514 million during 1997 to 1998 alone (more than is spent annually on bread, health and beauty care, books or rail travel), the public embraced the lottery with open arms, transforming the nature of the consumption economy almost overnight as they did so. Patterns of spending and recreation have changed: the lottery has created 12 million new shopping trips each week and sales in shops with terminals have risen by 20 per cent, due in part at least to the five thousand new customers brought in by the desire to purchase tickets. Central Statistical

Office figures show that the introduction of the lottery in 1994 increased consumer expenditure by 50 per cent from the previous year, even though it had only been in operation for half of that financial year (FitzHerbert *et al.* 1996). Leisure habits have also changed: Saturday night television viewing has increased by 20 per cent because of the televised draw (The Henley Centre 1995).

As well as the proliferation of lottery-type games such as scratch cards, given away, for example, with various products including packets of crisps, video games and newspapers, the lottery has had a 'knock on' effect on participation in other forms of gambling too. Its introduction initiated the deregulation of the entire gambling economy. Seeing its success and fearing its competition, other forms of gambling such as casinos and bingo companies demanded the same freedom to advertise and promote their 'product' as the lottery monopoly, with the result that the paternalistic strictures of the 1968 Gaming Act are gradually being repealed and the entire gambling industry is being opened up to the vicissitudes of market forces.

It is not only in economic life that the impact of the lottery has been felt, for it has dramatically and irrevocably altered the profile of British gamblers. Here the homogenisation of the gambling experience inherent in the commodification of games of chance is most strongly felt. Before the introduction of the lottery there were 15 million regular gamblers in Britain; now there are 25 million. In 1994 – the year of the lottery – around 90 per cent of the population took part in some kind of gambling activity, compared with 74 per cent the previous year. The increase is directly attributable to the lottery. Groups previously under-represented in gambling activities – the young, women and the middle class – are now becoming visible through their lottery participation. Traditionally a male pastime, playing lotteries like the pools was popular with skilled manual workers aged between 35 and 44. However, the lottery has attracted more young, female and affluent patrons, resulting in an increase in female participation in gambling activities from its pre-1994 figure of 70 per cent to 87 per cent, bringing them almost level with male gambling which stands at 89 per cent (Mintel 1995).

Remarkably little socioeconomic or geographical variation exists among lottery players; in fact, it has been remarked that the overall picture is one of 'unusual uniformity', with few differences between men and women, old and young and north and south (FitzHerbert *et al.* 1996). Traditional middle-class dislike of gambling has been overcome in this state-sanctioned activity, which further assuages uneasy consciences with the reminder of the 'good causes' that benefit from participation. The predilection of 'upmarket' ABC1 socioeconomic groups for the game is a source of pride for Camelot, which states: 'Guardian readers are just as likely to play as Sun readers' (*Guardian*, 22 March 1995, p. 2).

However, the ubiquity of participation and the inclusion of the young, middle class and female gamblers, while an important trend in the demographics of British gambling, should be interpreted carefully. Although effective marketing and distribution campaigns by private and state-run businesses have brought about the proliferation of lotteries and the expansion of their socioeconomic bases throughout the industrialised west, this tends to conceal another trend – the *concentration* of play among the poorest socioeconomic groups. The high incidence of participation among the poor, the under-educated and the old, and the increase in participation in times of high unemployment in countries with long-established lotteries, has been well documented (Kaplan 1978; Clotfelter and Cook 1989; Walker 1992), and this also appears to apply to the British case. Although 58 per cent of the population play, not all spend the same amount each week, much less a similar amount relative to their total incomes. The average of £2.08 per person per ticket conceals vast differences in the reality of play. Participation is highest (75 per cent) among skilled manual workers and those who left full-time education at age 15 or 16 living in the north, especially Scotland; and lowest (50 per cent) among managers and professionals and those who left education at age 19 or over living in the south-east of England (OFLOT 1998). Furthermore, it has been found that while high income groups spend only 4 per cent of their total leisure spending on the lottery, among poorer families the figure is 30 per cent (FitzHerbert *et al.* 1996). Although players come from a broad cross-section of the population, regularity and amount spent is concentrated among the poorest sections of society indicating that the historical trend towards the over-representation of the poor in lottery draws is substantiated today. Like the poor who played the lotteries of the sixteenth and seventeenth centuries, the unemployed, the low paid and the economically marginalised of today regard the distant possibility of winning as their best chance to escape poverty in what is essentially still an unmeritocratic social system. The very reasons that led to its outlawing in 1826 – its 'encouragement of a spirit of Speculation and Gambling among the lower classes of the people' – are the same reasons that assure its popularity today. Denied genuine opportunity, the poor are given a chimera; a vision of immense riches which only one in fourteen million will ever attain. Balzac's comment on the French lottery that 'No-one has realised that it was the opium of poverty. The lottery was the most magical fairy in the world: did it not nurture magical hopes?' (Balzac 1984, p. 88) is still as pertinent today as it was when he made it in 1841.

The advertisement for scratch cards in a Las Vegas casino shown in Plate 4 embodies the brutal exploitation of hope that is an integral feature of all lotteries. Instead of some redistribution of wealth, here money is taken directly from the impoverished as they cash entire pay cheques in the hope of instant riches.

It is ironic that, despite their over-representation in the purchase of tickets, those with the least to lose *do* in fact end up losing out in the distribution of stake money. At only 50 per cent, the return of the total stake as prizes is

Plate 4: 'Cash your paycheck and win!'
Source: Author

extremely low, and the impressive sounding 'good causes' which supposedly contribute to the wealth of the nation have turned out to be highly partisan – in effect, the pastimes of the affluent. While pennies are thrown at brass bands and school swimming pools, millions are plunged into the playgrounds of the middle classes – opera houses and art galleries, and those of their children – for example, the project to refurbish the sports grounds of Eton. So, although lottery participation is biased to the working classes in the north, proceeds are appropriated by the middle classes in the south. As a revenue-raising device then, the lottery is a particularly regressive form of taxation, with those on the lowest incomes paying far more than their wealthier neighbours.

In the US, state lotteries have passed the point where they generate revenue for only 'luxuries' and are now firmly ensconced in an area which the state has gradually backed out of – the provision of vital services. In most states, lotteries are funding larger and larger proportions of expenditure on health and education, and although (as in Britain) most deny such funding is intended to take over the state's share, it inevitably does so. For example, in Pennsylvania, rent assistance and medical rebates for the elderly were initially financed by the state and gradually shifted to the lottery fund as lottery revenues increased (Abt and Smith 1986, p. 31). No doubt the temptation to allow lottery players to 'voluntarily' pay for state-funded services will prove too much for Britain over the coming years; and, with the introduction of the New Opportunities Fund (NOC), whose 'good cause' is the funding of community projects in health, education and the environment, the process may already have begun.

The organisation and form of the lottery and its instantaneous cousin, the scratch card, have contributed to its easy integration into public life, and the broad social base of its support. Its form has remained virtually unchanged from that of its sixteenth-century predecessor and involves the selection of numbers which are chosen by a randomising device. The spatial organisation of the lottery is diffuse; tickets are available from many points and, because it is an integrated site, they blend almost seamlessly with their local environment. The very act of playing the lottery has become normalised, with tickets purchased as part of a daily routine along with the morning groceries or week-end shopping. There exists little spontaneity in this realm of pure chance: 80 per cent of lottery purchases are pre-planned with half the nation's players making special trips to buy tickets (*Guardian*, 22 March 1995, p. 2). Customers stand in a queue as they would for any other commodity, and, upon paying a pound, their bar-coded ticket indicates that they are now gamblers. It is perhaps in this prosaic ritual that the modern commodification of chance is most evident.

Because the lottery has a slow rate of play, every stage in the process of buying a ticket can be separated and stretched out to fill the time between draws. There is no sense of urgency in this kind of game: numbers need not be chosen at the same time or even in the same place as picking up the play slip, and once the ticket itself has been bought, another period of inactivity unfolds in the wait for the draw. In the interim, involvement is minimal, possession of a ticket being the sole measure of participation in an activity which is both spatially and temporally dispersed. The most distinctive characteristic of scratch cards on the other hand is their *instantaneity*, a feature emphasised in the advertisement 'forget it all for an instant'. This fast rate of play makes scratch cards an immediate form of gambling, whose instant result constitutes a large part of their appeal and contributes to their addictive effect (Griffiths 1995a).

The televised Saturday night draw is the climax of the protraction of lottery activity. In contrast to the leisurely stretched out time of the previous six days, the draw is over in seconds, characterised by a concentration of action in a short space of time. Six balls are ejected from a revolving drum, accompanied by drumrolls and fanfares in a game show hosted by various media celebrities and entertainers. Excitement peaks at this point as players at home anxiously check their tickets for the winning numbers. Thirty seconds later, it is all over for another week. The deflation of mood which inevitably follows such tension has for some been characterised as a unique new illness – 'lottomania' (*The Times*, 15 June 1995), or 'lottery stress disorder' (Hunter 1995). A doctor has described how patients presenting with the disorder show intense anxiety, which increases during the week and peaks on Saturday evening. It is often accompanied by 'unrealistic optimism and grandiose ideas' in which 'the subject experiences the delusional belief that great riches are about to befall him or her'. Inevitably, after the draw on Saturday, 'these feelings give way to rapid deflation of mood', and although recovery sets in at the beginning of the week, 'characteristically the pattern repeats itself over the coming week' (Hunter 1995, p. 875).

The distant relation of the player to the game, the high integration and the slow rate of play culminate in the *normalisation* of the lottery as a form of gambling. Such normalisation is so extreme that lottery players are often not regarded as gamblers at all, even by themselves. In Spain, where the state-run *El Gordo* is a national institution, most people deny they gamble but when asked if they take part in the lottery reply 'of course' (*Guardian*, 31 October 1994, p. 3). This perception is codified in language where, unlike gamblers in other games of chance, lottery players never 'gamble'; they merely 'participate' or enjoy an innocuous 'flutter' on a *sui generis* event. The idea of the lottery participant is not so much a euphemism as a reflection of the presentation of the lottery itself, and one which, for Walter Benjamin, means that 'an incorrigible patron of a lottery will not be proscribed in the same way as the gambler in a stricter sense' (Benjamin 1992, p. 137). Such a perception is descended from the lottery's sixteenth-century forebears when gambling was encouraged by the state as a patriotic duty and so defined as a philanthropic gesture, never a gamble. With its emphasis on the lottery's support of 'good causes' and 'heritage' the modern state once more sanctions betting and, thus legitimised, removes it from the arena of gambling proper.

The discovery already of a 'lottery pathology' serves to highlight the more general malaise which lies behind the official position on gambling. For every individual suffering from lottery stress disorder, there are thousands more whose poverty is exacerbated by overspending on tickets, and worse, by the removal of funds once provided by the state and now dependent on the vicissitudes of lottery revenue. State lotteries (and, to a lesser degree, *all* state-sanctioned and therefore taxable gambling) of the late twentieth and early twenty-first centuries are an indication of the degree to which governments are increasingly abnegating responsibility for the provision of services they once felt bound to provide. In the era of nascent capitalism, lotteries provided revenue for states whose infrastructures were insufficiently developed to collect taxes from every citizen. Now, the lotteries widespread among the most highly bureaucratised nations in the world function to raise an indirect and regressive form of taxation which their governments are politically unwilling to collect. As the presence of the state recedes in public life, that of the lottery grows, to the extent that every harmless 'flutter' heralds a further disintegration of the apparatus of state funding. The potentially pernicious effects of lotteries do not lie so much in the individuals who become addicted to the possibilities of instant riches, but rather in the governments who become addicted to the certain revenue they bring in. Such games can only be played to the detriment of society as a whole.

George Orwell's pessimistic vision of lotteries in the hands of the modern state is described in *Nineteen Eighty-Four*. Projected exactly ten years before the reintroduction of the British state lottery, it describes the cynical manipulation of hope by the Party in the form of a lottery whose prizes were 'largely imaginary' and where 'only small sums were actually paid out': 'The Lottery . . . was the one public event to which the proles paid serious attention. . . . It was their delight, their folly, their anodyne, their intellectual stimulant' (Orwell 1984, p. 77).

Bingo

Derived from the late nineteenth-century game of lotto, and the games of tombola and housey-housey played in the navy and army respectively, bingo is essentially a form of lottery, albeit a concentrated one. It occupies a separate site, is governed by a faster rate of play and is patronised by its own unique social group – predominantly working-class women. Nearly six million people play bingo in Britain, around half a million of them visiting some 850 bingo clubs every day (Dixey 1996).

As in the lottery, a bingo winner is declared when a randomly generated series of numbers matches those held by a player. However, unlike the lottery, in bingo players are present during the number-calling session, marking off the numbers in their books as they are announced. The rate of play of a game thus measures the time taken to fill in a book, and can be sped up by the player increasing the number of these books. Some experienced players can fill in several books simultaneously and so increase the intensity of the game. Intensity also increases as the game progresses. As more and more numbers are called, and more and more players find themselves waiting for a final, decisive number, anticipation mounts as the race to find a winner nears its end. Although unable to influence this game of pure chance in any way, players are fully involved at every stage by the need to vigilantly check their cards and keep up with the flow of numbers being called. Unlike the weekly draw of the lottery, bingo sessions are conducted in the afternoons and evenings of most weekdays in buildings which, despite being part of the local community, are essentially *separate* sites. Often situated in disused cinemas or town halls, entry into a bingo club is an entry into a distinct world, which is secluded from the one outside and governed by its own set of rules and conventions.

Enormous variations in levels of comfort, decor and amenities can be found between clubs, with new, custom-built premises in out-of-town leisure parks contrasting with those that occupy older, renovated cinemas or dance-halls in town centres. Dixey, for example, writes that 'the equivalent of sawdust and spittoon pubs can be found in the tombola clubs of the north-east, while the refurbished clubs of some of the major companies can be visually stunning, offering a very different kind of experience' (Dixey 1987, p. 208). The ambiance of a session can further vary, depending on whether it constitutes a 'Saturday night out', or whether it is scheduled on a midweek afternoon and fitted around the daily routine of children, housework and shopping.

Although Downes *et al.*'s 1976 survey found males and females to be equal participants in the game of bingo, subsequent research has found female participation to be far higher, and has pointed to the high degree of recruitment from working men's clubs in the original survey as the source of such an imbalance (Dixey 1987; Freestone 1995). The Gallup Survey of 1991 found that 83 per cent of players are women and 17 per cent men, with an average age of 53 (in Freestone 1995). The socioeconomic basis of bingo participation is predominantly working class, Downes *et al.* stating that '*not* being working class was practically enough to predict virtually no bingo playing' (Downes *et al.* 1976, p. 180).

Such demographics are the result of female patterns of leisure activity in postwar Britain. The schemes to rehouse the working class in new housing estates and high-rise flats in the 1950s and 1960s disrupted established communities and reduced the amount of semi-public space in which neighbourly interaction (especially among women) could take place. At the same time, the large-scale closure of cinemas in the 1950s curtailed the specifically female tradition of visiting the cinema, and so removed an important female meeting place. However, the reopening of cinemas as bingo halls during the following decade provided a new public space for women, and the 'natural' continuation of an already existing habit, assuring such clubs a place in the lives of working-class women. Thus a gendered space was created for women, allowing them to go out and socialise with each other in a secure environment (Dixey 1987). The sociable aspect of bingo is paramount then; four-fifths of Downes *et al.*'s (1976) female sample reported that they *never* played alone, while only 8.9 per cent of Dixey's (1996) sample played on their own.

Until recently, the bingo economy was bound by the restrictions of the 1968 Act which allowed the opening of only sufficient clubs to meet 'existing' not 'stimulated' demand. To this end, clubs were not allowed to advertise – even when their intention was to attract new members of staff – or to show any illustration of the inside of a bingo hall. Visitors to bingo clubs were required to be members, and had to wait twenty-four hours between joining a club and playing in it – a measure whose residual Puritanism was intended to eliminate any 'irrational' playing on impulse.

However, the general deregulation of the gaming industry has been felt quite markedly in the arena of bingo and has been codified in an Act of 1992 which lifted the ban on advertising and allowed clubs to invite the public to take part in their activities. Further deregulation in 1996 continued these first steps towards market integration by allowing bingo sites to exist without being 'members only' clubs and abolishing the twenty-four-hour 'cooling off' period. As a capitalist enterprise, bingo, like the lottery, is attempting to broaden its demographic base to attract younger and more affluent players. The renovation of older sites and investment in new, purpose-built venues often in leisure complexes and retail parks is deliberately intended to create a more 'upmarket' image, as is the introduction of various new technologies, such as a computer-linked National Game which joins together some 650 clubs in competition for a single prize of £50,000 (Freestone 1995, p. 6). Touch-screen computers have further modernised bingo, their digital screens sunk into tables rendering books of numbers redundant in many clubs. The option of a 'waitress call' button whereby players can order drinks at the touch of a screen is set to alter the constitution of the old-style bingo experience still further.

Already the physiognomy of bingo is changing, the deregulation of the industry and intervention of modernising technologies breaking down the traditional player profile. As more young people and more upwardly mobile social groups join in, the game, like the lottery, appears to be increasingly subject to the homogenising force of commercial interests.

Slot-machines

There are some 250,000 slot-machines or 'fruit machines' in Britain, which, because of strict licensing controls, occupy two types of gambling site: those in specially licensed premises or 'adult environments' such as public houses, bingo clubs, casinos and private members' clubs, and those which do not require a licence, known as Amusement With Prizes machines (AWP), which are found in various locations such as cafés, chip shops, sports centres and arcades. Both the number of machines and maximum prizes are regulated in these areas so that the top payment for AWP games is £4 in tokens, £8 cash, and £250 in 'adult environments' where the maximum number of machines is limited to two. The government-appointed Deregulation Committee has repealed some of the restrictions of the 1968 Gaming Act, making machines more widely available. Two machines are now allowed in betting shops, the number in casinos has been increased from two to six, and in bingo clubs from two to four, while cash prizes in arcades have been increased to £10 (Report of the Gaming Board 1994–1995, pp. 42–45; Deregulation Committee Ninth Report 1996, pp. vii–x).

Although this deregulation looks set to increase the integration of slots into everyday life, for the moment, British machines still occupy two distinct sites. Being spread out across large sections of public space, the organisation of machines in 'adult environments' is relatively diffuse. Although they must remain thinly spread, such slots penetrate deeply into the local social fabric and are more or less integrated with their surrounding neighbourhood. Amusement arcades, on the other hand, form concentrated sites which occupy their own separate gambling space. Found usually in commercial or tourist areas of towns, arcades exist slightly apart from their surrounding environment in buildings whose interiors are darkened and concealed from the outside world by blacked-out windows. One can enter the arcade in a way that it is impossible to 'enter' the diffuse slot-machine site.

From the elegant displays of lights and the soporific hum of hundreds of machines, arcades are possessed of a distinctive ambiance. Within their dimly lit interiors, rows of machines rattle out a cacophony of sound; a noise Tom Wolfe described as 'a random-sound John Cage symphony . . . much like the sound a cash register makes before the bell rings' (Wolfe 1981, p. 19).

The rate of play in slot machines measures the time taken for gamblers to insert their money, pull a lever or push a button, watch the display as the wheels rotate, carry out any commands and, if lucky, collect their winnings. This process lasts between five and twenty seconds, time that is animated by a bombardment of electronic sound and pulsating lights. Such a heady atmosphere is deliberately designed to seduce players into a rhythm of repetitive, continuous play. Although they can play at any pace they want, gamblers are carried along by this stream of noise and light which only stops when *they* stop, and play continuously, barely completing one round before inserting more money for the next.[4] Speeding up what is already a continuous rate of play, some gamblers play two or even three machines at once. Unlike the slow, stretched out rate of play of the lottery, then, the rate of slots is concentrated, grinding on with barely a pause between one game and the next.

Despite their impressive technological advancement, even the most sophisticated machines such as the microprocessor slots of Las Vegas, in which players insert a credit card, press a button and hope for a multi-million dollar jackpot, operate according to the same basic principles as their nineteenth-century predecessors. Like a kind of mechanised lottery, all slot-machines are basically random number generators. Play is straightforward: the gambler activates a machine by inserting money and wins a prize if a specific pattern or configuration of images is produced. Each machine is a self-contained gambling unit, accepting the player's stake and paying out a prize, and so rendering the presence of other players entirely superfluous.[5] Player involvement is direct and immediate with gamblers physically involved in play. Their presence is necessary to activate the machine and during the time spent playing it they must continually monitor their actions in accordance with its commands. They will be presented with a range of options for play and must decide whether to hold or nudge the reels, insert more money or collect their winnings. Such features create player involvement, which should not however be mistaken for influence, for despite the various 'skill' features which attempt to persuade players otherwise, slot-machines are games of pure chance.

It is perhaps at least partly their simplicity that contributes to slots' egalitarian appeal. Ever since the first penny arcades offered a wide public cheap entertainment in the late nineteenth century, slot-machines – both in and out of the arcade – have been patronised by the same cross-class clientele, and especially by the young. Generally, social class is not a significant factor in slot-machine play (Downes *et al.* 1976, p. 185; Ide-Smith and Lea 1988; Fisher 1991), the distribution of players being rather affected by the *age* and *sex* of participants. What Fisher calls an 'incoherent mish mash of legal rules and trade agreements' (Fisher 1998, p. 13) has meant that slot-machines are the only form of gambling legally available to young people. While it is legal for children of any age to play machines paying up to £5 in cash, only over-18s may play those paying £10. Since both types of machine are often located in the same premises and enforcement is usually left to the discretion of owners, the result is easy access and availability, and so widespread popularity.

The integration of slot-machines into their surrounding communities and their utilisation of the imagery of popular culture in designs which copy cartoon characters, soap operas and game shows makes them an everyday sight and further contributes to their popularity among the young. The situation of machines in chip shops, youth clubs and arcades also provides a favourable environment and opportunity for the young to gamble, with the result that the average age at which individuals begin slot-machine play is 10 or 11 years (Griffiths 1995a, p. 64). In this way, Fisher explains: 'amusement arcades . . . provide an important leisure environment for school age and unemployed youngsters' (Fisher 1993, p. 446; see also Fisher 1995). These arcades are cultural spaces where young people – particularly *males* – are free to engage in the rituals of adolescence; mixing with their peers and exploring their identities in an adult-free environment. Within these spaces, the machines themselves and the games played on them may be extrinsic to their function as a source of solidarity, status and a focus for group interactions.[6]

Players themselves can be further broken down into various categories depending on the motivations and orientation to play of specific subgroups. Fisher (1993) described the multi-dimensional nature of such gamblers, classifying the results of her ethnographic study into five discrete 'types': 'Arcade Kings', 'Machine Beaters', 'Rent-a-Spacers', 'Action Seekers' and 'Escape Artists'. The groups ranged in character from the sociable: the skilled, socially cohesive Arcade Kings and the Rent-a-Spacers, to the less sociable: the individualistic Machine Beaters who played alone in an attempt to master their machines, the Action Seekers who played for excitement, and the Escape Artists who played in order to escape their problems in the world outside. According to Fisher, none of these individuals gambled to win money: rather, the aim of winning simply provided a justification for involvement and so unified their activities.

The racecourse

The modern race-track still retains the aura of its aristocratic heritage, its legacy as the 'sport of the kings'. Although commercialisation in the nineteenth century meant that paying spectators were welcomed, the sheer size of race-tracks places them in relatively remote locations on the periphery of urban areas and has tended to militate against such a demo-cratising trend. This, along with a hefty entrance fee, works as a form of exclusion, effectively limiting regular attendance to those living nearby and/or with the financial means and leisure time to make a habit of spending 'afternoons at the races'. Physical enhances cultural separation, so that the subculture of horse-racing, where the natives are 'absorbed in unintelligible rituals and arcane wagering terminology' is a confusing and often incomprehensible experience to the initiate (Abt *et al.* 1985, p. 84).[7] Ultimately then, British racing is still a predominantly upper-middle-class form of gambling.

The architecture of the race-track itself is a monument to social stratification. The better quality seats in the clubhouse, traditionally reserved for the elite, are set slightly apart and are more expensive than those of the grandstand which, uncovered and commanding a less expansive view, are patronised by the 'commoners'. The modern race-track is thus a separate site and one which, despite the democratising commercialism of the past hundred years, still retains an air of privilege and exclusivity. In contrast, the dog track is still a separate site but one that is more integrated into its surrounding neighbourhood. Being smaller, it need not be situated on the outskirts of towns and is often located close to bettors' homes in working-class or industrial areas of cities. It is this that Downes *et al.* call the 'localised character' of the dog track, in contrast to the 'expeditionary character' of the horse racecourse (Downes *et al.* 1976, p. 143). Smaller, closer to home and with more races going on, the dog track can be seen as a miniature version of the racecourse; furthermore, free from the aristocratic heritage of the latter, it is a site that is occupied primarily by the working class.

Despite physical immediacy, the gambler's relation to play at the race-track is not one of involvement but immersion. The constant hubbub of activity, the smell of damp earth and horses all create a unique ambiance peculiar to the track. Despite this immersion, the gambler at the race-track, like the one in the lottery, is extrinsic to the gambling event itself. Unlike lottery players, who are neither involved nor present in the lottery, however, punters at the race-track are present during the race and so can watch the event upon which they are betting unfold in front of them.

Players' actual involvement with the race is dictated by the paraphernalia of the race itself. Having chosen their horse(s) they place their wagers at a betting kiosk, take a receipt and wait for the race to begin. Around the track, tote boards display times of races and odds on horses, while loudspeakers boom information on conditions and events. This information is vital for the study of form and for selection of horses, a complex activity which confers prestige on those skilled enough to undertake it successfully. The processes through which horses are selected at the race-track are the same as those governing selection at the betting shop, and will be discussed further in that section.

Races are held two or three times a month during the racing season, giving them a rate of play that can be measured, like the lottery, in long, slow cycles. Such cycles lack the absolute regularity of lottery draws however, for their periodicity can be interrupted by natural events such as bad weather or track conditions, resulting in the last-minute cancellation of races. Planned races such as the Grand National are much publicised, giving the punter time to find out who is running and what their past records are like. Unlike the lottery draw where the gamble – the event – is over in seconds, on a race day the gambling lasts all day long, broken up into three or four separate races.

The race-track is a concentrated site within which the concentration of action itself waxes and wanes in a series of stages. It peaks during the two to ten minutes of the race and declines during the periods of waiting in between. The rate of play is intimately connected to the players' relation to the game and to the concentration of action, a connection which is centred on the large amounts of geographical and temporal space at the race-track. After placing their bets, gamblers have a period of 'empty' time before them until the race begins. Because of its separation from the outside world, they cannot leave the track and so enter a period of waiting. During this time, punters' actions betray a certain purposelessness. From the distance, their collective milling appears like a particularly anxious form of Brownian motion. As the race is prepared, expectation mounts and a sense of direction gradually guides the disparate actions of individual punters into a focused movement towards the track and the stands. It is at this point that the panopticon-style design of the stadium becomes obvious: giant elevated grandstands surround the course and descend down in terraces lined with seats, so that the structure of the racecourse itself is built to extend vision from the periphery of the stadium to a concentrated point in the centre – the track. Corresponding to this temporal narrowing of distance is a physical one; with the race only minutes away, punters draw closer to their vantage points; the directionless flux becomes gathered, concentrated and stationary. Paraphrasing Merleau-Ponty, Scott writes that the individual at the track is so engrossed in the action that the reality of his field of consciousness 'is confirmed and thrust upon him with clearness and distinctness' (Scott 1968, p. 114). Just before the race begins, anticipation reaches a climax: the entire stadium is focused on the track, so that distractions are obliterated and the race is immediate in the consciousness of its spectators. Such charged, 'full' space contrasts with the 'empty', featureless space experienced in the period of waiting just before the race.

A period of quietude and deflation follows the completion of the race, during which time energy and individuals are again dissipated throughout the course. This whole cycle of energy and concentration, lassitude and relaxation is repeated several times throughout the day; a stage in the drawn-out recurrence of peaks and troughs that make up the rate of play at the race-track.

The bookmaker

The bookmaker is an ambiguous site and one that is in transition: concentrated but becoming more diffuse; separate but in many ways incorporated into its local environment.

Such ambiguity stems from a historical tension between the existence of racing as a legitimate aristocratic sport, and simultaneously as an illegitimate working-class one. As we saw earlier, this disparity was formalised in various historical statutes which effectively prohibited the poor from betting on races and outlawed betting shops. Commercial development proved a stronger force than moral outrage however, so that by the late 1950s bookmaking was legalised, allowing companies like Ladbrokes, Coral and William Hill to form and start making huge – and legal – profits from their ventures. Betting shops became visible and proliferated after the 1950s, especially in the working-class districts of urban areas. Despite being located on street corners and among conventional shops and public amenities, the terms of the 1968 Act required bookmakers to separate or distance themselves from their immediate surroundings. Blacked-out windows and double sets of doors were permanent fixtures, presumably to ensure that innocent passers-by would not inadvertently glance in and be corrupted by the debauchery going on inside! Such an extreme attempt at separation was complemented by a deliberately austere interior design. From their barren, brightly lit walls and rows of metal stools nailed to the floor to their dusty linoleum floors covered with cigarette ends and discarded betting slips, decoration was minimal. Every relentlessly functional fixture was designed to encourage gamblers to make their bets and leave. This project was effective, for the vast majority of patrons chose not to linger in such an inhospitable environment, remaining in the betting shop only for the few minutes necessary to place their bet.

Until the general deregulation of gambling, the artificial separation and deliberate austerity of the betting shop served as a testimony to the ambiguous status of working-class gambling; a token reminder of its clandestine past. However, in April 1995 the restrictions that forced them to be deliberately inhospitable were lifted, allowing bookmakers to have clear windows, to advertise what goes on inside and even display odds to passers-by. Restrictions on the maximum size of television screens allowed inside have been abolished, and bookmakers are licensed to sell refreshments. Carpets and seating areas are no longer frowned on by a government suddenly eager to throw open the closed shop of the betting world to a wider, paying audience. It remains to be seen, however, whether such deregulation will prove sufficient to alter the physiognomy of the bookmakers, and so overcome the cohesion of a social formation developed from centuries of social stratification.

Despite for decades being forced to separate themselves from their surroundings, bookmakers nevertheless became incorporated into the daily routine of their local neighbourhoods. Their situation and their opening hours (generally 9.30 a.m. to 5.30 or 7.00 p.m., now with the inclusion of Sundays) enables them to blend in with the rhythm of daily life around them, making it convenient for punters to drop in on their way home from work or on their way to the local pub. Downes *et al.* (1976) found that proximity leads to regularity: three-quarters of those regularly visiting betting shops lived only five minutes from one.

Their concentration in working-class neighbourhoods complements an overwhelmingly working-class and also an overwhelmingly *male* clientele. The working class use betting shops between five and twelve times as often as the middle class, with frequency increasing with descent down the class hierarchy, while males are eight times more likely to use the premises than females (Downes *et al.* 1976, p. 123). When women *do* bet on a race, Downes *et al.* found that they would often do so by proxy, asking a male friend or relative to place the bet for them, rather than entering the premises themselves (Downes *et al.* 1976, p. 122).

Of course, this apparently homogeneous betting population conceals a variety of subgroups with various motivations for and experiences of gambling. Recent research has documented this diversity (Rosecrance 1986; Saunders and Turner 1987; Bruce and Johnson 1992; Neal 1998), showing that punters gamble for a range of reasons – for excitement and intellectual challenge, as well as to socialise and for financial gain – and that these motivations are also related to the *times* at which individuals bet and the *types* of bet placed. Neal (1998) divided his sample of bettors into various categories. The 'morning flutter' punters were mainly pensioners who visited the betting shop every day as part of a sociable routine and placed low-stake multiple bets which allowed them to dream of a big win for a price that was within their means. The 'lunchtime punters' were made up of busy low- or semi-skilled workers who dropped in over lunchtime to place more expensive high-risk / high-return bets, thus relieving the monotony of the working day. 'Afternoon punters' were made up of non-routine workers such as waiters and bar staff, for whom the trip to the betting shop provided a routine and an outlet in which to socialise and exchange gossip. These punters tended to place individual bets, so maximising the excitement of a race, especially when many had the time to remain in the bookmakers to watch it as it was going on.

Within all this diversity, however, Neal came to a conclusion similar to Fisher's (1993) in her study of fruit machine players. The fundamental characteristic of all punters, he wrote, was that they invariably lost money, and, furthermore, that winning it in the first place was never a primary motivation to play. Rather, the activity itself contained social and personal rewards which gave it value regardless of the outcome of any particular game. The implications of this will be considered in Chapter 4.

But for the fact that punters at the bookmakers are not actually present to see the race, the conditions for the exercise of skill are the same for them as they are for the gambler at the racecourse. The 'arcane wagering terminology' of the race-track belies the complex frame of reference which underlies horse-race betting. Such a frame of reference, based on the art of handicapping, demands considerable skill and knowledge, for the list of variables which can influence the outcome of a race is vast, requiring the talents of a perceptive and experienced individual for effective interpretation. A wide range of betting options further increases the complexity of race gambling. Punters can decide which *type* of bet to place – single, double, treble or accumulator; choose the odds of the bet – favourite, outsider or in between; and select whether or not their bet is 'each way' or 'to win'. Such levels of complexity have elevated the practice of betting on horses into a virtual science with top punters regarded as skilled probabilists, admired and respected among their peers.

Like the long waves of lottery play, the rate of play in the betting shop is a drawn out, protracted affair. Punters put their money on races in leisurely cycles with pauses, consideration, even physical departure from the site altogether between bets. Generally hours, days or even weeks mark the temporal separation of bets, in contrast with, for example, the seconds of frenetic haste of the slot-machine player. The full immersion of the latter, surrounded by the action and physically participating in the repetition of successive bets contrasts with the gambler at the betting shop, who, displaced spatially and temporally from the action, slowly and carefully repeats daily 'long wave' bets.

Corresponding to the integration of individual sites into their local environment is the *diffusion*, among these separate sites, of a single concentrated site of action. Only the actual gambling event itself does not take place in the bookmakers. Everything else – from making a bet and watching the action unfold, to collecting winnings – is contained within its walls. Thus, as a scene of action in its own right, the betting shop is a concentrated site. However, insofar as it exists to receive an image of the race and to accept bets to and from areas outwith the actual scene of the action, it also exists as part of a larger whole. In this sense, it functions as a diffuse site, dispersing a single localised event throughout a wide area. The distinctive atmosphere of the race-track is removed from its geographical location, fragmented into hundreds of smaller races and flung on to television screens on the walls of betting shops across the country. The variable weather of the track is replaced by the static luminosity of artificial lighting, while the dynamic interplay of a single mass of individuals freezes into numerous groups of punters whose mobility is conditioned by their cramped surroundings and the necessity of maintaining the screen in their constant field of vision. The action of the race-track is, then, both *displaced* from its original location, and *diffused* among many new ones.

The betting shop is a site in transition; one which technological development is making ever more diffuse. In the nineteenth century, railways took bettors to the race-track; now, in the twenty-first century, technology brings the race to *them*. An innovation in computer linkage has brought the trend of automisation and privatisation in gambling to its logical conclusion. Pioneered by a company called Betpoint, this latest development will literally bring the betting shop into the living room in a package which links races and bank account details to a personal computer via a modem. With Betpoint, a bet is chosen from a menu of options and stakes are instantly taken from the punter's account. Any winnings are similarly credited when the race is over. Although not yet widespread, technologies such as these have the potential to link together millions of players, who need never interact with each other and who can gamble on a race going on many miles away without ever leaving their own home. The betting shop is here made redundant and the gambler isolated into a solitary gambling 'unit'.

Like the lottery, this increasingly diffuse site reaches deep into society. Its spokes are breaking down into ever smaller, individualised units which can penetrate the social fabric even further than the sociable aggregate of the betting shop. While the separation of the race-track works to encourage its exclusivity, the diffusion of the bookmaker encourages the opposite trend of democratisation, making races accessible to an increasingly wide audience.

The casino

The casino can be said to be the purest of the gambling sites, for it incorporates all the forms of gambling seen so far as well as many others of its own. The insulation of this 'ideal type' from the world outside and its accumulation of gambling forms *in*side make it a microcosm of gambling activity, for in the fleeting exchanges of the casino floor are contained all the varieties of gambling experience themselves.

Based on the very different societies they represent, significant differences distinguish the American from the British casino. However, it is instructive to compare the two, for in Britain proposed legislative changes are poised to move the latter closer to the American model. By relaxing the strictures of the 1968 Gaming Act, casinos would be given longer licensing hours, more slot-machines, and the ability, for the first time, to advertise themselves. Whether or not these changes materialise remains to be seen, but what is apparent is that, consonant with moves within the rest of the gambling industry, casinos are attempting to attract a wider section of the population and advertise themselves as a mainstream leisure activity. In this, Britain's multi-million pound casino business, in which eleven million people wager a staggering £18,000 million every year, appears to be moving towards the more libertarian models of its US counterparts,[8] whether aided by legislation or not.

This full-scale shift has yet to happen, however, and at present the character of the British casino is still defined by the relatively restrictive legislation from which it emerged. Consistent with a historical tradition which allowed the wealthy to gamble but forbade such a frivolous waste of time and money among the lower orders, the British casino attempts to re-create the air of exclusivity of the private clubs of the eighteenth and nineteenth centuries. To this end, a membership requirement and formal dress code reinforce class distinctions and create an atmosphere of glamorous refinement. The Stakis casino chain outlines its code of conduct in the most patrician language, stating that 'Only Ladies and Gentlemen of good social position and over the age of 18 years are eligible for Membership of the Club'. Assuming a tacit 'gentleman's agreement' between member and management, it reminds patrons that 'to maintain the desired atmosphere, we have, naturally, standards regarding dress and behaviour' (*Stakis Casino Guide* 1994, p. 3). These 'standards' are the standards of an elite, designed to insulate them from the rest of the world, and backed up by a government whose residual Puritanism aims to protect the gambler – and especially the working-class gambler – from the 'vice' of playing. Such an attitude is apparent in the innumerable obstacles that are placed in the way of immediate play. A forty-eight hour rule forces potential gamblers to wait for two days after joining to enter a casino, thus creating a 'cooling off' period in which they can reflect and come to a rational decision about their impulsive desire to play. Having decided that they do in fact want to play, hopeful players must apply for membership by visiting the casino in person, have a physical description of themselves taken and complete a form detailing, among other things, their occupation. A strict dress code of jacket and tie for men and evening dress for women further restricts spontaneous play, for the need to be 'appropriately dressed' generally requires planning and makes a visit to the casino something of an occasion. In this it differs markedly from, for example, the betting shop, which can be 'dropped into' on a casual basis.

Casino doormen wearing bow-ties and tails welcome members individually as they arrive, taking their coats, presenting them with the guest book to sign and showing them to the tables in an antiquated ritual that attempts to imitate the atmosphere and splendour of the luxurious clubs of the nineteenth century. The relatively limited facilities of the British casino (most clubs have no more than four different types of game) are licensed for approximately twelve hours a day, and gamblers are bound by a strict set of rules while they use them. They are forbidden to tip the dealers or to bring food or drink into the segregated gaming area, and men are required to wear their jackets while at the tables. The rules of the games themselves are designed to encourage moderation and sensible play, and, unlike American casinos, in British ones, players are allowed to sit at the gaming table without playing and are permitted to consult the rules of play which are printed (with tips for the gambler) on every table. The roulette wheel has only one zero, and 'sucker bets' in blackjack are not allowed. Unlike the casinos of Las Vegas, where a steady flow of alcohol dulls gamblers' judgement and encourages rash bets, coffee is provided free in British casinos in order to keep players alert and sentient.

The formalities of British casinos – while perhaps not in *reality* excluding lower socioeconomic groups from their membership – are nevertheless indicative of an overt attempt to attract a particular class of clientele. In comparison to those of the United States, British casinos are antiquarian establishments where the aura of tradition and social hierarchy emanates from every deferential doorman and every subdued fixture. In this they belong to a European tradition of gambling which reached its nadir in the aristocratic play of Louis XIV, and which today is exemplified by the unashamed elitism of Monte Carlo. Of this playground of the rich, Tom Wolfe wrote: 'At Monte Carlo there is still the plush mustiness of the nineteenth century noble lions. . . . At Monte Carlo there are still Wrong Folks, Deficient Accents, Poor Tailoring, Gauche Displays, Nouveau Richness, Cultural Aridity – concepts unknown in Las Vegas' (Wolfe 1981, p. 26).

Unlike its British counterpart, which actively works to reinforce class distinctions, the Nevada casino is a democratic social organisation which actually works to *eliminate* them.[9] Thus Mario Puzo writes of the 'ennoblement' of the customers as they enter the casino:

> One of the greatest Vegas tricks is to make every gambler a King.
> . . . If you just throw the dice or step into a casino, you're at least a duchess. The customer is immediately ennobled, made a Knight of the Garter, a Chevalier of the Legion of Honour.
>
> (Puzo 1977, p. 82)

While the British gambler has *already* to be a noble gambler before he can enter the casino, the American one is ennobled simply by virtue of *being* there.

True to the pioneer spirit in which it was built – Bugsy Siegel's famous 'come as you are' – there are no entrance restrictions in Las Vegas casinos. Literally anyone can walk in off the street and into some of the most spectacular buildings in the world. They will not be asked for credentials by any security staff and no one will notice what they are wearing or care if they are eating or drinking. Inside, in a general atmosphere of licence, they will be encouraged to indulge their every desire among an enormous variety of games which are available twenty-four hours a day. The absence of licensing regulations in Vegas casinos contrasts with Britain's paternalistic temperance; in the former, players are encouraged to drink as much and as often as they like at the tables; in the latter, the only indulgence is caffeine. While credit and debit mechanisms are strictly prohibited in British casinos, American ones make every effort to relieve players of their money, furnishing their interiors with so many cash card machines, phone-credit lines and *bureaux de change* that at times they resemble enormous banks.

A vast melting-pot in which social distinctions are dissolved in the desire to gamble, the Las Vegas casino is the embodiment of the American ideal. Its *laissez-faire* policy creates an ambiance of relaxed intemperance where everyone's dollars are welcome, whatever the station of their owner. This American dream is Simmel's nightmare, in which money is truly 'the frightful leveller' (Simmel 1971c, p. 329).

Las Vegas: capital of the twentieth century

Las Vegas is the epitome of the casino and, insofar as 'casino capitalism' exists as a metaphor for postmodern economies, it can also be said to epitomise the condition of postmodernity. If, for Benjamin (1992), Paris was the capital of the nineteenth century, then Las Vegas is the capital of the twentieth.

The form and organisation of Las Vegas is the form and organisation of the casino in macrocosm. All casinos are separate sites: 'timeless, hermetic environments of elaborate unreality' within which an intense concentration of play takes place (Abt *et al*. 1985, p. 79). Situated in the middle of the Mojave Desert hundreds of miles from the nearest town, Las Vegas presents such separation in extreme form. Isolated from the reality of the everyday world, the city appears to rise out of nowhere: a giant casino where the concentrated urge to gamble has pushed back the desert, annihilating its aridity in a flood of neon. Its remote location in such a hostile environment makes the city a uniquely tangible embodiment of Huizinga's abstract notion of play; a 'magic circle' within which the player 'steps out' of real life and adopts new roles and identities (Huizinga 1949, p. 9).[10]

The visitor to Las Vegas does in fact 'step out' of real life and into a new world. The energy of a city sustained by gambling surrounds and overwhelms individuals the moment they arrive. There are slot-machines in the airport, in the hotels, in the hospitals and sunk into the bars. People play the souvenir toy machines on sale in shops, and keno slips nestle between the salt and pepper pots in restaurants. In this labyrinth, all the relations which anchor the visitor to familiarity and routine are severed, and, cast adrift, they enter a play world of illusion and unreality. Mario Puzo knew the sensation well: 'It is all a dream. It has nothing to do with reality . . . and it's somehow fitting and proper that the city of Las Vegas is surrounded by a vast desert. A desert which acts as a *cordon sanitaire*' (Puzo 1977, p. 21). It is easy to imagine that the oasis of Las Vegas is in fact a particularly beguiling mirage. Looking out of the plane just after take-off, back in the real world, the visitor sees nothing but desert.

The city of the spectacle

> The present age . . . prefers the sign to the thing signified, the copy to the original, fancy to reality, the appearance to the essence . . . illusion only is sacred, truth profane. Nay, sacredness is held to be enhanced in proportion as truth decreases and illusion increases, so that the highest degree of illusion comes to be the highest degree of sacredness.
>
> (Feuerbach 1957, p. xlix)

Feuerbach's comment on the predilection of the modern age for the illusory over the real is used by Debord (1987) to open his essay on *The Society of the Spectacle*. It can equally well be used to illustrate the spectacular nature of Las Vegas, for here, spectacle defines the form and content of the city. This feature has been created by the city's rapid artificial growth and its internal constitution which is made up of a relatively small resident population of one million inhabitants and a huge transient one of twenty-four million tourists per year. It is the fastest growing city in America, attracting around 120,000 new residents every year, most of whom come to work in the multi-million-dollar resort hotels, the casinos and the 'entertainment' industry. Collectively, these leisure centres will relieve tourists of some $10 billion per year: $25 billion wagered on games of chance, $5 billion of that lost, and another $5 billion spent on other leisure activities. Built at breakneck speed purely for the purpose of gambling, Las Vegas is less than a hundred years old and has no conventional economic infrastructure, no personal taxation and no existence without the gambling economy which created and sustains it. It creates nothing and produces nothing, simply recycling millions of dollars in losing wagers through its spectacular casinos. Based almost entirely on the provision of services, and sustained by almost unlimited consumerism, it is an ideal example of a post-Fordist economy: a giant monument to the excesses of capitalist materialism.

Lacking an indigenous cultural tradition of its own, Las Vegas mimics the activity that gives it form, and so the repetition of play corresponds to the city's repetition of other cultures in the hotels and casinos of the Strip. As a city without substance and without history, its profusion of neon signs conceals the fact that it is similar to the *Invisible Cities* described by Calvino in which 'Memory is redundant: it repeats signs so that the city can begin to exist' (Calvino 1979, p. 18). Las Vegas as an entity engages in repetition on a grand scale – the repetition of events and images, plucked out of historical narrative and re-created in the form of spectacular themed resort hotels. In their desire to attract customers, these self-contained 'mini worlds' provide every convenience for their guests, including a number of enormous casinos housed under one huge thematic roof. Hotels now boast of being destinations in their own right and tourists talk of 'going to Caesar's Palace' or 'going to Excalibur', as much as of 'going to Las Vegas' itself.

In its creation of themed worlds, Las Vegas acts as a giant sponge, absorbing the most fecund images from world history and drawing them into its lush desert playground. Its indiscriminate borrowing results in a bizarre pastiche of cultural appropriation: the jousting knights of medieval England in Excalibur, the basilicas and statues of the Roman Empire in Caesar's Palace, the pyramids of ancient Egypt in Luxor and south seas piracy in Treasure Island. Every one is a representation of the ancient within the modern. In their themed worlds, the resort-casinos surround gamblers with a fantasy; an imaginary world in which they can escape the monotony of real life. Las Vegas is built on simulacrum and reproduction and, in creating itself from a spectacular and arbitrary collage of historical images, has proved that, in late modern society, 'technology can give us more reality than nature can' (Eco 1995, p. 44).

Playgrounds

In these miniature worlds of play, the boundary that separates inside from out, night from day and the casino from the city breaks down in a city so saturated with gambling that it itself comes to resemble a giant casino. Inside and out merge into a vast gaming emporium, so that like Benjamin's Arcades, Las Vegas casinos are 'houses without exteriors' (Benjamin, in Buck-Morss 1990, p. 271). See the breakdown of exterior and interior, night and day, in the dazzling casinos of the Strip and in the self-contained universe of Excalibur, in plates 5 and 6.

In blending the immediacy of the slot arcade with games like keno (a concentrated lottery), table games and sports betting, no single rate of play and no definitive relation between players and games exists in the casino. Instead, both are contingent on the specific game being played. The outcome of a round in games of pure chance like roulette, baccarat and craps is resolved in the time it takes for a wheel to spin, cards to be turned over or dice to be rolled, so that a single bet can be won or lost in a matter of seconds. Games of skill such as poker and blackjack, on the other hand, tend to last longer, due to their greater degree of player involvement. Here, a round is lengthened by the gambler taking time to make decisions and choose between alternatives,

Plate 5: Excalibur by day and night
Sources: Las Vegas Tourist Board (above) and author (below)

Plate 6: Las Vegas inside and out
Sources: Las Vegas Tourist Board (above) and author (below)

so that a game of poker can last for hours, blackjack for up to ten minutes. The crowdedness of the table further affects the length of a game, simply because the greater the number of players, the greater the time taken dealing cards, collecting bets, making pay-outs and so on. A crowded roulette table may have more than ten people counting out chips and shuffling them around the board as they make up their minds about their bets, and when the outcome of a spin is resolved, the dealer will have to remove and pay out chips for all of them. Meanwhile, at a less busy table, a game will be over almost as quickly as it takes to spin the wheel. The size of the stake in relation to a player's bankroll also affects the length of a game: obviously (the vagaries of luck aside), players gambling for low stakes with a large bankroll will be able to stretch out their playing time longer than those betting high stakes with small bankrolls. So, in the timeless void of the casino, the length (or rate of play) of a game thus becomes gamblers' measure of time, constituting their own internal 'clock', and is determined by factors such as the structure and degree of skill in a game, the crowdedness of the table and the size of the stake in relation to the player's bankroll.

The heart of the casino – the gaming hall – is pure spectacle, a dizzying emporium of noise, movement and colour. Upon entering, gamblers find themselves plunged into another world that is insulated in a timeless void from the flow of everyday life outside it. Casino light is not susceptible to the rhythms of night and day, for the exclusion of clocks and windows banishes daylight and, in a perpetual twilight, all measure of time is lost and the time of the casino set apart from that of the everyday world. Artificial luminescence obliterates the sense of time passing, and disorients the gambler in both space and time, contributing to what Tom Wolfe called Las Vegas' 'quixotic inflammation of the senses' (Wolfe 1981, p. 20).[11]

Despite their direct participation in table games, casino gamblers appear to each other as anonymous, transient individuals, for their relation is with their invisible opponent in every game – the casino – and not with each other. The perpetual twilight and labyrinthine organisation of the casino discourages social contact and contains a mass of individuals who, although noisy, are seldom seen actually communicating with each other. When not playing, gamblers tend to wander singly from table to table, so that little contact, beyond that regulated by play, goes on. Even the social focus of the refreshments bar is dissipated by waitresses serving drinks to members as they play. Casino design itself works to reinforce this asocial atmosphere, creating an apparently chaotic and disquieting landscape, whose confusion is mitigated only by play. Rows of tables and machines run into each other, forcing gamblers to retrace their steps time and time again and making travel in a straight line impossible. There is nowhere to sit – the only seats are around the tables – and nowhere to stand without being swept along by a tide of people wandering haltingly in all directions. Crowds mill around in chaos, bumping into each other as they side-step machines, squeezing through narrow rows of slots and navigating around banks of tables. The distraction created by this lack of organisation and design makes it very difficult for the individual to *do* anything – except, of course, to gamble. And it is in this action that order and regularity emerge out of the sensory maelstrom of the casino floor. In the repetitive rituals of play, the world becomes organised again. Although initially, the solemn actions of blackjack players appear to the novice as some kind of esoteric ritual, players soon realise that it is one into which they can be easily initiated, for the semicircular table is laid out with geometric simplicity: squares for card places, circles for chips and insurance pay-off odds printed in crisp white on the smooth surface. Cards are dealt out in a speedy arc to players evenly spaced around the crescent table; turned over and collected and chips swept backwards and forwards across the green baize in a ritual that is hypnotic in its simplicity. Focusing on a single machine, it becomes apparent that even the amorphous babble of the slots is made up of distinct voices, each with its own tone. The coins are dropped, the handle pulled, the machine lights up and wheels revolve then stop, and the action is repeated, interrupted only by the occasional rattle of a pay-out, without variation, all 'day' and all 'night'.

The ritualised action of the tables and machines and the fixed expressions of dealers and players signifies regularity and contrasts sharply with the chaotic formlessness of the casino floor. Out of its labyrinthine confusion, the gaming tables emerge as oases of order with a soporific appeal of their own. As players gravitate towards them, their attention and actions become focused and the imperatives of the game gradually relieve them of the responsibility of deciding what to do. All they need to do is sit down and play and, in the simplicity of this resolve, the world becomes ordered again.

www.casino.com

If Las Vegas, with its concentration of casinos, was the gambling capital of the twentieth century, then the Internet, with its diffusion of gambling opportunities, will surely be the capital of the twenty-first. As we head into the new millennium, gambling is beginning to move into cyberspace: the action has gone on-line. Every type of gambling discussed so far is available on the Internet, although in a peculiar, new – 'virtual' – form.

Although legal only in Liechtenstein, Gibraltar and certain Caribbean countries, gambling in cyberspace has grown exponentially in the past five years and is predicted to become a $10 billion-a-year industry by the year 2000 (McGuigan 1997). There are now some three hundred sites in existence, from casinos such as Virtual Vegas (http://www.virtualvegas.com/) and the Caribbean Cyber Casino (http://www.ccasino.com/) to on-line lotteries, sports betting and bingo 'halls'. Some are reasonably permanent but many more are extremely transient: appearing, flourishing and then vanishing in a matter of weeks or even days. It is difficult to keep track of such sites, and impossible to control them. State regulation cannot halt their growth, for the borderless, lawless nature of the Internet means that promoters simply transcend the restrictions of any individual country by giving their site an address which is outwith its jurisdiction. Profits made by operators are not subject to the stringent laws that control mainstream gambling, or to taxation; a loophole which, given the massive turnover of an industry still in its infancy, represents a significant loss of revenue for states. In this, Internet gambling presents us with the strange meeting of the tightly regulated gambling industry with the virtually unregulated Internet.

Internet gambling (or 'nambling' as it is colloquially known) transcends geographical and temporal boundaries in a giant global casino: an environment in which individuals are free to bet, unhindered by any of the restrictions associated with terrestrial games of chance. By offering immediate access and instant credit, it links together players from all over the world, twenty-four hours a day. The instant transfer of cash adds to the immediacy of games. Players generally buy credit by credit card or electronic funds transferred from the casino 'bookie', and then play with virtual money backed by this deposit. When it runs out, they simply repeat the process. However, the Internet also has its own 'currencies' specially designed for on-line transactions, such as DigiCash or CyberCash, which are drawn from on-line banks and permit gamblers to remain anonymous (McGuigan 1997).

In this diffuse 'site', gamblers are completely absent from the action: there is nothing they need do and nowhere they need be to allow a game to go ahead. All that is required is a credit card and a computer. In fact, these players are only gamblers at all in the sense that they demonstrate interest in the event through their wagers, which are sufficient to include them in a distant ritual which can then go on without them. Players 'interact' with each other in sites which may be thousands of miles apart – if there are any other players there at all that is, for, since virtual casinos can simulate games to cater for lone gamblers, the presence of others is completely superfluous to the action. The real players would never know the difference.

It has been observed that the Internet creates an alternative reality, immersing users in an activity in which they are subject to altered states of consciousness (Griffiths 1995b), and, in the activity of gambling, this state appears in an extreme form. A combination of sophisticated animation, sound effects and carefully calculated links to selected sites draws casual surfers and committed players alike into a virtual reality where they are seduced by the easy click of a button, the repetition of continuous play and the possibility of instant wins. For example, along with dazzling graphics and wild promises, a fairly typical website, CasinoLand, based off-shore in Antigua, advertises itself in the following terms:

> Move over Las Vegas. . . . Make way Atlantic City. . . . CasinoLand
> has arrived! With multiple casinos, exotic themes, and twenty eight

international games, CasinoLand provides the widest variety of gambling, twenty four hours a day. And for the gambler with an erotic taste, CasinoLand also offers the finest in adult gambling casinos! Just download the easy to use software and you're home free. CasinoLand brings the excitement of real money wagering right to your doorstep! What other Internet casino offers Blackjack, Roulette, Gold Rush Slots, Magic Hat Slots, Jacks Video Poker, Jokers Wild Video Poker, Deuces Wild Video Poker, King of the Deck Video Poker, Pai Gow Poker, Red Dog, Battle Royale, Baccarat, Victory Pachinko, Dragon Spirit Pachinko, Video Mah Jong, Sic Bo, Crazy T Video Bingo, Crazy L Video Bingo, Crazy U Video Bingo, Super Video Bingo, Free Ride, Craps, and Caribbean Poker?

(http://www.casinoland.com/)

In the spectacle of players staring at their computer screens, engrossed in an anonymous, solitary activity, we have an image of a pure form of gambling. With the distractions of time, place and money stripped away, we find an intensification of gambling, in which certain features of the gambling experience are laid bare. These will be considered further in Chapter 4.

In the transient, fast-changing world of the Internet, developments are under way which could dramatically change the way gambling is organised. Major European companies are constructing websites which will offer on-line gambling to domestic customers and will be bound by national legislation, pay taxes and screen out children. G.Tech Holdings, the world's largest lottery operator, has recently established a unit to set up Internet lotteries, while the bookmakers Ladbrokes and William Hill are about to launch websites which will enable their customers to gamble in an interactive environment beyond the betting shop. It has been suggested (Reeve 1998) that these developments will lure existing customers away from casinos, lotteries and betting shops and out into cyberspace, so dramatically changing the profile of gamblers. However, given the material factors which restrict access to the Internet, and the nature of the gambling experience itself, this seems unlikely.[12]

As very little research has been conducted into the activity,[12] the player profile of these gamblers is largely unknown. Around 7.5 million Internet users exist in Britain: 16 per cent of the total population (*Internet Magazine*, October 1998: http://www.internetmagazine.com/news/oct/02a.htm), although it is difficult, if not impossible, to estimate how many of those gamble on the medium. However, even with limited information, certain assumptions regarding participation can be made. Although no one is excluded from the 'freedoms' of the Web (including, by definition, children wielding their parents' credit cards), it could be argued that the prerequisites for participation of a computer, credit and Internet connection would effectively limit the access of the lowest socioeconomic groups. Furthermore, as we have seen, gambling on Internet games offers quite a different experience to that of gambling on their terrestrial cousins, to which they are often related in name only. Although it can be said to represent an intensification of the experience, such gambling is nevertheless a distinct *type* which lacks the sociable aspect of many other forms. For these reasons it seems likely that, rather than simply 'poaching' players from existing games, a specific subgroup of gamblers will emerge from the Internet, drawn to it for its particular experiential component.

To sum up: we have seen in this chapter that the gambling sites are quite distinct, each one governed by its own peculiar order. Each provides a different experience of gambling, which attracts a variety of social groups for different reasons. The phenomenon of gambling is multi-faceted: an exciting leisure activity, a mundane form of consumption, a means of socialising with others, an opportunity to display skill, a hobby which offers the possibility of winning money. The heterogeneity of games is matched by the heterogeneity of players and motives, so that the experiences and motivations of a working-class woman playing bingo in the afternoon are very different to those of a millionaire high roller gambling in a plush casino, which again are different from a teenager truanting in order to meet up with friends and play the machines in an amusement arcade or a 'nambler' betting on the Internet.

But – within all this diversity, the phenomenon of gambling nevertheless retains an essential character, possessing certain features that are fundamental to the nature and experience of games of chance. So, having described the physiognomy of individual sites and the experience of gambling peculiar to each, it is time now to look in more detail at those features which are common to the experience of play *in general*. This will be the subject of Chapters 4 and 5.

4

THE EXPERIENCE OF PLAY

THE EXPERIENCE OF PLAY

So far we have been talking about gambling as a material phenomenon: in various ways as consumption, as leisure, as something that is bought and sold in capitalist enterprise as though it were just another type of commodity. But it is more than this. It *is* a form of consumption, but it is a special *type* of consumption, with a unique experiential component. It is the purpose of this chapter and of Chapter 5 to provide a description of the nature of this experience. This takes us from an analysis of the formal properties of particular types of games to an examination of that which is general across all forms of gambling. Obviously, such a portrait is bound to be, to a certain extent, an ideal type – an attempt to go beyond the specific and the particular to discover something about gambling which is general and fundamental. Therefore many of the assertions made will not apply to all gamblers or to all forms of gambling, but it is hoped that they will at least say *something* about them which will reveal the common features which link their varied historical expressions.[1] In a very broad sense then, these two chapters will focus on the experiential aspects of gambling in an attempt to provide some kind of answer to the question: What is it *like* to play at games of chance?

This question can be approached by a phenomenological analysis of what Kant called the fundamental categories of perception: those of time, space and cause. It is through these 'building blocks' of consciousness that our relationship with the world is mediated: whatever we experience affects or is affected by them so that together they can be said to comprise a Gestalt: as Ey puts it, a 'total structure of experience' (Ey 1978, p. 94).

However, despite our general dependence on these categories, they are not fixed and absolute but rather vary according to a range of factors. Certain situations and environments can affect them and so alter the nature of subjective experience – and of course, in a reciprocal relationship, the categories of time, space and cause can also affect that experience itself.[2] Conditions such as physical and psychological illness (Strauss 1968; Charmaz 1992), stress-related disorders (Straus 1966; Minkowski 1970; Ey 1978), states of extreme tension or excitement (Bergson 1910, 1911), addiction (Reith 1999) or even incarceration (Cohen and Taylor 1972) can have a dramatic effect on the way individuals perceive their surroundings and even their own self-identity. In these situations, the world appears to take on subtly different nuances: for instance, when we are happy, it appears to be open and expansive, but in states of pain or fear, our attention narrows and our surroundings accordingly seem to contract. This is exemplified in the state of depression for instance, which, Straus tells us, is characterised by an alteration of the basic structures of space and time in which 'Familiar surroundings become estranged, everything shows a new, bewildering physiognomy' (Straus 1966, p. 290).

From all this we can see the fundamental relativity of consciousness – the fact that our relation to the world is not fixed and unchanging, but rather depends very much on how we feel, what we are doing, where we are. As William James put it, 'the world of our present consciousness is only one out of many worlds of consciousness that exist, and those worlds must contain experiences which have a meaning for our life also' (James 1982, p. 519). It should therefore come as no great surprise to find that the perceptions and consciousness of gamblers are similarly conditioned by their situation, for the gambling arena imparts its own peculiar qualities to consciousness.

This is in part caused by the nature of the gambling environment itself, which has been extensively commented on by many writers. Although, as we saw in Chapter 3, every gambling site forms its own separate world with dramatic variations in the nature and experience of play in each, the gambling sites are, in a broader sense, united by certain common features which have been described by Huizinga (1949), Caillois (1962) and Goffman (1961, 1963) in their delineations of the formal properties of 'playgrounds'.

For all three writers, the 'peculiar character' of games is characterised essentially by their *separateness*, both temporally and spatially, from everyday life.[3] They involve both a physical and a mental crossing of a threshold out of the ordinary world and into the world of play. For Huizinga, this involves a 'stepping out of "real life" into a temporary sphere of activity with a disposition all of its own' (Huizinga 1949, p. 8). In the same way, Goffman describes them as 'world building activities' whose events constitute 'a field for fateful, dramatic action, a plane of being, an engine of meaning, a world in itself, different from all other worlds' (Goffman 1961, p. 25). Play is also separated by strict temporal limits which 'end as inexorably as the closing of a parenthesis' (Caillois 1962, p. 43), so necessitating the constant repetition of games. Furthermore, just as the play world is animated by a different set of rules from those which govern everyday life, so players within it are animated by a different set of motivations from those of their everyday routines in which they are free to experiment with new roles and to temporarily adopt new identities.

Its essential feature of 'separateness' means that the gambling arena forms a self-contained realm of activity, set against the world of utilitarian goals, with its own rules and conventions and within which the gambler's orientation to the everyday world is altered. In fact, for Gadamer, so extreme is this feature that he argues that the play world actually constitutes a specific mode of *being*. Thus 'play does not have its being in the consciousness of the attitude of the player, but on the contrary draws the latter into its area and fills him with its spirit', meaning that ultimately, 'the player experiences the game as a reality that surpasses him' (Gadamer 1975, p. 89). In this way, the basic perceptual categories of time, space and cause become distorted, for submersion in an environment of chance creates a kind of experiential chaos in which players cease to perceive their surroundings in the ordered, logical manner of 'rational' consciousness, but as a barrage of information, or, to use Cassirer's phrase, in a 'rhapsody of perception' (Cassirer 1953, p. 21).

At this point, it will be evident that the type(s) of enquiry used in the previous three chapters cannot provide us with an adequate tool for gaining insight into the nature of the gambling experience, which brings us to a methodological problem of all social investigation: how to describe something as intangible as a state of consciousness; a phenomenon which by definition we have no access to. This is a problem that has long occupied the traditions of phenomenology, existentialism and hermeneutics, and has found resonance in the disciplines of philosophy, psychology and sociology. Edmund Husserl established the phenomenological method of enquiry when he attempted to undertake the pure inspection of consciousness and the objects of that consciousness. Although Husserl was more interested in the intellectual forms of mental life, existentialist philosophers such as Heidegger, Kierkegaard and Sartre applied the phenomenological method to questions of being and existence and specifically to the understanding of mental states. Their ideas were influential in social science, where Schutz's focus on the manner in which individuals construct and interpret their everyday existence introduced them into sociology, and Minkowski's and Binswanger's analyses of the varieties of conscious experience brought them to clinical psychiatry. Hermeneutics and interpretive understanding are frequently utilised in the methodological application of these insights. Ever since Dilthey stated that we can only understand (*verstehen*) the world in terms of the meanings and intentions which individuals attribute to it, it has been recognised that the understanding of 'lived experience' requires a special method of analysis. For Weber, this *verstehnde* method involved the interpreter placing him/herself in the position of the interpreted, while other researchers emphasised the gaining of knowledge more through a process of emotional participation and empathetic understanding of their subjects' world.

It is within this broad phenomenological tradition that the nature of the gambling experience and the mental life of the gambler can best be understood. In this context then, Chapters 4 and 5 will draw on the comments and experiences of players themselves, as well as on the insights of various writers who were also gamblers and who can therefore provide an articulate window into that 'inner life' so sought after by phenomenologists. We are fortunate in that the world of play has captured the literary imagination of many great writers, including Alexander Pushkin, Honore de Balzac, Charles Baudelaire and, of course, Fydor Dostoevsky.[4] The latter is perhaps its most eloquent spokesman, for as well as being a great analyst of human motivation, Dostoevsky was an inveterate gambler who thus wrote from the privileged position of having actually experienced first-hand that which he described. His disastrous tour of the gambling capitals of Europe was fictionalised in the novel *The Gambler*,[5] and revealed with dramatic insight the 'rhapsody of perception' experienced within the gambling arena. This position lent his description of the gambling experience an authenticity and verisimilitude that is absent from subsequent, more 'scientific' accounts.

In this section then, the various components of the general experience of play will be examined, followed by a consideration of the perception of the specific categories of time and space, and of the medium of the gambling world, money. The nature of the perception of cause will be considered in Chapter 5.

Excitement

The adventure – dream state

When they enter the gambling arena gamblers temporarily step out of the real world, leaving their everyday concerns and routines behind and embarking on an adventure which, as well as being exciting, is also experienced as a state of dream-like dissociation from their surroundings. Their shared feature of separateness means that both gambling games and adventures can assume the properties of dreams, a peculiarity which is caused by the occurrence of the adventure outwith the usual stream of life. Just as, for Huizinga, the world of play is a 'stepping out' of real life, so the adventure for Simmel is a 'dropping out of the continuity of life' (Simmel 1971b, p. 187). The 'otherness' of the play world lends to it the quality of an adventure, while the strangeness of the stimuli inside contributes to the dream-like nature of the experience within it.

While immersed in a game, gamblers tend to shut out the world around them, leaving everyday life behind and narrowing their field of attention to concentrate on the action immediately in front of them. Leiseur (1984) called this a 'twilight zone' or 'dream world', while Jacobs (1988) and Brown (1994) have described this feature of gambling as the experience of *dissociated states*. These can include feelings of depersonalisation and *déjà vu*, trance-like or hypnotic states, somnambulism and fugue and even the experience of mystical religious states and multiple personality. Common to all these states they found a quality of 'separateness' or 'disconnection from the normal flow of mental life' (Brown 1994, p. 3), in which players often felt disembodied or 'outside' of themselves, as though in a trance, watching themselves play.

We can regard these dissociated states as a specific form of consciousness which Ey calls 'oneiric states' and in which individuals are in a condition of 'pathological dreaming'. Neither asleep nor awake, they experience a kind of 'awake dream' in which they feel disembodied; as if a spectator, watching themselves from without (Ey 1978, p. 65). As he succumbed to this dream-like absence of mind, Dosteovsky's gambler Alesky also lost awareness of himself as subject, and could not recall what had happened. He related: 'I lost track of the amount and order of my stakes. I only remember as if in a dream' (Dostoevsky 1992, p. 241).

The thrill of play – vertigo

One of the most striking aspects of the experience of gambling is the tension or 'thrill' of the game: the irresistible seduction of money and chance which Balzac called the *Spirit of Gaming*: 'a passion more fatal than disease' (Balzac 1977, pp. 22–26). This affective experience is generated by the creation and resolution of the tension in a game, and centres on the risk faced by the individual while awaiting the outcome of their stake. It begins the moment the bet is placed and ends when the outcome of the round is known. In between, the gambler waits in anticipation, and in this state of suspended animation 'the conflicting valences of fear or hope run in tingling arpeggios up and down his spine' (Devereaux 1949, p. 699). One gambler described the sense of expectation characteristic of his encounters with chance in a part-icularly vivid metaphor: 'Imagine going into a dark room. When the lights are turned on the room could be empty or it could be filled with the most extraordinary objects you've ever seen. A game of cards is like that' (*Observer*, 25 June 1995, p. 12). It was a similar state of tension upon which another gambler's experience of play was founded: 'My feelings when I play roulette are of tension – partly painful, partly pleasurable and expectant' (in Bergler 1970, p. 83), and which defined the exquisite agony of Tolstoy's relation with roulette, of which he wrote: 'it is a long time since anything tormented me so much' (in Barnhart 1983, p. 110).

The apex of the gambling experience is the moment when excitement peaks and gamblers are gripped by the fever of play, playing on and on, oblivious to their surroundings, to their losses, to the passage of time and even to themselves. This is the experience of what Caillois calls *ilinx*. Derived from the Greek 'whirlpool' or 'vertigo', it is a governing principle of Dionysian or pre-rational societies, and can also be found in a type of play which consists of an 'attempt to momentarily destroy the stability of perception and inflict a kind of voluptuous panic on an otherwise lucid mind' (Caillois 1962, p. 23). In it, players are unaware of what is going on around them and oblivious to fatigue. It is this state that is responsible for some of the marathon gambling sessions of popular gambling folklore, such as the forty-eight-hour game in which Lord Sandwich refused to stop playing, inventing the sandwich as a means of having food brought to him without leaving the table.

Baudrillard explains the hypnotic appeal of this vertigo in terms of the gambler's challenge to fate:

> By itself each throw produces only a moderate giddiness, but when fate raises the bid . . . when fate itself seems to throw a challenge to the natural order of things and enters into a frenzy or ritual vertigo, then the passions are unleashed and the spirits seized by a truly deadly fascination.
>
> (Baudrillard 1990, p. 147)

In this sensory maelstrom, perceptions of time and space are shattered. Time freezes, and gamblers become absorbed in a total orientation to the immediate Here and Now. In this state they become creatures of sensation; seeing, but not really being aware of their surroundings; perceiving, but not truly cognisant of what is going on. One punter described his thoughts, shattered into incoherence by the tension of the game: 'I thought I'd gone mad; I'd completely flipped . . . I don't think I've ever come close to another experience that produced as much adrenaline . . . it was a near death experience.' Utyeshitelny, in Gogol's *The Gamblers*, was similarly shaken, saying: 'The loss of money is not so important as losing one's peace of mind. The mere agitation experienced during play, people may say what they like, but it obviously shortens one's life' (Gogol 1926, p. 228).

It is during this stage that physiological changes such as increased respiration, heart rate, blood pressure and adrenaline have been found to occur in gamblers, changes which provide the strongest evidence for those who argue that gambling can be a physiological addiction. Having staked – and won – at roulette, Dostoevsky's Alesky experienced a degree of excitement so intense as to be a visceral sensation: 'I was a gambler; I felt it at that very moment. I was trembling from head to foot, my head was throbbing' (Dostoevsky 1992, p. 203). He goes on to give perhaps the definitive account of vertigo in the description of Alesky's penultimate bet at the roulette tables. Alesky stakes everything, flinging his money down at random; then there is 'one moment of waiting in which my impressions were perhaps similar to those experienced by Madame Blanchard when she plunged to the ground from a balloon in Paris' (Dostoevsky 1992, p. 241).

His choice of the plunging analogy is revealing, for it is also the one used by Caillois to describe the sensation of vertigo. Children's spinning games and whirling dervishes, he writes, create states of ecstasy, disorientation and hypnosis, as do physical activities like rapid accelerations and falling through space (Caillois 1962, p. 24). Alesky's feeling of hurtling through space is the sensation of such vertiginous disorientation; a mental sensation transposed into a physical one and caused not by physical exertion but by the sheer excitement of play.

In such moments of intense physical and perceptual disorientation, gamblers' links with reality are tenuous, and loosen still further as they surrender to the immediacy of the present. For Boyd, such an individual is 'lost in a world of his own. . . . There is no longer an outside reality. . . . Even time is non-existent, and in a certain sense he is insane' (Boyd 1976, p. 372). Madness is a recurrent theme in the gambling literature. Alesky certainly wondered if he had gone mad during one particularly intense session: 'Had I taken leave of my senses at that time, and was I not sitting somewhere in a madhouse and perhaps that is where I am now' (Dostoevsky 1992, p. 225), while the narrator of *The Mahabharata* observed a similar effect on gamblers 'drunk with playing dice' who 'prattle[d] like madmen of things they had not seen asleep or awake' (*The Mahabharata* 1975, p. 136).

The alteration of identity – transcendence

From among all this disorientation comes one of the most frequently discussed aspects of gambling – its ability to act as a conduit for the alteration of identity. Its separation from the routines of everyday life as a kind of fantasy world means that, while engaged in it, individuals are temporarily released from the strictures which usually govern their actions. Freed from habit in this way, they are able to imagine themselves in other identities and to explore alternative ways of being. Caillois (1962) and Goffman (1969) have pointed out that all games consist in becoming an illusory character; of temporarily adopting a new identity which endures for the duration of the game. Jacobs (1988) described such states, in which gamblers underwent a shift in persona, as part of the more general phenomenon of 'dissociated states', while Rosenthal (1986) reported that many individuals in his study often talked of becoming someone else when they played, and even went so far as to call each of their play 'selves' by a different name.

This fluid 'gambling identity' is one in which the everyday self is left behind and another persona, more pertinent to the ritualised social situation in which gamblers find themselves, is adopted. With the interruption of habit and routine and the removal of familiar surroundings, the reference points of the personality disappear. As the traditional categories of orientation loosen and shift, so the gamblers' axes of identity become less fixed and allow for the investigation and creation of new roles. As Caillois explains, when players leave the everyday world behind they also leave *themselves* behind: 'In one way or another, one escapes the real world and creates another. One can also escape oneself and become another' (Caillois 1962, p. 19). The most radical illustration of this is probably Luke Rhinehart's famous creation, *The Dice Man* (1972), an individual who lived out the ultimate existentialist fantasy by surrendering his life's decisions to the roll of a dice. Cinematically, the protean gambling identity has also been portrayed in Fritz Lang's eponymous film of *Dr Mabuse, The Gambler*. Mabuse is depicted as an individual with no fixed character, appearing in every scene in disguise. Just as the gambler of the eighteenth century was perceived as an individual of 'no distinct physiognomy', Mabuse's constant changes reveal his chameleon-like personality, his refusal of any fixed characteristics.

Goffman (1969), Zola (1967), Herman (1967, 1976) and Newman (1972) have all focused on the gambling arena as a site in which qualities and abilities not normally utilised in the outside world can be given free rein. Goffman describes the 'rules of irrelevance' which delimit the gambling situation, and signify the freedom from needing to act for 'real'; the licence to 'play act' or behave out of character according to the situation at hand. Zurcher (1970) described a similar feature: the 'ephemeral role' which is specially designed and created by the individual to 'fit' the gambling occasion and then discarded once it is over. In this way, gambling provides the opportunity to present an idealised identity to the self and others (Holtgraves 1988). Through the display of skill and knowledge, gamblers in games such as horse-race handicapping or poker can become experts within their social group and so win the respect and admiration of their peers. The taking of risks, or as Goffman puts it, exposing oneself to fate, that is involved in gambling contests creates a social situation in which character – or 'face', qualities such as self-discipline, courage and integrity – can be displayed and abilities and skills not otherwise used can be exercised. By virtue of the fact that they are solely responsible for their own actions, that they *make things happen* in the consequent unfolding of a game, gambling confers a degree of autonomy on players, and, according to Kusyzyn (1990), it is this that affirms gamblers' self-worth and makes gambling a site in which one's existence can be confirmed. As one player put it: 'gambling is a replacement of the fantasies [we] have as children. . . . For me, the fantasy in gambling is not monetary. It's a question of fulfillment: being who I really am, doing things well, being involved – just feeling good' (in Alvarez 1991, p. 138).

Boredom

Just beyond the 'kind of pain' of play hovers another kind of pain – boredom. The tension of a round is short-lived, for a sensation of such intensity can only be sustained for a few fleeting moments. In the inevitable let-down that follows, reality appears dull and colourless; the gambler is deflated, for the converse of the vertigo experienced during gambling is the torpor felt when *not* at play. Thus Shohnev, in Gogol's *The Gamblers*, describes how, between games, a gambler feels 'just like a general when there is no war! It's simply a deadly interval' (Gogol 1926, p. 224).

Stepping outside of the gambling arena, players find the real world unutterably dull in comparison to the one they have just left. Pascal recognised the threat of boredom that lingered behind the excitement in games of chance, warning, 'a man enjoying a happy home-life has only to spend . . . five or six pleasant days gambling, and he will be very sorry to go back to what he was doing before' (Pascal 1987, p. 51). That is why, for Pascal, gambling was such a useful, but dangerous, diversion from boredom; useful because it agitates and so diverts us, dangerous because it exacerbates the tedium of the initial condition.

For de Jong, the problem of boredom is intrinsic to modernity, and has its roots in the nineteenth century when the breakdown of a sense of meta-physical order gave birth to the distinctive feature of the modern age – the syndrome of intensity. The desire to experience intense sensation – of which gambling is typical – replaced the pursuit of meaningful activity and had as its converse the existence of apathy and boredom (de Jong 1975). Benjamin was among the first writers to realise the true horror of this contemporary malaise, declaring after Strindberg: 'Hell is not something which lies ahead of us, – but *this life, here*' (Benjamin 1985, p. 50). By secularising it and changing its temporal location from the remoteness of the afterlife to the immediacy of the present, Benjamin brought hell to earth and announced boredom as a fundamental condition of modernity.

As the chief poet of modernity, Baudelaire understood very well the existence of boredom as a kind of secular hell:

> Nothing is slower than the limping days
> when under the heavy weather of the years
> Boredom, the fruit of glum indifference
> gains the dimension of eternity.
> (Baudelaire 1982, p. 75)

He also recognised the desire to banish its aching emptiness in its polar opposite – excitement, and in particular, the excitement of gambling. Baudelaire's gamblers are essentially degraded characters, and desperate to feel *anything* rather than nothing. What he calls these 'ancient whores' with their 'lipless faces' and 'toothless jaws', are possessed of a 'stubborn passion', a 'deadly gaiety':

> Horrible that I should envy those
> who rush so recklessly into the pit,
> each in his frenzy ravenous to prefer
> pain to death and hell to nothingness!
> (Baudelaire 1982, p. 101)

Pushkin's portrayal of *Eugene Onegin* also draws on the association between gambling and boredom. Eugene is a 'superfluous man' who has no place in the rush of modern life and despite all his travels and distractions finds himself supremely bored:

nothing caused his heart to stir
and nothing pierced his senses blur.
(Pushkin 1983, p. 52)

Like Baudelaire's gamblers, Eugene occasionally escapes boredom through play; the one thing that can pierce his 'senses blur':

pursuits of a monstrous breed
begot by boredom out of greed.
(Pushkin 1982, p. 149)

The continued association between boredom and excitement is encapsulated in gambling. Just as gambling embodies de Jong's intensity cult, so it embodies the converse of intensity: boredom. Seeking release from monotony, gamblers plunge into the tension of a game, only to come face to face with the everyday world and all its attendant tedium when they re-emerge from play.

Repetition

Their fleeting nature, and their vacillation between excitement and boredom, makes repetition an intrinsic feature of games of chance. Put simply, because a game ends so quickly, it must be repeated, and this is one of the most essential features of play. The gambler plays in order to experience the tension and expectation of a game, but because it is over almost as soon as it begins, it must be continually repeated. The gambling sites reverberate to the drum of this steady repetition. In the casino, bets are made, cards shuffled, dealt and collected over and over again; dice are shaken and rolled *ad infinitum*, just like Nietzsche's 'iron hands of necessity' shaking 'the dice box of chance for an infinite length of time' (Nietzsche 1982, p. 81). Roulette wheels spin for eternity on unchanging, regular axes, while balls tumble out of the lottery drum week after week and month after month in a ritual which, like all those of the gambling sites, is unflinching in its exact repetition of what went before.

For Gadamar, repetition is the essence of play: 'The movement which is play has no goal which brings it to an end; rather it renews itself in constant repetition' (Gadamar 1975, p. 93). By creating a formal structure which is absolute and unchanging, it confers order on the random play of chance events, and so removes the burden of initiative from the player (see Huizinga 1949, p. 10; Caillois 1962, p. 5).

Baudrillard sees, in this tendency to repeat, something which is more than simply a definitive feature of games of chance but a movement which annihilates the relation between cause and effect. 'Their true form is cyclical or recurrent. And as such they . . . put a definite stop to causality . . . by the potential return (the eternal return if one will) to an orderly conventional situation' (Baudrillard 1990, p. 146). This eternal return, for Baudrillard, is an important factor in the generation of vertigo, for the desire to know the result of the next round, to put one's fate to the test once more entices the gambler to play on, and so creates 'the vertigo of *seduction*' (Baudrillard 1990, p. 148).

Walter Benjamin shares with Baudrillard the image of gambling as a phenomenon whose fundamental structure denies the relation of cause and effect. However, the implications of this denial are very different for Benjamin, for while Baudrillard sees a seductive vertigo as the mode of experiencing an a-causal universe, Benjamin's universe is made up of the austerity of hard work and the divorce of gamblers from the fruits of production. Such a distinction can be seen as analogous to the different responses of the Protestant-bourgeois and the gambler to chance which we saw earlier. For Benjamin, repetition is the factor which connects gambling with the production line. The former shares with the latter:

> the futility, the emptiness, the inability to complete something which is inherent in the activity of a wage slave in a factory. Gambling even contains the workman's gesture that is produced by the automatic operation, for there can be no game without the quick movement of the hand by which the stake is put down or a card picked up.
>
> (Benjamin 1977, p. 179)

The lines of slot-machine players, adeptly operating their machines, is a panorama which Benjamin could never have seen, and yet it is the visual apotheosis of his comparison. He goes on:

> The jolt in the movement of a machine is like the so-called *coup* in a game of chance. The manipulation of the worker at the machine has no connection with the preceding operation for the very reason that it is its exact repetition. Since each operation at the machine is just as screened off from the preceding operation as a *coup* in a game of chance is from the one that preceded it, the drudgery of the labourer is, in its own way, a counterpart to the drudgery of the gambler. The work of both is equally devoid of substance.
>
> (Benjamin 1977, p. 179)

Although he effectively highlights its repetitive, insubstantial nature, Benjamin is mistaken in equating the drudgery of work with the excitement of play. For him, all gambling is like the punishment inflicted on Claudius: 'useless labour . . . an illusory hope of gratifying some desire' (Seneca 1986, p. 232). Benjamin's mistake stems from his implicit conflation of games of chance with those based on skill for, as we shall see, if anything it is the calculation and self-restraint involved in games of *skill* that represent such drudgery. Certainly, both unskilled labour and games of chance involve repetition, but here the similarity ends, for games of chance are animated by the affective excitation of the thrill; a sensation entirely lacking from the dull routine of factory labour. Thus the category of repetition does *not* bring gambling into the realm of work, since such work as Benjamin outlines and the structure of gambling share only their repetitive *forms*. The subjective response to each is quite different, and, as Kierkegaard (1983) has pointed out, repetition contains the qualities of self-realisation and transcendence, which make it amenable to a response of seductive vertigo rather than austere drudgery.

THE CATEGORIES OF PLAY

In the arena of play, the articulation of the gambler's field of consciousness breaks down so that perception of the fundamental categories of space — according to Kant, the form of our 'outer experience', time — the form of our 'inner experience', cause and (unique to the gambling world), money are distorted. The basic categories of the gambler's world thus assume a bewildering new physiognomy, which constitutes a perceptual Gestalt and in which the passage of time freezes into repetition, space contracts, and the value that accrues to money is obliterated.

Time

The perception of time is crucial to the experience of play, for

> time is the material into which the phantasmagoria of gambling has been woven.
>
> (Benjamin 1992, p. 137)

Since Bergson's distinction between two different 'types' of time — 'homogenous and independent Time' and 'true duration, lived by consciousness' (Bergson 1911, p. 275) — it has become a phenomenological axiom that the experience of time is a medium for experience in general. The former absolute, Newtonian time is the time of the scientist. Broken down into quantifiable units and applied equally to everyone, this 'clock time' is exemplified in modern life in the almost ubiquitous habit of wearing wrist-watches. The lived time, the *durée*, which we experience, is quite different however, and is unique to the individual and their particular position in the world at any one moment. Bergson thus opens up a *relativistic* notion of time, the experience of which is contingent on different states of consciousness. As Proust put it: 'for certain people, the *tempo* of Time itself may be accelerated or retarded' (Proust 1983, p. 986). The gambler is one such individual.

The case studies of phenomenological psychologists such as Eugene Minkowski and Erwin Straus illustrate the non-homogeneous nature of personal, 'lived' time. It can pass quickly or slowly depending on the situation, actions and mood of the subject. For example, on a boring day time seems to drag, whereas on one filled with activity and interest it appears to pass quickly. The perception of time has an *active* and an *affective* component; how we experience it depends on what we 'fill' it with, what we are doing, and how we feel about it. In turn, experience itself 'receives its specific significance, its specific value, from its temporal position' (Straus 1966, p. 292). Experience in general, and the experience of time in particular, exist in a dynamic relation, each one containing and affecting the other. Minkowski describes a case in which a patient conflated his personal time, his *durée*, with homogeneous time, and, regarding his watch as the literal embodiment of the latter, shot it with a revolver in order to 'kill' time (Minkowski 1970, p. 15)! This gesture, which we would regard as symbolic, highlights the distinction which we take for granted between the two 'types' of time separated by Bergson.

As an example of the effect of temporal position on experience, Straus cites imminent death: 'With such transitions from indefiniteness to finality, everything changes its physiognomy' (Straus 1966, p. 292). He does not elaborate, but we know from Raskolkinov's walk to give himself up in *Crime and Punishment* that the subject, seeing the world for the last time, is fully aware of its every detail, avidly drinking in the minutiae of life and engrossed in every fleeting second (Dostoevsky 1951, pp. 535–536). This example is particularly illuminating in the gambling context, for many gamblers themselves choose a similar analogy. The protagonist Raphael in *The Wild Ass's Skin* experienced a similar moment of clarity to that of the condemned man on his way to execution, in which he felt as if he had just escaped certain death. Despite the noise of the casino – 'the buzz of voices', 'the chink of coins' and 'the strains of the orchestra' – Raphael related that: 'thanks to a privilege accorded to the passions which gives them the power to annihilate space and time, I could distinctly hear what the players were saying' (Balzac 1977, p. 95). Dostoevsky too described these moments of lucidity during intense play, and, as someone who had experienced such moments of finality during his mock execution as a political prisoner, was well placed to relate the two experiences to each other. His description of gambling is imbued with the sense of urgency and intensity which he would have felt during what he thought were his final moments; a sensation he re-created at the gambling table.

Like any other individuals, gamblers' time is 'true duration, lived by consciousness', and its nature is dependent on what they are doing and their emotional state while they are doing it. In turn, their experience of play receives its specific value from its temporal position. In this way the nature of time in the gambling arena is twofold. On the one hand, it is a perception in the mind of individual gamblers, measured by their rate of play and dependent on factors such as the type of game they are playing, the size of their stake in relation to their total bankroll and the crowdedness of the table. As we have seen, a gambler with a limited bankroll, playing high stakes at a deserted roulette table, will have a shorter experience of play than one with a large bankroll, playing low stakes at a busy blackjack table. Since the experience of time is coloured by the situation of the subject, they will perceive it moving quickly or slowly depending on the length of their period of involvement in play. Such a perception of time is unique for each gambler, distinguished ever so slightly from all their other games and those of all other gamblers by the particular combination of many factors.

Over and above the *specific* nature of time in each game played can be discerned a *general* experience of time; a set of characteristics that come to light through the frequent playing of many games. This perception of time, common to all gamblers in all games, is of a *constant repetition of a fleeting present*.

In games of chance, the present is all-important. The field of gamblers' attention is defined by the unfolding of the event on which they have their stake. However long the rate of play, the resolution of the risk is over in an instant. It is the moment when the lottery ball bounces out of the drum; the moment when the dice fall; the moment when the roulette ball slips into the pocket. In an instant, the uncertain becomes known; the future becomes the present. It is this instant that the gambler lives in; the time of the eternal present, in which the gambler Jack Richardson felt he 'existed in a sharp, exhilarating present that refreshed itself over and over again' (Richardson 1980, p. 86). Because it has no bearing on the present, the past and the future are irrelevant to the experience of the round being played at any particular moment. In the frozen instant, in which the gambler lives only for the moment, time has lost its articulation. This is the moment Benjamin talks about, in which 'gambling converts time into a narcotic' (Benjamin 1992, p. 54). The narcotic effect is experienced as an isolated and fleeting moment which is constantly repeated in every round of play.

This state of perennial expectation, in which the future is rendered obsolete, is an instance of what Straus would call a 'pathology of becoming'. The 'normal' experience of time, Straus tells us, occurs in individuals who are in a state of *becoming*. However, when their temporal perception becomes so disoriented that 'the context and continuity of time crumbles', a disjunction between individuals and their orientation to the world opens up, and a 'pathology of becoming' exists (Straus 1966, p. 293).

This essential transience is captured by Baudelaire in *The Clock*, where, for him, it also encapsulates the nature of modernity:

> Thirty six times in every hour
> The second whispers: Remember! and Now replies
> In its maddening mosquito hum: I am Past,
> who passing lit and sucked your life and left!
> (Baudelaire 1982, p. 82)

The problem of the fleetingness of the present has occupied philosophers since Augustine, and was partially resolved by Bergson's notion of *durée*. This 'lived time' contains the past, as memory, within the future. His *durée* involves both 'past and present melting into one another and forming an organic whole' (Bergson 1910, p. 128). For Bergson then, the present is not an isolated instance, but part of an organic 'melting' of past, present and future. The role of memory is instrumental in this process, for it is the mechanism by which 'the past tends to reconquer, by actualising itself, the influence it had lost' (Bergson 1911, p. 169).

Unfortunately, Bergson's solution is completely inapplicable to the gambler. While at play, the latter's experience of time lacks the historical element of *durée*, for in games of chance, Bergson's all-important past has no place. Each round is a self-contained island in time, existing independently of what came before or what will come after. The perception of time that arises from this is made up of a succession of unrelated instants and absolutely opposed to the flowing organicism that is the lived time of the *durée*.

The past can never 'actualise' itself in gambling, for it requires the operation of memory to do so, and the abolition of time in gambling means the abolition of memory too. In a world of chance, the past has as little relevance for the future as the future does for the past. The only thing which can transcend the timelessness of this contingent world is the passage of time itself – realised in the repetition of games – whereupon the law of large numbers can take effect and some semblance of order be restored. This uncompromising law of probability is given lyrical expression by Baudelaire:

> Remember! Time, that tireless gambler, wins on every
> turn of the wheel. That is the law.
>
> (Baudelaire 1982, p. 82)

Gamblers, however, caught in the particular instant, are, by their simple corporeality, denied such a vantaged position. Forever bound to the outcome of a single round, of a single moment of play, they exist as individuals without memory. The nature of chance means that 'gambling invalidates the standards of experience' and betting works as 'a device for giving events the character of a shock, detaching them from the context of experience' (Benjamin 1992, p. 136).[6]

Experienced in a timeless void, the thrill of gambling is an essentially *insubstantial* sensation, and one which leaves no traces for the gambler to hold on to and recollect. Nothing is produced, nothing changes, nothing really happens – there is therefore nothing to anchor memory on to in play. It is because of this feature that Mr Astley observes of Alesky by the end of *The Gambler*: '"You've become dull . . . you've not only renounced every aim whatsoever in your life, you've even renounced your memories"' (Dostoevsky 1992, p. 269). But then this is all part of the fascination, part of the *enchantment* of gambling – the 'crystalline passion that erases memory traces and forfeits meaning' (Baudrillard 1990, p. 135).

The advertising campaign of the British lottery's scratch cards utilises the appeal of this feature in a particularly apposite slogan: 'Forget it all for an instant[s]', which encapsulates the instantaneity of the gambling experience in tones of hedonistic abandon.

The repetition of the ever-same in the mind of the gambler corresponds to the repetition of the ever-same in the economic realm of play. Nothing is ever produced in gambling, and in lieu of any such creative activity we have the endless circulation of money. It changes hands, but nothing substantial is ever produced, and the endless cycle of this money in the economic sphere is perceived as an endless cycle of the ever-same in the mind of the gambler. The constant repetition of the ever-same implies a cycle of no real change. Nothing occurs to distinguish one night in the casino, one day at the book-makers, from any other. Nothing out of the ordinary disturbs the ebb and flow of winning and losing; no landmarks appear to signify change in the monotonous sea of repetition. With the absence of any real change, it becomes impossible to measure the passage of time, and so play goes on, suspended in a timeless void. The narcotic effect of gambling which Benjamin talks about is experienced as an escape from time.

This state of timelessness reaches its apogee in the removal of clocks from the casino. Clocks exist as markers of a shared, objective temporal consensus, imposing order on the flux of human relations and their surroundings. In this, they symbolise the victory of absolute Newtonian time over human time. However, the order of such scientific time is absent from the casino, banished since the nineteenth century as a distraction from the world outside. In a London club of this period, two gamblers playing *ecarte* were asked to leave after closing time. 'Their only answer was to stop the clock, an irritating reminder of the fleeting hours' (Neville 1909, p. 19). With the removal of the clock went the last vestige of the outside world, and the last fragment of memory tying the gamblers to it. In the twenty-first century, no such removals have to be made, for clocks are never present in casinos. Their absence signifies the breakdown of temporal articulation altogether. Unchartered by measurement and with nothing to differentiate it, the experience of time is of an eternal present, recurring at various speeds, in the mind of the gambler. In giving licence to the experience of subjective temporalities, the casino exists as a physical embodiment of the dramatic action of the patient who shot his watch with a revolver in order to 'kill' time.

In the gambling arena players close off the outside world, shed their personality and forget their past, thus freezing themselves in a present which, without reference to the past and without enjoying real change, is empty. Simmel recognised, in their lack of memory and invalidation of experience, the uniquely modern nature of gamblers as an extreme example of the ahistorical individual: 'On the one hand, he is not determined by any past . . . nor on the other hand, does any future exist for him' (Simmel 1971b, p. 196). This is the type of individual with whom Benjamin was concerned when he described how the conditions of modernity were distorting the experience of temporality; eroding genuine experience and replacing it with an experience of a present, 'a *Now* which is incessantly emptying, always already past' (in Spencer 1985, p. 61).

The insubstantial time of the gambler is thus an extreme instance of the empty time of modernity: cut adrift from past and present, it is perceived more as a succession of fleeting, fortuitous moments than as the organic wholeness of Bergson's *durée*.

Space

Spatial perception is a fundamental mode of existence which, according to Merleau-Ponty, resides at the core of the subject's being and provides 'a communication with the world more ancient than thought' (Merleau-Ponty 1981, p. 254). Contrary to the Cartesians who spoke of a 'natural geometry', spatial perception must be grasped *from within*. There are a great many ways of experiencing this kind of space, for lived space, like lived time, is not a homogeneous, geometrical construct, but is rather heterogeneous and relative to the experience of the individual. It can be conceived as a 'field of consciousness', or to use Husserl's term, an 'inner horizon': 'that zone of indeterminacy and ambiguity found in lived experience' (Ey 1978, p. 90).

In fact, the experience of space is inextricably linked with the experience of time, with the former defining our 'outer' and the latter our 'inner' experience. Thus in games of chance, the perception of space undergoes a distortion similar to that of time: the cessation of duration has its counterpart in the contraction of space in the mind of the gambler. Just as time freezes and loses its articulation, so space shrinks and loses *its* articulation.

Gamblers' experience of space is conditioned by the parameters of the game being played; their inner horizon stretches no further than the circumference of the roulette wheel. In the excitement of a game, the perception of space contracts to encompass no more than the physical dimensions of the highly charged area of play. Such spatial disorientation is inherent in the nature of intense sensations themselves, which contain, for Bergson, 'the image of a present contraction and . . . of a compressed space' (Bergson 1910, p. 4). This concentration destroys the harmony of perspective to the extent that the centre of the visual field is magnified and the surrounding space of the periphery obliterated – a sensation which most of us have had when intense concentration momentarily blocks out our immediate surroundings. When tension peaks, all that is perceived is that which contains the action, and it is because the gambler's gaze is so limited in this way that the stage upon which the spectacle of gambling is played out is so correspondingly small.

Just as time needs the unfolding of events to mark its passage, so space requires points of orientation to delimit its parameters, for an empty space is also a formless space. However, with everything external to the action obliterated, gamblers are oblivious to the passage of time, to their surroundings and even to themselves. Absorbed to such an extent in the game, they are subject to a degree of indissociation with their surroundings, a phenomenon which is apparent in one individual's description of the experience of the play world in general: 'You are so involved in what you are doing, you aren't thinking of yourself as separate from the immediate activity . . . you don't see yourself as separate from what you are doing' (in Csikszentmihalyi 1975, p. 46).

Since spatial perception is a primary mode of existence and guarantees the security of the body in space, when it breaks down or becomes distorted, disorder reigns and the sensation of 'plunging', so common to gambling, is experienced. Merleau-Ponty describes how the instability of perception 'produces not only the intellectual experience of disorder, but the vital experience of giddiness, and nausea, which is the awareness of our contingency and the horror with which it fills us' (Merleau-Ponty 1981, p. 254). This disorientation is experienced in gambling as the sensation of 'plunging', and was described by Dostoevsky as a feeling of actual immersion in the game. Rootless in space and time, he felt as though he was being swept along by the roulette wheel, in a 'whirlwind which caught me in its vortex . . . spinning, spinning, spinning' (Dostoevsky 1992, pp. 225–226).

The primacy of *movement* in the field of spatial orientation has been emphasised by many phenomenologists, but is given perhaps its simplest expression by Ey when he stated that space 'is in movement . . . is nothing but movement' (Ey 1978, p. 104). Physical mobility is a means of orientating oneself and establishing a direct spatial relation with the world, and as such 'is on the same footing as perception' (Merleau-Ponty 1981, p. 111). However, one of the most striking features of gamblers in action is their indifference to their surroundings and to their own physical comfort; an indifference manifest in immobility. Most will not tolerate interruption and ignore, with single-minded concentration, the distractions of the world around them. At one time, legend has it, Las Vegas almost became the scene of a disaster when players, oblivious to fire alarms, had to be forcibly removed from a burning downtown casino! Slot-players are frequently so stationary for long periods that when they eventually move they suffer excruciating cramps and dizziness. During one particularly tense game, one punter described how he felt immobilised in an out-of-body state, saying: 'You get what's called a "red mist". You can't leave the table; you're frozen to the table . . . you can't move.' We can see from all this that gamblers' space is *not* a dynamic one conditioned by movement, but is rather characterised by a *breakdown* of such movement; by stasis. The gambler does not move and does not avert his/her gaze from the immediate spectacle of the action in front of him/her, with the result that the surrounding space loses its extensity and its articulation. This is a part of the breakdown of the articulation of space in which the latter shrinks into a single point and loses its extensity and, in this sense, we can describe the experience of space in games of chance as conditioned by a 'pathology of being'.

The perception of space is related to other modes of experience, and in particular the shrinkage of space affects the perception of causation. This is apparent in the gambling arena when, in the heat of the moment, the usual relations between cause and effect become disjointed in the gambler's mind. The particular form of this disjunction will be considered in the following section; for now it is sufficient to entertain it, after Merleau-Ponty, as a possible mode of perception:

> The shrinkage of lived space . . . leaves no room for chance. Like space, causality, before being a relation between objects, is based on my relation to things. The 'short circuits' of delirious causality, no less than the long causal chains of methodical thought, express ways of existing.
>
> (Merleau-Ponty 1981, p. 286)

Money

Although Benjamin thought that 'it is obvious that the gambler is out to win' (Benjamin 1992, p. 136), most gamblers do *not* in fact usually play to win.[7] Nor, as psychoanalytic theory would have it, do they play out of a masochistic desire to lose. The intentions of gamblers are not to be found between these two extremes, for they are generally indifferent to the possibility of winning or losing *per se*. The aim of gamblers is simply to experience the excitement of the game, and so the main goal is thus the indefinite continuation of play. As Spanier expresses it, 'win or lose, everyone feels the thrill' (Spanier 1992, p. 13).

Although, as we saw in Chapter 3, the motives for gambling can be almost as heterogeneous as the variety of games themselves, with sociability (for example, with women in bingo and young people with slot-machines), financial gain (for example, in lottery play) and the exercise of skill (for example, in horse-race handicapping) cited as important elements of different gambling experiences, underlying all this variation is a common element – the quest for excitement, or the thrill of the game, as an end in itself. This is present, to a greater or lesser extent, in *all* forms of gambling, and fundamental to it is the devaluation of money and the indifference to winning or losing. Even lottery players, who, it could be argued, are the group of gamblers most interested in financial gain, are not immune to this common feature. As evidence, we can cite the existence of players who continue to play even after winning enormous jackpots. In a study of Ohio State lottery winners, Kaplan (1988) found that no one actually stopped playing after winning, and that, on the contrary, most players had actually gone on to *increase* their expenditure on tickets. In other forms of gambling, such as horse-race betting, winning is important not so much for the sake of money itself, but rather for what a successful outcome shows about a gambler's skill and ability. Money here is associated with social rather than financial rewards; with factors such as recognition, status and peer approval being paramount.

Despite the fact that gamblers do not play primarily to win it, the *presence* of money in play is nevertheless important: it is vital for the game to be meaningful, as it is the medium through which participants register involvement in a game. In modern gambling, money is both a means of communication and a tangible symbol of the player's presence. The ritual of risk, penalty and reward is couched in the language of money so that in games like poker it eloquently expresses 'every subtle nuance of meaning' (Alvarez 1991, p. 174). In this sense, its presence is vital for the unfolding of a game, for it is the universal equivalent, the dynamo of play. Money is necessary for the generation of the affective tension – the excitement – in games of chance, for at stake in a game is not simply the financial value of the wager, but what it represents – gamblers' opinion, their judgement, their very identity. With the placement of a bet, gamblers become vicariously involved in the game: the fate of their wagers becomes a test of character, and players who manage to control themselves and shrug off their losses in the face of adversity demonstrate strength of will or what Goffman calls 'face' (Goffman 1969).

Any game can be played with a measure other than money, but the thrill will not be the same. Playing poker for matchsticks is perceived as child's play because without the existence of an authentic measure of value, gamblers cannot enter wholeheartedly into the game. As a measure of the degree to which they are prepared to back their opinion, the wager is a measure of the gamblers' integrity, and so must be represented by something worthy of them – hence Richardson regarded his chips as the embodiment of himself, his 'tokens of specialness' (Richardson 1980, p. 121). To have themselves embodied in something as worthless as matchsticks would be demeaning, for it would be to render the player equally as worthless, an object of ridicule. Insofar as money exists as a measure of self-esteem, winning validates gamblers' self-worth. It is in this sense that Rosenthal writes: 'the more money one has, the more substance to oneself, the more one *is*' (Rosenthal 1986, p. 112).

The role of money in gambling however, is ambiguous. On the one hand, it can be seen to be vital, both as the language of play and as a constituent of the thrill. On the other, it is not a sufficient reason for play itself and, paradoxically, once *in* a game, it becomes instantly devalued. Such a contradiction led Baudrillard to state: 'The secret of gambling is that money does not exist as value' (Baudrillard 1990, p. 86). What then *does* it exist as? To answer this, we must look at the effect of money on the gambler at play.

Dostoevsky was adamant that 'The main thing is the play itself. I swear that greed for money has nothing to do with it' (Dostoevsky 1914, p. 119), while Richardson gave a more considered account of his relation to money, writing that gambling had invested it with 'the quality of a medium necessary to the conditions of life. It was not that I wanted to *do* anything with it, any more than I wanted to *do* something with oxygen or sunlight; it was simply that cash had become the element I needed for my personal evolution' (Richardson 1980, p. 75).

It would appear then that gamblers do not play to win but play *with* instead of *for* money. In fact, when they continue to win in games that offer little real challenge, they become quickly bored. Jack Richardson went through such a period of playing poker solely for gain. The result? – 'I grew tired of winning every day. . . . The game had become nothing but empty labour' (Richardson 1980, p. 201). Without the element of chance, the risk of losing all, the game lost its thrill and became mere monotonous work. This effect is evident in the behaviour of top poker players who, after winning large sums of money through concentrated effort and skill, frequently go out and lose it betting on things they have no control over, such as craps and roulette.[8]

Pascal was well aware of the ambiguity of money in games of chance, realising that it was not *only* the money or *only* the play itself that made gambling such an effective antidote to boredom. In the *Pensées* he imagined a hypothetical life in which boredom lurks at every corner:

> A given man lives a life free from boredom by gambling a small sum every day. Give him every morning the money he might win that day, but on condition that he does not gamble and you will make him unhappy. It might be argued that what he wants is the entertainment of gaming and not the winnings. Make him play then for nothing, his interest will not be fired and he will become bored, so it is not just entertainment he wants either.
>
> (Pascal 1987, p. 70)

Money must be present in games of chance, but it cannot be important. In fact, contrary to its status in the outside world as a desirable medium of value, in play, money is apprehended as a thing that is virtually worthless in its own right. As such, it is *devalued* in the mind of gamblers. In order to play without reserve, they must be unconcerned with money for its own sake. As they play, a gulf opens up in their minds between the value of money in the world outside and its value (or lack of) in play. As this gap widens, and the 'real' value of money recedes ever further from the game, gamblers are able to play with increasing insouciance. Chip Reese explains the mechanism of this devaluation:

> Money means nothing. If you really cared about it you wouldn't be able to sit down at a poker table and bluff off $50,000. If I thought about what that could buy me I wouldn't be a good player. Money is just the yardstick by which you measure your success. You treat chips like play money and don't think about it 'til it's over.
>
> (In Alvarez 1991, p. 42)

This devaluation is one of the 'tricks' which gambling plays on value, and it is in this, according to Baudrillard, that its truth is to be found. Gambling, he says, is 'immoral' because it explodes the relation between money and its embodiment of value. This is the crucial relation for 'In gambling, money is *seduced* . . . [it is] no longer a sign or representation once transformed into a stake. And a stake is not something one invests; but as we have seen, it is something which is presented as a challenge to chance' (Baudrillard 1990, p. 139). Removed from the realm of material necessity, money becomes a part of the means of play; a plaything devoid of economic value. Its seduction is even embodied in the language of gambling where stakes, wins and losses are always euphemistically couched in the neutral adjectives of volume and weight as 'heavy', 'large' or 'small', thus avoiding the harsh imperatives of economic reality, of financial profit and loss.

Such devaluation is instrumental in creating the sense of unreality that is a feature of the general tension of games of chance, and is exemplified in the use of 'currencies' such as DigiCash in Internet gambling, and chips in the casino. In the latter, money is changed into chips at the beginning of play; and chips back into money at the end. In the interim the chip is the unit of value. A piece of plastic, with no exchange value outside the casino, inside it is nevertheless the medium of play; the currency of chance. Money – the ultimate measure of value in the world outside – is dethroned in the gambling exchange. It is worthless, its magical effects on the everyday world are redundant here and, its role thus inverted, it must be transformed into chips for play to commence. The act of changing money into chips changes the way the gambler thinks about the latter for the duration of play. As if by magic, the arena of play transforms the prosaic character of money into something fantastic and strange, a process that is described by Alvarez as 'like a conjurer's sleight of hand that turns . . . a necessity of life into a plaything, reality into illusion' (Alvarez 1991, pp. 44–45). The value of the real world, measured in drab green and brown paper, becomes a toy of the play world measured in shiny bright plastic. Looking at the chips on the table in front of him, Richardson 'felt for a moment that they were radiant things. Gold, green, orange, they encased, like pearls in amber, rusty undulations of colour beneath their surface, gay fusions of light and shadow that made one's thoughts reckless and playful' (Richardson 1980, p. 254).[9]

In games, chips are regarded as things which are not quite real, and as a result gamblers tend to lose track of the value of the flow of coloured discs streaming through their hands. When money is turned into plastic in this way it is no longer perceived as an efficacious part of the real world[10] but as an inconsequential counter in a play world, and so players find it easy to let go of their usual pecuniary reserve and abandon themselves to the flow of play. The use of money is here not directed by an awareness of needs which may arise in the future, but by the imperatives of the next round of play in the immediate present.

In the moment of staking, the economic value of money is far outweighed by the excitement it creates in play. Here the gambler is like Simmel's spendthrift, for whom 'the attraction of the instant overshadows the rational evaluation of either money or commodities' (Simmel 1971a, p. 182). For Simmel, the immoderation of both the miser and the spendthrift stems from the same source, the same 'daemonic formula' whereby every pleasure attained increases the desire for more in a spiral that can never be satisfied. Such a formal identity suggests a 'capricious interplay' between the two tendencies, which explains why 'miserliness and prodigality are often found in the same person, sometimes in different areas of interest and sometimes in connection with different moods' (Simmel 1971a, p. 186). This is a tendency also found in gambling, where the inversion of its value lends a dual nature to money in the mind of the player: a 'capricious interplay' of miserliness and prodigality. Gamblers frequently refuse to 'waste' money on necessities, instead hoarding every penny to save enough for enormous bets on games of chance. This orientation was recognised by Balzac, who described the 'strange indifference to luxury' in people who came to the casino to 'perish in their quest of the fortune that can buy luxury' (Balzac 1977, p. 23). Such a blend of parsimony and extravagance is institutionalised in Las Vegas, where casinos absorb the hundreds of thousands of dollars saved for high-stakes play by gamblers living in budget motels and eating only the cheapest food.

As a measure of play, money is also a measure of time, for the two exist in an intimate relation. Low intensity play (i.e. long games with low stakes) makes money, and therefore playing time, last longer. Leaving aside the vicissitudes of luck, a player can gamble longer at a table which costs £1 a game than at one which demands £500. This relation is strikingly evident in the casinos of Las Vegas, which reward time spent at play with a sliding scale of free goods and services. At the Flamingo, breakfast is free for gamblers who have played a $5 slot-machine for an hour or a 25-cent machine for eight hours. They are presented with a complimentary hotel room after four hours on the $8 machine or twenty hours on the 25-cent one. Table awards range from a complimentary room for placing $10 bets for four hours, to free room, food, beverages and health spa for gamblers and their guests for playing for four hours at a table which takes $500 bets. The casino draws attention to its policy; its guide inadvertently articulating the conflation of time and money in play: 'Excess playing time reduces the average bet requirement and higher average bets reduce the playing time requirement. Consideration for airfare reimbursements are based on a minimum of twelve hours playing time' (*The Flamingo Casino Guide*).

It can be seen then that money is necessary as the dynamo of gambling. As the currency of the world of play, it comes to assume magical properties, becoming an insubstantial chimera that contributes to the sense of unreality and the affective tension experienced by gamblers during play. Once in a game however, it is immediately devalued, becoming merely a means of sustaining or prolonging the action. As one player explained: 'The whole point of money is to allow you to remain in the action. Once you have no money, it's axiomatic. You're out of the action' (in Martinez 1983, p. 361). The repetition of play is evidence of this goal for, even when winning vast amounts, gamblers tend to continue playing anyway. As we have seen, repetition is an intrinsic element of both the form and the content of play, and one that prevails whether the outcome of a round is loss or gain. A common sight in slot-machine arcades and the casinos of Las Vegas is slot-machine players emptying their winnings from a previous round back into the machine, thrusting handfuls of coins in as fast as they pour out, in the pursuit of further play. Even multi-million-dollar lottery winners play on, one remarking wistfully: 'It'd be nice to get one more win.'

THE VARIETIES OF GAMBLING EXPERIENCE

Unproductive expenditures

This devaluation highlights one of the most striking characteristics of play: its essentially *unproductive* and non-utilitarian nature. No wealth or goods are ever created in its endless circulation of money, and in this sense 'Play is an occasion of pure waste, waste of time, energy, skill and often money' (Caillois 1962, p. 5). Despite the tone of residual Puritanism in many statements about its unproductive nature, it is undeniably true that with its flamboyant squandering of money, gambling *is* such an occasion of pure waste, or what Bataille calls 'unproductive expenditures': activities which are pursued for their own sake and whose principle is pure consumption. Contrary to bourgeois rationality which recognises 'the right to acquire, to conserve and to consume rationally' (Bataille 1985, p. 117) exists the notion of non-productive expenditure – the waste, destruction or conspicuous consumption of wealth in activities which have no end beyond themselves. This expenditure exists as the converse of wealth creation and production and represents the fundamental human need to 'use up' wealth (Bataille 1985, p. 121). Bataille cites sacrifice, potlach and gambling as examples of this broadly non-utilitarian, anti-bourgeois approach to wealth, and it is an approach which we saw earlier in the gambling orgies of the seventeenth-century aristocracy. The obligation to expend accompanies the possession of wealth, and, he says, the two have always existed harmoniously until the 'fairly recent' ascendancy of the bourgeoisie in economic life, when such obligations broke down as the principle of 'restrained expenditure' began to dominate. Now 'everything that was generous, orgiastic and excessive' has disappeared, overtaken by a bourgeoisie who 'having obtained mediocre or minute fortunes, have managed to debase and subdivide ostentatious expenditure, of which nothing remains but vain efforts tied to tiresome rancour' (Bataille 1985, p. 124).

By 'restrained expenditure', Bataille means the rationalist orientation developed by the bourgeoisie in the seventeenth century, coming to power out of the humiliating shadow of a more powerful, noble class. This orientation defined the nature of the bourgeoisie: 'This rationalism meant nothing other than the strictly economic representation of the world', with the result that their hatred of expenditure became 'the *raison d'être* and the justification for the bourgeoisie' (Bataille 1985, p. 124). Their narrow economic rationality opposed the excesses of aristocratic display, making the existence of the bourgeoisie 'a sinister cancellation' of all that had gone before: 'the shame of man' (Bataille 1985, p. 125).

Bataille's notion of expenditure is the economic counterpart to the excitement generated by gambling. It represents the desire to 'plunge', realised in primitive and feudal social groups, and negated in the economic utilitarianism of bourgeois society. Gambling can be seen as an arena in which a non-capitalist disregard for money prevails and where bourgeois rationality, dominant since the seventeenth century, is inverted. While playing, gamblers' orientation to wealth is contained in the notion of this type of 'unproductive expenditure'. Without concern for the rational accumulation of wealth, they play rather for the sheer sake of play itself; for self-realisation, status and pure enjoyment. The nobility of the seventeenth century demonstrated honour in their wholehearted pursuit of play, and in their disinterest in its base, pecuniary potential. In the same vein, modern gamblers demonstrate character and realise their selves in their pursuit of play: an unproductive expenditure; an activity in and for itself.

Gambling, chance and status

Plunging into a game is not the automatic response of *all* gamblers however: we only have to remember Dangeau and his 'bourgeois' play at the court of Louis XIV to be aware that different styles of play exist, each with its own rationale and social affiliation.

The polarisation between 'bourgeois' and 'aristocratic' play which emerged in the seventeenth century produced a form of gambling based on a patrician disdain for money and display of honour, as well as a 'bourgeois' mode of play whose aim was pecuniary gain. In the nineteenth-century wave of commercial and democratic expansion, another style of play emerged whose dynamic was based neither on winning nor on the ostentatious display of wealth, but simply on participating in the game. As we have seen, aspects of both types are also present in contemporary gambling: in the latter, in games which are pursued for their own sake, simply for the pleasure of participating; and in the former, in games where status and character can be demonstrated in facing up to the challenge posed by risk itself.

Dostoevsky is illustrative of the opposition between what can be termed bourgeois or utilitarian play for financial gain, and the type of gambling that is pursued purely for its own sake, for although he was involved in the latter camp, he remained unaware of the existence of such an opposition. At first he appears to demonstrate a remarkable lack of awareness of the laws of probability, and even of the rules of gambling themselves, for he is convinced that with prudence and calculation he can win and that it is only when he becomes excited that he gets 'carried away' and loses. This may be useful advice for those playing games of skill, but Dostoevsky was playing roulette, where such tactics would have made absolutely no impression on the outcome of a game. This gambler's (mis)application of the betting ethos to games of chance which can only be *played* is interesting, less for what it tells us about his knowledge of probability than for what it reveals about his notion of the nature of play itself. In the catalogue of disaster that is the content of his published letters, Dostoevsky explains the infallibility of his system:

> I have observed as I approached the gaming table that if one plays coolly, calmly and with calculation *it is quite impossible to lose*! I swear – it is an absolute impossibility! It is blind chance pitted against my calculation; hence I have an advantage over it. . . . If you gamble in small doses every day, it is impossible not to win.
>
> (Dostoevsky 1987, pp. 345, 346)

Dostoevsky is convinced of the efficacy of his system: to win, one must simply remain calm and rational; his problem is that he quickly loses his reason when he plays: instead of holding back he plunges into the game – and into disaster. Having won a small amount by staking one or two gulden at a time and sensibly allowing his profits to accumulate, he reflects that that was the time to have stopped, but he could not restrain himself: 'I lost my composure, became tense, started to take chances, became exasperated, laid my bets haphazardly because my system had broken down – and lost' (Dostoevsky 1987, p. 246).

Dostoevsky aspired to the success of Dangeau – 'the scientific man, the average man, the economic man' – and thought he knew how he could achieve it. By maintaining the bourgeois imperative of reason in the face of disorder and passion, he believed everything would fall into place and the world and, more importantly, the *game*, would become as ordered as he was. The problem for Dostoevsky however was that he could *never* play in this way, for he despised such 'bourgeois mentality', and was repeatedly overcome by his disregard for winning and desire for excitement, for risk. This orientation meant that he would always 'plunge', always lose control and experience the excitement of gambling instead of remaining aloof, holding back and coolly calculating his gains. He chose (as does any gambler who experiences the thrill) the excitement of play itself over pecuniary gain, abandon over restraint, the 'aristocratic' over the 'bourgeois' ethic. Lamenting his losses to Anna Suslova, he wrote:

'What could I possibly have done to deserve this? Is it my disorderly ways? I agree I have led quite a disorderly life, but what is all this *bourgeois morality*!' (Dostoevsky 1987, p. 219). The true gambler, he believed, played 'simply for the sake of the game itself, only for amusement . . . not out of a plebeian desire to win' (Dostoevsky 1992, p. 138).

In this style of play, we see a disregard for money, a deliberate seeking out of risk and chance, and a realisation of the self: values which are encapsulated in Nietzsche's allegorical 'dice throw'. In a philosophy which rejects as slavish the values of bourgeois morality and which upholds the masterful ones of aristocratic excess, the dice are thrown on to the earth and fall into the sky; 'for the earth is a table . . . trembling with . . . the dice-throws of the gods' (Nietzsche 1969, p. 245). The good player must be as anti-rational as Zarathustra, repudiating reason and logic and actively *courting* chance. Rules and systems must be abolished and chance affirmed in one, single, all-or-nothing throw. In terms of the master–slave dialectic, the gambler who risks all and 'plunges', or affirms chance, is the stronger, while the one who holds back and whose object is pecuniary gain is subject to the slave mentality. For Nietzsche, to play successfully is to affirm chance, an approach which will necessarily produce the winning number. Players lose because they do not affirm strongly enough, counting on a great number of sensible, cautious throws to win:

> Timid, ashamed, awkward like a tiger whose leap has failed: this is how I have often seen you slink aside. . . . A *throw* you made had failed. But what of that, you dice throwers! You have not learned to play and mock as a man ought to play and mock.
>
> (Nietzsche 1969, p. 303)

Gambling in twentieth-century Las Vegas, Richardson displayed an almost intuitive understanding of his role as a modern dice thrower. While ostensibly aware of probabilities and odds, in a more profound sense he felt that *real* winning, as opposed to the various rational calculations which ultimately only ever amount to loss minimisation, could only be achieved by a single, brave gamble. In keeping hold of himself, he wrote: 'I thought I was displaying admirable self control but I was really afraid to face the risk of a large gamble, to submit to the full force of chance and feel my entire being at stake in the encounter' (Richardson 1980, p. 153). He could not find the strength to affirm chance strongly enough: 'I kept demanding to win, but still could not find the courage to make winning possible' (Richardson 1980, p. 168). Thus he lost, over a period of days, his entire bankroll.

In a sense, Nietzsche is right: given finite funds in commercial games of chance, one all-or-nothing bet at least contains the possibility of a big win. Otherwise, the longer gamblers play with small stakes, the longer the house edge has to eat into their bankroll, gradually taking its cut and reducing them to penury. One large bet at least has the chance of winning a sum untouched by this steady, relentless erosion.

The affirmation of chance provides an opportunity to demonstrate character, to display courage and honour in the face of risk. In this way the affirmation of chance is also an affirmation of the *self*. It is here that the relationship between gambling and status, risk and ennoblement, is most obvious. Alesky found redemption through his gambling, for Dostoevsky writes of him that 'deep down he feels that he is despicable although the need to take *risks* ennobles him in his own eyes' (Dostoevsky 1987, p. 186). He set an arbitrary test for himself, betting his last money on the turn of the roulette wheel, to decide whether he was 'a man or a nothing'. The risk paid off: 'I had achieved this at the risk of more than my life, I had dared to take the risk and now I was *once again among the ranks of men*!' (Dostoevsky 1992, p. 267; my italics). A similar sentiment was expressed by Gogol's Utyeshitelny, who declared: 'the chief zest lies in the risk. Where there is no risk, anyone is brave; if the result is certain, any paltry scribbler is bold' (Gogol 1926, p. 236).

It is not only the plunging into chance that has this effect; games of skill also provide a stage for self-realisation. Although, as we saw in Chapter 3, the orientation involved in the two is different (with games of skill utilising calculation and planning), crucially, the element of risk is still paramount. The similarity derives from the fact that it is mainly social rewards, not financial ones, that derive from the taking of such risks. Exposure to risky or uncertain situations provides individuals with the opportunity to display courage and integrity, and so to earn the respect of their peers. As top poker player Jack Strauss explains, it is not mathematical ability but 'heart' – 'the courage to bet *all* their money' – when the odds are in their favour which is the criteria by which a player is judged (in Alvarez 1991, p. 31).

Despite their manifold differences, games of chance and those of skill are united in their common disregard of financial gain. In neither one is money the primary motive for gambling, rather it is the aspiration to be a 'dice thrower': the demonstration of character and courage and the consequent affirmation of the self that makes the play meaningful. Despite the victory of the bourgeois ethos, represented by the winnings of Dangeau, subsequent generations of gamblers like Dostoevsky and Richardson have *not* played to win, but rather for the continued experience of the game itself. The orientation of the modern gambler can be seen to be inspired not by the 'rational' goal of financial gain, but rather by ever-renewed play, and it is here that the relationship between gambling, self-realisation and, as Goffman puts it, 'face', is most striking. Thus the abandonment of reason embodied in Dostoevsky's plunging parodied the bourgeois style of play; a style eternally constrained by the discipline of self-consciousness over oblivion and restraint over excess. By not risking all, such gamblers will never lose all, but nor will they ever gain anything of value. Their greatest reward will be a few pennies, carefully won in an eternity of sensible, cautious play.

Play-in-itself

The rationale of the repetition of play, and the fundamental aim of gamblers, is the ever-continued pursuit of play. They attempt to sustain the fleeting sensation of the thrill by repeating their actions, striving for a state that cannot be – the *continual* sensation of the thrill. For Gadamer, the essence of all play is that it is divorced from the realm of utilitarian ends and pursued entirely for its own sake. Thus 'the being of all play is always realisation, sheer fulfillment, energia which has its telos within itself' (Gadamer 1975, p. 101). Win or lose, play is all; it is an end in itself and so the goal of the gambler is simply to remain in play. The outcome of a game is not so important as the possibility of its being brought to a conclusion, for this means that that particular round is over. So, having won or lost, gamblers are frustrated by having brought the game to an end and to re-create the sensation of play must repeat their actions again and again. The repetition of such activity so engrosses players that their very *being* becomes absorbed in it; as Steinmetz puts it: 'the gamester lives only for the sensation of gaming. . . . All the rays of [his] existence terminate in play; it is on this centre that his very existence depends' (Steinmetz 1870, p. 49).

In trying to hold on to this elusive sensation, gamblers are caught in the eternal repetition of the ever-same. Time freezes, space contracts, and players hang, it could be said, in a state of suspended animation. They possess no past, and are unable to consider the future beyond the next round. Forever pursuing the fleeting sensation of play – a sensation which vanishes almost as soon as it is reached – they are caught in a state akin to what Schopenhauer describes as a state of becoming and never being. For Schopenhauer, it is not the end but the sensation of striving for a goal that satisfies us. Any pleasure we experience ceases as soon as we reach it and so the more distant it is the better, for its very distance gives us the illusion that its eventual attainment would satisfy us. He writes that 'we take no pleasure in existence except when we are striving after something in which case distance and difficulties make our goal look as if it would satisfy us (an illusion which fades when we reach it)' (Schopenhauer 1970, p. 54). Thus by the time a game has been won or lost, it is over, the thrill is dissipated and the gambler must begin again to re-create it. Such a frustrating predicament underlies all gambling, and was well understood by Balzac when he described the typical player as a 'modern tantalus, one of those men who live just out of reach of the enjoyments of their times . . . a kind of reasoning madman who consoles himself by nursing a chimera' (Balzac 1977, p. 25).

5

THE MAGICAL-RELIGIOUS
WORLDVIEW

THE REJECTION OF PROBABILITY

Having examined the disruption of perceptions of time, space and money, it is now time to look at the perception of causation in the world of play. To do this, we shall focus on the beliefs held by gamblers, for games of chance encourage a distinctive cognitive outlook among players. Unlike games of skill which are governed by a more straightforwardly 'rational' framework based on prediction and control, games of chance tend to engender alternative types of belief. Despite the knowledge of random events, percentages and odds generated by that tool of chance – probability theory – gamblers on the whole tend to ignore its insights; continuing to play when the odds are against them, behaving as though they could influence games of pure chance and stubbornly expecting to win in the midst of catastrophic defeat. Thoughts banished from the outside world as superstitious and irrational are here given credence and provide a framework which organise and explain the vagaries of play and the outcome of games. These include a broad range of magical and quasi-religious beliefs: there is the notion of 'luck', the idea that cards, dice or tickets can somehow be influenced by the gambler, and the idea that the outcome of games is decided by providential forces such as 'fate' or 'destiny'. All these beliefs are popular currency in games of chance, and exist to provide a system of thought which is uniquely adapted to the nature of the gambling environment. It is in this cognitive outlook that the tension of the gambling situation – the dynamic between uncertainty and order, chance and meaning – is to be found.

The rejection of probability has caused consternation among psychologists trying to uncover some rationale for gamblers' behaviour. The latter's determined disregard for modern mathematics flies in the face of conventional rationality, with the result that gamblers have been accused of suffering from a variety of 'irrational beliefs' (Gadboury and Ladoceur 1988), including an 'illusion of control' (Langer 1975) and a 'biased evaluation of outcomes' (Gilovich 1983). Langer described the 'illusion of control' as a belief that games of chance could be influenced or controlled by gamblers merely by virtue of their participation in them. Subjects in her experiments believed themselves more likely to win when they were allowed to participate in games, for example, by selecting their own lottery tickets or throwing their own dice. The overestimation of skill is concomitant with this illusion of control, since it is through their supposed skill that gamblers believe they can influence games of pure chance by their own efforts alone (Furnham and Lewis 1983). Griffiths found this tendency particularly marked among fruit machine players, who believed a variety of 'skills', such as knowing how to utilise the 'hold' and 'nudge' buttons on machines, were relevant to play (Griffiths 1993). Linked to the overestimation of skill is what is described by Gilovich (1983) as a 'biased evaluation of outcomes'. The author found that gamblers attributed different causes to the outcome of races depending on whether they had lost or won. Wins were attributed to skill and effort whereas losses were put down to factors outwith their control, for example, distractions and bad luck.

These 'pathology' models inevitably treat gambling belief as an individual disorder of cognition designed to 'cope' with an untenable situation. As Devereaux put it: 'to fill the gaps in positive knowledge . . . and hence overcome the inhibiting anxieties induced by a feeling of ignorance and helplessness' (Devereaux 1949). While they contribute something to our understanding of individual gamblers' behaviour, these models provide only piecemeal explanations for actions which inevitably appear as sporadic, *ad hoc* solutions to difficult situations in which gamblers 'find' themselves. Such impulsive reactions can only appear irrational. However, we know that gamblers do not simply 'fall into' the gambling situation, but actively seek it out and, moreover, through systematic action, expect to win while in it. The determination of most players actually stems from their firm conviction of the possibility of winning – certainly not from feelings of 'ignorance' or 'helplessness'. A more comprehensive framework must therefore be sought; a 'cognitive map' in which the various actions, expectations and beliefs of the gambler may be located. In order to do this, we must look at the *context* in which these beliefs flourish: in other words, at the nature of the gambling environment itself and, by extension, at the most striking feature of that environment: the pervasive presence of chance.

Few concepts are as alien to human thought as the notion of pure chance – the idea that events have no identifiable cause and no particular meaning. Probability theory – the apologist of this secularised chance – is equally alien. Probability creates order out of randomness, but not for the gambler. As with classical scientific enquiry in general, it is concerned solely with establishing causal relations between separate events which then form the basis of universal explanations. But, as we saw in Chapter 1, since it cannot predict any single outcome, its secular insight is ultimately just as emotionally meaningless as the chaotic operation of pure chance. There is, in fact, something strangely counter-intuitive about probability theory, and its laws are misunderstood by most people – gamblers and non-gamblers alike. It tells us not to look for patterns or sequences, and informs us that the fact a card or a number has come up many times in a row does not make it any more or less likely to come up in the next round. The fact that, for example, in roulette, the number five has come up in the previous ten games does not make it any less likely to appear in the next one: the odds are still exactly the same – 36 to 1. There is no apparent logic to these short-term sequences: they cannot be predicted or worked out,[1] they simply have to be accepted. The existence of bizarre coincidences (with which gambling folklore is littered) does not help gamblers to resign themselves to its laws. Among such coincidences is the individual cited by Kaplan (1978) who won two prizes on the same New Jersey lottery ticket. He first won a $10,000 'runner-up' prize, then, less than an hour later, the jackpot of $1 million. The odds of this happening, calculated by surprised statisticians, were worked out at 334 trillion to one! What William James called the cold generalisations of scientific explanation, which are oblivious to 'human anxieties and fates' (James 1982, p. 491) cannot explain this. The security offered by numbers breaks down at this level of reasoning.

As we saw in Chapter 1, gamblers' interest in the gambling event is focused on the unit event, the next round, the specific individual outcome of a game and its relation to their wagers. However, probability theory – and particularly the law of large numbers – speaks only of the general, the many and the long term and is 'forever mute' as to what is most crucial: what will happen next. This is representative of the scientific rational consciousness, and is, according to Baudrillard, 'a statistical response . . . [a] dead response' to chance; an approach which is, he says, quite simply 'demented' (Baudrillard 1990, pp. 145–146). The gambler obviously agrees, and consequently rejects its explanatory force, regarding the gambling event, not scientifically as one among a broad dispersal of indifferent occurrences, but as an exceptional individual event imbued with meaning in its own right. The distinction is that between the scientific and the magical-religious worldview; between a relation to the world expressed in general, 'objective' laws, and one which focuses on the subjective meaning of individual events. As an example of the contrast, Cassirer (1953) cites the instance of the death of a man. The scientific explanation can give us medical reasons as to why a body should die, but this is emotionally unsatisfying at another level. It does not – cannot – 'explain' the specific instance, 'namely the here and now of the particular case, the death of precisely *this* man, at *this* particular time' (Cassirer 1953, p. 49). It is this level of meaning that concerns gamblers – the outcome of *this* game at *this* time – and so they look away from the explanations offered by scientific thought, inclining instead towards that which explains and makes meaning-ful the specific event. Thus, for gamblers, as for their historical predecessors engaged in religious divinatory drama, there is no such thing as chance. The random event is rather taken as a *sign*, and both groups search for its meaning and ultimate significance outwith the immediately given. In this worldview the random and the unpredictable once again come to indicate the existence of some higher meaning. Thus gamblers disregard probability theory, within whose formulae chance became a constituent part of the modern world. Removing it from the equation that gave it ontological status, the gambler personalises the outcome of a game and elevates chance to transcendental significance so that it is no longer 'an abstract expression of statistical coefficient, but a sacred sign of the favour of the gods' (Caillois 1962, p. 126). It is in this way, as Simmel explains, that gambling belief operates to draw chance into a teleological system, 'thus removing it from its inaccessible isolation and searching in it for a lawful order, no matter how fantastic the laws of such an order may be' (Simmel 1971b, p. 191).

We can here make a distinction between 'rational' or scientific thought (which includes the theory of probability) and what can be termed 'magical-religious' or mystical thought – beliefs which operate to make sense of uncertainty. We know from phenomenology that 'knowledge' is socially constructed and adapted to meet the requirements of particular situations, and it is in this sense that the gambler rejects the type of knowledge provided by probability theory, adopting instead another type, more relevant in an environment of chance. It is this latter system that provides a means of understanding the gambling situation and a rationale for action while in it. Within this context, far from being simply and prosaically 'irrational', the worldview of gamblers appears as a framework of thought uniquely adapted to the peculiar nature of their environment.

Two overlapping currents of belief can be discerned running through this general orientation: one magical, the other what can be termed broadly religious. The specifically magical dimension of the gambler's worldview is concerned with efficacy in general and the efficacy of the individual gambler in particular. Such efficacy refers to the impersonal power of the subject; in other words, to a power or powers possessed by the individual. It encompasses a range of ideas described by anthropologists as the notions of *mana* (or luck), animism, and beliefs about the efficacy of dreams and omens. The religious aspect of the gambler's worldview is concerned with the operation of power outwith the subject. In this orientation, power is regarded as a thing imbued with moral and metaphysical properties, not merely as an impersonal force, and is conceived as some kind of providential authority: fate, destiny and sometimes even God. Both of these currents of thought are based on a rejection of the secular basis of probability theory, and the adoption instead of an alternative, 'sacred' order of belief. In the discussion that follows, they will be considered separately.

THE MAGICAL WORLDVIEW:
PARTICIPATION

Magical ideas such as the belief in luck, animism (the notion that inanimate objects are imbued with animate properties), and ideas about prophetic dreams and omens derive their efficacy from their shared characteristic of *participation*.

The notion of participation is fundamental in magical-religious thought, and refers to a basic state of indissociation between the individual and the world (van der Leeuw 1967). Within it, individuals are literally a part of the world around them in the sense that not only can it affect them, but they can also affect it through thoughts and will as much as through physical effort. This, van der Leeuw tells us, is an attitude deeply rooted in human nature – 'an underlying current of waking-day thinking within every modern' (van der Leeuw 1967, p. 545) – even if we are not always aware of it. It emerges when the boundary between the self and the external world 'becomes momentarily vague and uncertain' (Piaget 1977, p. 184), and has been described as characterising the consciousness of various groups: children (Piaget 1977), compulsives (Freud 1939), poets (van der Leeuw 1967), natives (Levy-Bruhl 1966), and even ourselves, when we dream (Straus 1966). The experience of dreams, in which we can influence things, cross distances and move around in time, without any regard for the strictures of reason or cause, is representative of the participatory worldview. The consciousness involved in it is not concerned with dissection or abstraction, but with totalities and wholes – in fact, there are no 'parts' *to* dissect, since each 'part' of the world participates in every other 'part'. Such a lack of differentiation of the constituent elements of the world has far-reaching implications for notions of causality, for since a 'true indifference' between the whole and its parts exists, neither can be singled out and granted causal priority. Thus 'there is in fact no "other" in any actual sense, just as there is no such thing as chance' (van der Leeuw 1967, p. 381). Applied to the gambler, such an orientation implies a rejection of the rational causation behind probability theory, and an alternative understanding of the world through *magical* notions of causation instead.

The depiction of this type of worldview has been criticised (for example, by Evans-Pritchard 1965) for attributing a 'misapplication of ideas' – the mistaking of an ideal connection for a real one – to the individuals involved in it. However, to a certain extent, such criticism misses the point by overlooking the essentially pragmatic role that the possession of magical ideas can have, whether 'believed', in the strictest sense, by their owners or not. Furthermore, it is not being suggested here that the beliefs about to be discussed are based on a misunderstanding of the world; rather, the more limited argument that this type of approach simply provides a fruitful means of understanding the beliefs of those engaged in the gambling situation.

In his classic study of the Trobriand islanders of Melanesia, the Polish anthropologist Bronislaw Malinowski (1935, 1948) illustrated how magical beliefs fulfilled a particular function by providing a basis for action in situations of uncertainty, and it is in this sense that the magical worldview of gamblers should be understood. Malinowski demonstrated that a magical orientation to the world could exist alongside a more conventionally scientific or 'rational' one, and that recourse to magic was made in situations where individuals had little control over their environment and where knowledge and skill were of limited use. For example, when fishing in the relatively calm waters of the lagoon, the Trobrianders utilised their skills and knowledge of relevant conditions to ensure the success of an expedition. When faced with the more unpredictable waters of the open sea however, they supplemented technical expertise with magical rituals. It was not that the efficacy of magic was confused with technical knowledge here, but rather that it was brought in when the limits of such knowledge were felt. It was the *possession* of magical beliefs rather than the magical acts themselves that provided the sensation of security and a means of dealing with uncertainty in an emotionally satisfying way.

For gamblers, immersed in an environment of chance in which the limitations of scientific knowledge are most keenly felt, the possession of alternative, magical beliefs are similarly efficacious. As we shall see, such beliefs work to make sense of the gambling situation and provide a framework for action while in it. Broadly speaking, they include ideas about dreams and omens, about animism and the omnipotence of thoughts, and the widespread belief in the existence of the magical qualities of 'luck'.

Dreams and omens

Omens

Because events in the magical worldview are not subject to normal causal laws and are not separate in time and space, the possibility of gaining foreknowledge of those events, and also of influencing them, exists. Many players cite premonitions, visions and psychic and religious experiences as forces that alerted or guided them to their impending win (see e.g. Kaplan 1978). Nothing, then, happens 'by chance', and players see meaning in everything: 'everything . . . is full of significance, everything can be interpreted' (Freud 1939, p. 318). Clues to the outcome of a game can be found everywhere, and are particularly evident in the beliefs in dreams and omens.

Apparently fortuitous events can be regarded as omens which are full of significance, conveying some kind of private message to the gambler about the future course of a game. A sudden win on the slots just as he was about to stop gambling altogether convinced Richardson that he was the recipient of an *ex machina* intercession: 'Naturally, it was not the amount, but the way of obtaining it, that made me feel certain I'd been given the sign I'd waited for during the weeks of slow, grinding descent' (Richardson 1980, p. 170). Omens can also indicate the course which a game will take, and to this effect gamblers frequently make associations between some symbolic event or action and the outcome of a game. Like diviners, they view the satisfaction of certain ritualistic criteria as prophetic for the future course of events – 'if x happens, then I'll win, if y, I won't.'

The literature on gambling is full of examples of this tendency. One bettor declares, 'If I see a car from New York I'll bet the Giants tomorrow. If I don't, that's a bad omen. Don't bet 'em. Sick' (in Leiseur 1984, p. 32). Cohen (1972) describes a player whose decision-making ritual bears a striking resemblance to the Azande's consultation of the termite oracle. The gambler would place a spider in a matchbox, one side of which was painted red, the other black. He then backed which ever colour the spider crawled out of. In a similar procedure, the Azande would dig a stick into a termite mound, and depending on whether the termites ate it or not, interpret their answer accordingly (Evans-Pritchard 1991, p. 165).

The efficacy of omens derives from the peculiar nature of causation in the magical consciousness. In the latter, as we have seen, 'cause' and 'effect' are not distinguished and so these rites or omens function as both cause *and* effect at the same time. The prophetic ritual and the event it is concerned with exist in an indissoluble relation so that what happens in one will happen in the other. Using our terminology of cause and effect, Levy-Bruhl explains how omens function as both in certain tribes, writing that good omens 'not only announce the desired success; they are a necessary condition of it. They guarantee it and they effect it' (Levy-Bruhl 1936, p. 47). In this way, important ventures will not be undertaken until the requisite signs have appeared. The good omens upon which gamblers base their decisions are thus important, not simply because they reveal what will happen, but rather because they also *cause* the event to happen. In this way the fulfilment or non-fulfilment of the rite is both sign *and* cause.

It is not only natives with whom gamblers share a belief in the efficacy of these prophetic rituals, for Piaget has shown that they are common among children, who also possess a participatory outlook. Like gamblers, this group frequently associate the outcome of an activity with the fulfilment of some later condition. Piaget quotes one individual who, as a child, to succeed in some activity such as winning a game, would test himself by engaging in a certain pattern of behaviour. If successful in this, he felt assured of success in the other, more important area, explaining: 'I would hold my breath and if I could count up to ten . . . I felt sure of gaining what I wanted' (Piaget 1977, p. 160). In these examples, the operation of counting is both sign and cause, just as it is for a gambler who set 'walking races' with unwitting individuals on the way to the betting shop. Like the child who failed his 'test', this gambler would censure his bet if he lost his race: 'If the rival reached a preset point . . . before the gambler then the selected horse would lose and the bet was not placed' (Scolarios and Brown 1988).

With our continued enactment of what Huizinga called the 'futile auguries' of childhood, we also, at times, share this belief in omens, with avoiding the cracks on pavements while walking perhaps being the best known – and most commonly practised! – example. Piaget lists instances of 'spontaneous magical ideas' in adults (Piaget 1977, pp. 184–189), while Rousseau found himself prey to one he described somewhat shamefacedly as both childish and insane, in his *Confessions*. One day, throwing stones at trees, he decided to draw 'a sort of omen' from it, to allay his anxiety about the course of his life. If he hit the tree, he decided, all would go well with the rest of his life; if not, it would not (Rousseau 1967, p. 231).

To succeed in the situation we have set up for ourselves is the fulfilment of a ritual which is indissolubly linked with the successful realisation of a more important one – for the gambler, the outcome of a game.

Dreams

Tatyana shared with full conviction
the simple faith of olden days
in dreams and cards and their prediction.
(Pushkin 1983, p. 134)

The belief in the significance of dreams and the practice of oneiromancy is ubiquitous, occurring throughout history in almost every part of the world. In the modern world Freud emphasised the importance of dreams as messages from the subconscious mind, an emphasis quite unlike that placed on them in ancient thought where their content was believed to derive from *outwith* the conscious self. Whatever their origin however, the nature of dreams was generally perceived as being more expressive than the experiences of waking life. In worldviews in which involuntary gestures and 'accidental' occurrences were regarded as being imbued with deeper significance, dreams appeared as vehicles of supernatural meaning. Gamblers possess a similar worldview, and as such, dream interpretation has existed throughout history alongside games of chance, with players assiduously analysing their nocturnal visitations for what they might reveal about the outcome of future gambling contests. The Huron Indians, for example, would fast before a gambling contest in an attempt to induce dreams which were then regarded as divine pronouncements on the result of the game. An individual who dreamt of winning would be given a central role in the proceedings; chosen to shake the dice, pass the sacred gaming implements and arbitrate in any disputes (Levy-Bruhl 1936, p. 163).

Among modern gamblers, dreams are no less valued for their prophetic insights. In Pushkin's *Queen of Spades*, Hermann was convinced of success when the dead Countess Fedotovna appeared to him in a dream-like visitation and gave him the secret of the winning cards. In the waking world of life, nothing would compel the Countess to reveal the secret; it was only in the twilight world of dreams and the dead that she finally did so. Few dreams are as obliging to the gambler as Hermann's however, in which the Countess simply appeared and recited the winning combination, and so the technique of dream interpretation has been developed into almost an art-form. In this way, significance can still be derived from dreams which do not specifically refer to gambling through the translation of their individual images into numbers, the latter of which are then deemed efficacious in number games like lotteries. The *National Lottery Magazine* hints suggestively at the possibility: 'Perhaps you HAVE seen those winning numbers before – in your sleep!'

Despite Freud's insight that dreams *do* have a meaning that can be interpreted – albeit one that is to be found within the dreamer – gamblers still search for their significance outwith the self. Myriad methods for 'calculating' the numbers in dreams exist. 'Dream books', for instance, interpret the 'meaning' of dreams and convert their visual representations into numbers, which are believed to be propitious for the dreamer in games of chance. The form of these books has remained virtually unchanged since the very earliest lists of dreams and their interpretations which were used around the second century AD for divinatory purposes (Cryer 1994, pp. 220–221). The seventeenth-century explosion of numeracy saw the assignation of specific numbers to dream images, and the establishment of the definitive form of dream books for the next three centuries. Today, dream books for lottery and 'numbers' players are published throughout the western world and often sold alongside horoscopes and lottery tickets. In a worldview in which every 'meaning' is reducible to number, these books offer, for the personal, fleeting images of dreams, knowledge expressed in the quantifiable universals of number; a process which, one dream book boasts, takes the 'raw' dream and realises its significance in a 'sophisticated computer algorithm'! By some arcane process, it somehow manages to convert a dream involving 'sauerkraut' into the combination 9–10–17–19–30–38 (*Dream Script* 1994, p. 23)!

Animism and the omnipotence of thought

Tylor (1871) regarded animism as the most basic category of religious belief, while Freud attributed it to the projection of subjective states on to the outside world. He considered it to be the first human *Weltanschauung*, and cited Hume's identification of it as a fundamental trait in human thought. In his *Natural History of Religion* Hume wrote, 'There is a universal tendency among all mankind to conceive all beings like themselves, and to transfer to every object those qualities with which they are familiarly acquainted and of which they are intimately conscious' (in Freud 1985, p. 134).

Such animism is also a feature of gamblers' belief, and can be witnessed in their attribution of 'dispositions' or 'natures' to material objects which reside in all the paraphernalia of play: cards, dice, tickets, roulette wheels and slot-machines.

Henslin studied a group of craps players who believed that they were able to 'control the dice by verbal and non-verbal gestures, by words and actions' (Henslin 1967, p. 319). This control was possible through the gambler's knowledge of their capricious natures and moods, for the dice were granted a will, inclinations and the rudiments of character (Henslin 1967, p. 319). To get the point (number) they wanted, players had to 'persuade' the dice to supply it. One advised Henslin, 'Talk to 'em! Talk to 'em when ya shoot!' In this way, obtaining the desired number was attributed as much to the 'nature' or 'mood' of the dice as to abstract features like chance or the way that they were thrown.

Slot-machines are notoriously subject to the most extreme forms of animistic – and even anthropomorphic – belief, as is apparent in the attribution of human characteristics to them. Some are regarded as generous – 'hot', some parsimonious – 'cold', in their payouts. As they play them, alert gamblers gradually 'get to know' their nature: manifestations of the iron laws of probability become idiosyncrasies of an entity which reveals its personality in the outcome of every spin. Players frequently talk to their machines, and attribute motivations to them. 'The machine's laughing at me now'; 'it knows what I'm thinking' (Griffiths 1990, 1994). After a long sequence, one gambler was convinced the devil was in the machine and had spelled out 'SATAN' on the screen (Walker 1992, p. 74). After a time, gamblers can develop a 'rapport' with their machines, believing them to be surrounded by an aura and jealously guarding them from other players. Such personification is vividly apparent in this comment from Hansant: 'What is more, they [slot machines] assume human traits, like the greedy mouth, the pot belly and the sphincter from which spills a diarrhea of coins' (in Walker 1992, p. 68).

The corollary of the attribution of wills to inanimate objects is the possibility of then influencing those objects by words or magical thoughts, for as Freud put it: 'the technique of the animistic mode of thinking is the principle of the omnipotence of thoughts' (Freud 1985, p. 143). Such attempts at magical control are most often expressed in language, and can be seen in the way that many gamblers talk to, cajole and reprimand a whole range of gambling equipment as if it were alive and responsive to their will. Hence the efficacy of the utterances of Henslin's craps players. Their most effective verbalisation was to command the dice to deliver the point by uttering the desired number: '"Five it" or "Six it" or "Eight it Dice!"' (Henslin 1967, p. 320). Similarly, Richardson observed a roulette player who leaned over the wheel and 'would scream orders at the small white ball as it bounced along the numbered grooves; shouting last minute warnings and reminders' (Richardson 1980, p. 246). Such specific directions rely on the omnipotence of words within what Mauss calls 'sympathetic magical rites' in which 'it is only a matter of naming the actions or things in order to bring about the sympathetic reaction'

(Mauss 1972, p. 54). Because of the idea that they can exert their will over the objects with which they are playing, gamblers will tend to bet less money *after* the fall of the dice, without knowing the result, than beforehand, for once it has fallen, the opportunity to influence it no longer exists (Strickland *et al.* 1966).

Piaget noticed a similar tendency to act as though the world could be modified by words or thoughts among adults, listing five pages of examples, including the specific case of card players. He attributed this to the existence of states of tension in which the desire for something to happen encouraged animistic and participatory thinking. Very often, it was also accompanied by the idea of a hostile fate, which the individual attempted to propitiate and influence through magical thinking. He wrote:

> it is generally sufficient ardently to desire something outside our control (such as good weather or anything depending on luck or chance) in order to have the impression of a sort of hostile power seeking to mock us. The desire thus becomes hypostatised in the things, and by projection personifies fate [which is] sufficient to cause any number of magical tendencies.
>
> (Piaget 1977, p. 186)

We can see this tendency in gamblers who can be said to 'ardently desire' something outwith their control – winning – and dependent on luck or chance. They too are prone to the idea that the outcome of a game is determined by some potentially hostile force, and may deliberately think the opposite to what they really want as if to court the caprice of fate. Scodel interviewed one gambler who would try to 'trick' fate, saying, 'If I pretend that I am going to lose, Fate will be placated and will be kind and I will win' (Scodel, in Herman 1967, p. 162). Another punter would place her bets at the roulette table, and then deliberately collect up her remaining chips and prepare to leave the table as if she had lost. She did this before the ball had even come to rest, before the outcome was known, as if *anticipating* a loss would somehow improve her chances of winning. She explained these actions by saying, 'if you half think you're not going to win, it's more likely you will . . . if you sit there and wait to win, you probably won't; it often works out like that; you've got to pretend you don't care.'

The belief in luck

Of all the magical notions involved in gambling, the belief in luck is perhaps the most pervasive. It is the centre around which magical notions of efficacy gravitate, and it is luck which guides gamblers through every game they play, absolutely certain that *this time* they will win. The belief in the power of their own luck is a tireless guide and support to players who *know* that the laws of probability are stacked against them, but, on another level, also *know* that their good fortune can overturn them.

Wagenaar (1988) explains these types of belief with reference to a subtle distinction between chance and luck in the minds of players. Both, he argues, are causal concepts and both determine the outcome of games, but luck has greater valence. The outcome of a game is governed by chance and is therefore immutable, but it is luck that determines how gamblers will bet on a game, inducing them to make the right choice. Luck is therefore a force which provides the gambler with foreknowledge of the outcome of a game. Powerful enough to overcome chance, such luck is essentially an order of knowledge and implies a reversal of causation in time: 'a belief that through luck, future outcomes may determine choices' (Wagenaar 1988, p. 102).[2]

Mana

The anthropological notion of *mana* describes the vital aspects of this belief in luck. First used by a nineteenth-century missionary to describe 'a power or influence, not physical and in a way supernatural' (van der Leeuw 1967, p. 24), it has since passed into common anthropological usage, referring, for van der Leeuw, to the embodiment of power and for Mauss, to the embodiment of the sacred. Among the ancient Germans, *hamingia*, the guidance of an unseen hand, or luck, was a 'quantitative potency'. Soldiers fought by inciting their luck against their enemy, and only lost because their *hamingia* had deserted them (van der Leeuw 1967, p. 24). *Mana* operates as an indiscriminate power: it can be positive or negative, signifying good or bad luck, and can be possessed in varying quantities. It can also reside in both animate and inanimate objects, and be passed on from one to the other as though it were contagious.

Lucky people

When choosing their tickets, their horses or their numbers, gamblers behave as if they can somehow influence games of pure chance; as though the force of their luck can overcome the odds against them so that somehow they *will* win, the game *will* bend to their wishes. Even mathematical laws are susceptible to gamblers' luck, and are forced to exclude the latter from their relentless determination of the world. Winning is no longer the impersonal outcome of the distribution of a probabilistic equation, but the uniquely personal expression of the individual gambler's power. In the case of the former, the winner can be anyone; in the latter, it can *only* be the lucky individual. Bolen likens the gambler's state of mind to that of the magician: 'The modern gambler behaves as though he . . . can control or contradict the laws of probability by certain types of thought or action. He is not unlike the sorcerer who has similar ceremony and paraphernalia' (Bolen 1976, p. 8).

In this frame of mind, one gambler wrote that, while playing, he was 'sustained by a conviction, akin to mystical belief that I was endowed with an extraordinary inner power – an ability to reverse the iron laws of probability' (Spanier 1992, p. 1).

Dostoevsky presents us with a figure who always believed that he was in control of a game, and that winning was due to himself alone. His wife lamented his belief in his own powers, which were so often to drag her to penury, when he had promised to win a certain amount one night 'in a tone of complete conviction, as if his winning or not winning depended on him alone' (Mme Dostoevsky, in Koteliansky 1923, p. 867).

Although it cannot be deliberately shared or exchanged, the good and bad luck that resides in people can sometimes emanate from them in a force that influences those around them. In this way, *mana* can be passed on involuntarily, and can be said to be contagious. This belief in the contagious properties of *mana* can encourage individuals to attach themselves to lucky people and avoid unlucky ones. In all traditional communities, writes Levy-Bruhl:

> the natives range themselves, as if instinctively, on the side of the man favoured by fortune. They think that they can thus participate in his good luck, and the favourable influences exercised on his behalf will extend to his companions. The mere fact of being with him implies such participation.
>
> (Levy-Bruhl 1966, p. 55)

Among gamblers, this belief is manifest in the perceived attraction of lucky people – usually winners, or those who are involved in some way with winning. Kaplan (1978) reports instances of lottery winners fêted for their luck – asked to rub tickets, touched and sometimes even mobbed by hopeful players! The case of Charles Wells, who broke the bank at Monte Carlo, is a typical instance of one such charismatic player. After a series of spectacular wins, Wells' table ran out of money, whereupon huge crowds gathered and surged around him, trying to touch him 'for luck' (Allcock 1985, p. 186). Slot-machine players often behave in a similar fashion, encouraging winners to touch their machines to pass on their luck, while discouraging losers from doing the same. Physical contact, however, is not always necessary for the transmission of *mana*: mere presence can suffice, as Dostoevsky reported when he had a run of luck at roulette. His wife wrote:

> Behind him stood an Englishman who staked on the same numbers that Fedja did, and Fedja observed that each time he made a stake and looked at the Englishman, he won without fail: Such a lucky face that man has. Fedja says that the Englishman's face is so good and kind that it is bound to bring luck.
>
> (Mme Dostoevsky in Koteliansky 1923, p. 82)

Here Dostoevsky engaged in a sublimated form of divination, for in 'reading' in the player's face signs of good fortune, he participated in what Benjamin identified as the interpretation of fate through physiognomic signs, a process in which 'modern physiognomics reveals its connection with the old art of divination' (Benjamin 1979, p. 131).

Lucky things

Luck is often thought to reside in objects, which can then be used as mascots or charms to influence the course of a game. Levy-Bruhl described the use of items which are full of positive *mana* in traditional societies and which resemble the use of lucky objects or mascots among gamblers. If a divination ritual yielded favourable results, the object which had been used to 'cast the lot' would be used for making amulets which were considered especially efficacious and which would protect the wearer from harm (Levy-Bruhl 1966, p. 189). Gamblers frequently display a desire to play with items that have just won; a tendency which was noted as early as 1708 by the probabilist Montmort, who wrote: 'There are those who will play only with packs of cards with which they have won, with the thought that good luck is attached to them' (in David 1969, p. 143). Children often hold similar beliefs, as is illustrated in one of Piaget's studies of a boy who attempted to win at games of marbles by playing with the marble which had last won. It was, Piaget informs us, 'as if the player's skill gave the marble permanently good qualities or as if the marble was made particularly good by the player's luck' (Piaget 1977, p. 166). Gamblers often carry an array of such 'lucky mascots': lucky coins, clothes or toys whose presence and unique personal meaning inspires them with the confidence – the *certainty* – of winning. As well as the personal mascots unique to their owners are the standardised ones of gambling folklore – such as borrowed money and four-leaved clovers. The design of Fitzgerald's casino in Las Vegas is an architectural reification of the idea of luck. Its neon sign promises 'luck available' as though it were a commodity that could be bought, while its interior resembles a museum of lucky artefacts – 15,000 four-leaved clovers carpet a special enclosure, surrounded by giant horseshoes and beaming 'lucky' leprechauns!

Lucky places

Many gamblers prefer to play in their favourite places which they consider lucky and feel uneasy if forced to sit or play somewhere else. Downes *et al.* (1976) found that lottery players usually have one specific kiosk or newsstand from which they buy their tickets because of its 'lucky' properties. Certain seats in casinos, bingo halls and slot arcades are also sought out by gamblers for their lucky properties time and time again.

The affinity between gamblers and 'their' lucky places represents a propitious combination of which they are made aware by an original win, or some early run of luck, while positioned there. Shops which have sold winning tickets often become extremely popular with subsequent players who flock briefly to the sanctified spot, keen to buy more tickets from such a lucky place. One bingo player who always sat in the same place stated: 'When I changed seats after my first win, I lost and went back to my old position and won again, so I'm not taking any more chances' (*Observer*, 19 February 1995, p. 22). What was regarded as the bad luck residing in certain places compelled gamesters to move even in the seventeenth century, when Pepys observed:

> the different humours of gamesters to change their luck when it is bad – how ceremonious they are as to call for new dice – to shift their places – to alter their manner of throwing; and that with great industry, as if there was anything in it.
>
> (Pepys 1976, vol. 9, p. 3)

There *is* something in it however, for these lucky places are not merely 'places' to gamblers. One seat or one kiosk is not identical with any other but is imbued with significance. It is not simply one of a number of interchangeable places, but is the only one of its kind, and is sought out by players for its unique possession of luck or *mana*. In this, we can see that gamblers do not perceive space as a homogeneous mass, but as a thing possessed of differing qualities. The non-homogeneous experience of time corresponds to the non-homogeneous experience of space during play, for parts of space, like instants of time, 'have their specific and independent value' (van der Leeuw 1967, p. 393). What Cassirer (1944, 1953) calls 'primitive' or 'mythical' space is a space of action, fraught with emotional and affective elements. Such space is syncretically bound up with its subject, and so, far from being objective, geometrical and abstract, can exhibit egocentric and anthropomorphic characteristics. Thus the table or kiosk at which the gambler plays is organised and familiar – it 'makes sense' to him/her in a way others of its kind do not. In this way, it is possessed of *mana*, or, to use van der Leeuw's expression, it is a 'position': an area which is subjectively meaningful and therefore particularly efficacious to the individual (van der Leeuw 1967, p. 393).

Once they have chosen their lucky places, gamblers are understandably reluctant to give them up and will try to occupy them every time they play, with, for example, slot-machine players becoming notoriously agitated if prevented from doing so. This tenacity was abundantly evident in the 1981 poker final, when, in the full glare of media attention, the world's most skilled poker players, playing for hundreds of thousands of dollars, petulantly refused to change seats. Eventually they were persuaded and moved reluctantly, muttering and indignant, for, Alvarez confides, every one was 'obscurely afraid of what a new seat at a new table might do to them' (Alvarez 1991, p. 162).

Lucky times

The existence of lucky people, places and things alone is not sufficient to assure luck, for they are dependent for their efficacy on opportune moments. Like space, time is not a homogeneous mass but is made up of separate intervals, each with its own unique value. Certain times therefore are more favourable than others and for luck to befall a player it is important that it occurs at the right time.

As we saw in Chapter 1, this notion of 'timeliness' is designated by the Greek *kairos*: 'the time of the due situation: the time of grace' (van der Leeuw 1967, p. 384). The 'due situation' is the time of the unfolding of luck, and gamblers must be present when it occurs, otherwise their own luck and that of the things around them will be redundant. The power of the propitious moment overrides that of the *mana* in things, for it must be present for the latter to have efficacy.

Richardson was well aware of the effects of inopportune moments on players. Most gamblers, he wrote, know when it is not their lucky day, and they ignore this intuition at their peril. Should they do so, they will be gambling while 'disconnected from propitious flows and patterns', stubbornly trying to force a return of the luck they enjoyed earlier. When this happens they 'become nothing but an item of desperation, someone doomed to be unloved by fortune and destroyed by mathematics' (Richardson 1980, p. 127). On the other hand, most players have a strong sense of when it is their lucky time, manifest in notions of the 'lucky streak', 'run of luck', and being 'on a roll'. In this state, having won once or twice, they feel certain they will continue to do so until 'their' time – *kairos* – passes. One punter was convinced of the potency of these lucky times, saying: 'If it's my night I've won a fortune on stupid things, but if it's not my night . . . can't do a thing.' When immersed in this time of grace, gamblers play on, convinced that its influence will safeguard their every move, and eager to make the most of it before it runs out. When a woman had a lucky run at craps, winning several throws in a row, an envious bystander described 'the streak a gambler spends his waking hours trying to find and ride to glory'. On this lucky roll, time itself seemed to stop, and order and meaning emerged from chance. The awestruck onlooker continued his commentary, writing that this gambler had 'stopped time for one mythical, magical moment, [and] saw everything fall neatly into place' (Vinson 1988, p. 57).

Lucky numbers

The phenomenon of gambling is saturated with numbers. The trend which saw the emergence of highly numerical types of wager in the seventeenth century and the development of games of chance along similarly arithmetical principles in the nineteenth is continued today, with number forming the basis of all modern commercial games of chance.

Gambling can be said to represent the apogee of our modern obsession with enumeration, and, moreover, the *dual nature* of this obsession; for both the scientific and the mystical forms of knowledge afforded by number converge here. The mechanics of play – the calculation of odds and distributions of wagers – is governed by the theory of probability, and lies within the domain of objective scientific knowledge. However, the relation of the gambler to play is governed by a different order of knowledge altogether. In the scientific worldview, like the phenomenon of chance, number is regarded as an explanatory force in itself, while in the magical-religious it signifies something else. What the scientific mind sees as a secular, explanatory power, the mythical one perceives as a sacred sign of the workings of some 'foreign demoniac power' (Cassirer 1953, p. 144).

Since most of their attention during play is concentrated on specific numbers, the latter come to assume enormous significance in gamblers' subjective maps, and, more than any other facet of play, are regarded as being imbued with magical significance and specific powers, or *mana*. In most games, possession of the correct number or series of numbers is the key to winning, and so players are constantly searching for that elusive digit in which the winning formula is stored.

In this sanctification of number, gamblers participate in a long western tradition originating in the classical world in which numbers were perceived as the intermediary through which earthly and divine, or mortal and immortal, communicated with each other (Cassirer 1953, p. 144). From divine messenger to divine harmoniser, for the Pythagoreans order was ultimately reducible to number. Observation of the heavens led to the concept of a celestial harmony that was mirrored on earth in quantifiable amounts. Everything in the universe could be expressed in the language of numbers, for 'the cosmos is isomorphic with pure mathematics' (Schimmel 1993, p. 13). In Pythagorean number mysticism, the universe was divided into numerical categories, each with different 'natures' or attributes. It is in this tradition that gamblers are engaged when they study numbers as bearers of power and meaning. A variety of methods of number selection exist, most operating on the Pythagorean assumption that every earthly phenomenon can be expressed as a number and that the relations between numbers produced this way will possess a certain harmony. The dream books that translate dreams into numbers also transform events and objects into a series of digits imbued with metaphysical meaning. Drake and Clayton describe such a translation for an American lottery: 'People want "hot" numbers. Numbers and combinations of numbers derived from lucky situations are much more powerful, have much more of what anthropologists call *mana* than ordinary run-of-the-mill, garden variety numbers' (Drake and Clayton 1967, p. 7). Numbers may also appear of their own accord, announcing their presence with their own peculiar qualities or natures. Thus Puerto Rican lottery players, like the Pythagoreans, attribute such characteristics as 'beautiful' or 'ugly' to them (Sullivan 1972, p. 83).

Similarly, the poker-playing brothers Flower and Stone in Paul Auster's
The Music of Chance are very aware of the 'natures' of numbers. Stone explains:

> after a while you begin to feel that each number has a personality of
> its own. . . . A twelve is very different from a thirteen for example.
> . . . It's all very private, but every accountant I've ever talked to has
> always said the same thing. Numbers have souls and you can't help
> but get involved with them in a personal way.
>
> (Auster 1990, p. 73)

They selected their winning lottery numbers in a manner that utilised their
harmonious balance, and so realised their lucky potential. Like the Pythagoreans,
the brothers favoured prime numbers:

> It was all so neat and elegant. Numbers that refuse to co-operate, that
> don't change or divide, numbers that remain themselves for all
> eternity . . . 3, 7, 13, 19, 23, 31. . . . It was the magic combination,
> the key to the gates of heaven.
>
> (Auster 1990, pp. 73–74)

This notion that they have 'natures' is also the expression of what Cassirer
calls 'affective tonality': the idea that certain numbers have specific qualities
that are more significant than their mere designation of quantity. For gamblers,
such affective tonality depends on the personal significance of a number
marking it out from the undifferentiated insignificance of all others. Numbers
which have some association with the player's life are recognised as having
peculiar qualities *for that player*, which will be carried into the game as an
executive power. In this way, numbers which are derived from events or relationships in gamblers' lives, such as their age, their children's birthdays or their
telephone numbers, are regarded as particularly lucky.

For Freud (himself intensely superstitious about numbers), this tendency
could be explained by displacement. Although their meaning was to be found
in the subconscious, he argued that gamblers, like all superstitious people,
saw the significance of numbers as emanating from *outside* the self. For such
individuals, meaning is external: 'everything . . . is full of significance,
everything can be interpreted' (Freud 1939, p. 320). An instance of this
affective tonality, or displacement, is demonstrated in the case of one gambler,
Angela V, who became reluctantly aware of the mysterious forces in numbers
when some that were significant for her began 'appearing' in her life. The
number in question was 226 – the abbreviated form of February 26 – her
mother's birthday. The night before the birthday, she dreamed of her mother,
and the following day she saw the number four times. Initially, she was
worried by the coincidence – 'that bothered me . . . I was upset' – but,
becoming aware of the hidden significance contained in the digits, decided

to play the number in the lottery. After she won, more numbers flooded into her consciousness, and, highly sensitised, she was in no doubt as to their significance and began to act on what she regarded as their prophetic quality:

> other numbers began to bother me in the same way . . . I would see them three or four times in a couple of days and I would bet the number and win . . . I was afraid, I thought it was some kind of an omen, a message.
>
> (In Custer and Milt 1984, pp. 151–152)

Here, number is conceived similarly to chance in the mind of the gambler, as a sign imbued with metaphysical meaning.

THE RELIGIOUS WORLDVIEW: TRANSCENDENCE

The worldview of gamblers is a complex one. On the one hand, they are absorbed in a world of magical participation whose efficacy – 'luck' – derives from within themselves. On the other hand, they are also concerned with the operation of a power that lies *outwith* the self, and which determines the course of a game and also has wider implications for their life in general. The distinctions between these two orders of belief are often not clear-cut and their spheres of efficacy can overlap so that most of the phenomena so far designated as magical also possess quasi-religious connotations. It is to this specifically *religious* dimension of gambling belief that we now turn, for it is here that the dynamic of the gambling situation – the tension between uncertainty and order, chance and meaning – becomes apparent.

The dualism of luck

The dualism of gambling belief is perhaps clearest in the notion of *mana*, which exists, somewhat ambiguously, in the mind of the gambler both as a neutral power residing in things, and also as something else – a power which is bestowed from without; a metaphysical sign. It thus has both magical and theistic connotations. Mauss emphasised its transcendental aspect when he wrote of the magician: 'if he thinks about it, he may even come to the conclusion that his magical powers *are quite separate from him*' (Mauss 1972, p. 138; my emphasis). The externality of the power of *mana* is most evident in its formulation as *hamingia* – the guidance of an unseen hand. This 'guiding hand' is a constituent element of gamblers' conceptions of their own luck: a semi-conscious apprehension of a guiding force. The idea of power resident within them is still there, but its *origin* is outwith themselves. In this sense, a patient of Bergler felt sure of himself when he played, but this was not

174

simply the apprehension of his own *mana*, but rather 'a strange sensation that I am an executive agent of something beyond my control' (Bergler 1970, p. 45). It is the same guiding force that the gambler who 'threw fistfuls of chips at random on the table, accepting where they came to rest as fateful places' trusted in (Richardson 1980, p. 232). Like ancient diviners with their bundle of divining sticks or *astragali*, this individual believed in the significance inherent in the random pattern made by his chips, for he believed in the mysterious intentions of the power that put them there.

When the grandmother in Dostoevsky's *The Gambler* won, she too attributed her luck to an external force: '"Look, look", grandmother quickly turned to me, all radiant and happy. "You know I told you, I told you. And it was the Lord himself who gave me the idea of betting two gold pieces"' (Dostoevsky 1992, p. 202). The idea of this guiding hand is perhaps best demonstrated by the imagery of the original British national lottery advertisement. As a constellation of stars in the shape of a giant hand descends from the heavens, this literal depiction of the hand of fate extends an enormous finger to one lucky individual and thunders its celestial pronouncement: 'it's YOU!'

The apprehension of their luck can be experienced by gamblers as a transcendental or religious sensation, for when winning, their self-worth – their very existence – is confirmed. Mario Puzo – by no means a religious individual – certainly experienced his luck in this way:

> A winning streak inspires belief in your own infallibility. . . . What non-gamblers do not know is the feeling of virtue . . . when the dice fall as one commands. And the omniscient goodness when the card you need rises to the top of the deck to greet your delighted yet confident eyes. It is as close as I have ever come in my life to a religious feeling. Or to being a wonder-struck child.
>
> (Puzo 1977, p. 134)

Fate and destiny

Time and time again, gamblers imply that the unfolding of a game is overseen by some kind of 'higher power', hinting that events in the gambling arena are predetermined in some mysterious way. This is the impersonal, providential power faced by gamblers when they play, and is conceived variously as fate, destiny, fortune and sometimes even God. It is what Duryodhana referred to when he declared in *The Mahabharata*: 'if we gamble, the heavenly gate will be nearer' (*The Mahabharata* 1975, p. 123), and is the subject of what Gogol called the 'higher mysteries' of cards (Gogol 1926, p. 216). The Chevalier Menars in E.T.A. Hoffman's *Gambler's Luck* also described such a force when he advised his friend to make the most of its favourable orientation to him by gambling:

'Fate', he said, 'Drops hints to us as to the path along which we should seek and find our salvation. The higher power that rules over us has whispered in your ear: if you wish to acquire money and goods go and gamble, otherwise you will remain forever poor, indigent, dependent.'

(Hoffman 1963, p. 222)

It is this force that gamblers are most keen to propitiate, since it is this that determines their fate in any particular round, in any game – and more, for by participating in a game, players are engaging in a ritual in which the uncertainties of their life are symbolically played out in microcosm. The testing of luck in this way has implications far beyond the immediate game being played, with wins and losses being interpreted as pronouncements on the course of the gambler's life in general.

Questioning

In playing, then, gamblers are doing more than simply engaging in a game, but are, in a sense, questioning their destiny. The query 'will I win?' takes on metaphysical significance, far transcending the outcome of the game and amounting to the gamblers' questioning of the basis of their very existence. According to Devereaux, for the player who asks 'am I lucky?': 'the answer seems somehow to promise a solution to the whole problem of his personal relation to the supernatural powers that govern the universe' (Devereaux 1949, p. 981).

The luck conceived as the personal possession of power or *mana* here takes on religious significance as a sign of external favour. Gamblers want simply to *know* their status. In an inner dialogue, Richardson debated his motives for gambling: '"I want to know, I finally want to know", he asks, and his inner voice retorted "what do you so badly want to know?" And I would answer, "whether I am to have any grace in this life"' (Richardson 1980, p. 25). To find out their status, gamblers must simply *play*, and to this end, the formal structure of a gamble creates an arena for a ritualised dialogue with fate. It is in these rituals that we see evidence of the oracular origins of gambling. Just as the modern gambling sites can be said to resemble the specially demarcated 'magic circles' of the ancient diviners, so the instigation by the diviner of an action whose outcome was interpreted as an expression of destiny can be said to resemble the gambler's pursuit of an activity whose outcome is similarly considered as the unambiguous verdict of fate. As we saw in Chapter 4, gamblers' wagers represent themselves and, by staking them, they are offering these wagers – and vicariously, themselves – up to fate to dispose of at will. The outcome of the game determines whether they lose this wager or are rewarded by winning more money: whether they are deserted or favoured by fortune. This is the element of redemption bestowed by the taking of risks which we saw in Chapter 4. By hosting this confrontation, the gambling site becomes the arena of a ritualised encounter, where gambling itself becomes a symbolic activity in which 'the player asks for a decision that assures him the unconditional favour of destiny' (Caillois 1962, p. 73).

This oracular dimension of gambling belief has been particularly emphasised within the psychoanalytic tradition. Freud's analysis of Dostoevsky's passion for gambling was founded on the assumption that the activity functioned as a cycle for the purgation of guilt, with losses masochistically courted by gamblers as punishment for their sins. Reik's comments on the article developed Freud's analysis into a more compelling argument which took into account the specifically religious dimension of gambling belief. Reik postulated that the overriding concern of gamblers was not that they *had* sinned, but the uncertainty as to whether or not they would be punished for it. Their concern simply became to *know* their fate, and so their actions assumed the form of a question addressed to destiny. Ultimately, gambling became a divinatory activity: 'a modern form of consulting the oracle' (Reik, in Halliday and Fuller 1974, p. 80).[3] A patient of Bergler confirmed this theoretical perspective when he outlined what for him was the dynamic of play: 'For me, gambling is a question I ask Fate. The question is simple – am I your favourite?' (in Bergler 1970, p. 83). For Richardson, writing from within the Protestant tradition, the expression was slightly different: 'gambling provides the answer to what all men want to know, namely which of us are the elect' (Richardson 1980, pp. 21–22). The answer is communicated unambiguously in the outcome of a game with winning a sign of approval, and losing, disapproval. Organisers are keen to encourage these kinds of beliefs, as were those of a lottery held in 1572 in Paris who spelled out Divine favour on winning tickets. *Dieu vous a elu*: 'God has chosen you' was the phrase written on winning tickets; *Dieu vous console*: 'God comforts you', on losing ones (in Brenner and Brenner 1990, p. 9). The British national lottery advertisements also tap into these beliefs, depicting an image of a lucky winner specially chosen from millions of others by a starry miasma which erupts from the cosmos. For one moment, the heavens open and the gambler is assured of his/her status and showered with beatitude and grace.

A kind of circular causation similar to that described by Wagenaar permeates the notion of luck as the favour of fate or state of election. If a gambler wins it is because they are lucky, and if they are lucky they will win. Within this tautological system, luck or favour, once bestowed, are impossible to lose. Conversely, they are also impossible to attain if *not* bestowed. Puerto Rican lottery players adopt a philosophical approach to this dilemma, saying, 'if a person is meant to have luck, it will find him. If he's not there's no use looking for it' (in Sullivan 1972, p. 83). When a gambler is singled out in this way, they can do no wrong. As a roulette player we saw earlier stated, once 'your time is up', you can act with impunity, secure in the knowledge that you cannot lose. This punter's statement can now be revealed in full to indicate what he regarded as the transcendental origin of such empowerment: 'Well, I think it's 'im up there and if 'e says it's your night, it's your night and whatever you do you can't lose . . . if it's my night I've won a fortune on stupid things, but if it's not my night . . . can't do a thing.' In the same way, Flower, in *The Music of Chance*, described the luck that befell himself and his brother after winning the lottery:

> Good luck continued to come our way. No matter what we do, everything seems to turn out right. . . . It's as though God has singled us out from other men. He's showered us with good fortune and lifted us to the heights of happiness . . . at times I feel that we've become immortal.
>
> (Auster 1990, p. 75)

As the external favour of Fate or Destiny, luck cannot be cultivated by gamblers. Just as Protestants had a duty to consider themselves elect, so, to play with confidence, gamblers also have to presume their chosen status. Winning in games of chance is taken as confirmation that the player is favoured by destiny; it is the apprehension of grace or election. For the poker player in Auster's novel a kind of Pythagorean harmony reigns, described evocatively as 'the music of chance'. He explained:

> Once your luck starts to roll, there's not a damn thing that can stop it. It's like the whole world suddenly falls into place. You're kind of outside your body and for the rest of the night you sit there watching yourself perform miracles. It doesn't really have anything to do with you anymore. It's out of your control . . . everything is in harmony . . . everything turns into music.
>
> (Auster 1990, p. 137)

This, then, is the order that can be found in chance once it is removed from its 'inaccessible isolation' as a secular category and interpreted instead as a sign of some higher meaning.

Repetition

We saw in Chapter 4 how the temporal limitations of a game have their counterpart in repetition, and how gamblers tend to play over and over again, regardless of whether they are winning or losing. Now we can develop the deeper significance of this repetition, for it is out of these repetitive rituals that the order, rhythm and harmony of the play world are created. According to Huizinga, play 'creates order, *is* order. Into an imperfect world and into the confusion of life it brings a temporary, a limited, perfection' (Huizinga 1949, p. 10). For Kierkegaard, it has an even broader significance both as a category of existence in its own right and as a religious category, for it confers order and meaning on the world. This conceptualisation has particular resonance for gambling, for Kierkegaard writes that without repetition, 'all life dissolves into empty, meaningless noise' (Kierkegaard 1983, p. 149). This is lived out in gambling, where, without the repetition of highly structured rituals, the game dissolves into the chaos of untamed chance.

The repetition of gambling derives from the dynamic between fear and faith – gamblers' certainty that they are favoured alongside the simultaneous fear that they are not. The decision of the game is final. They cannot challenge it but nor can they altogether accept it, so their only option is to repeat it in the hope that their status will change. This repeated supplication of fate in the face of rejection resembles the behaviour of diviners and augurs when they failed to attain the answer which *they* required. As we saw earlier, in this situation the enquirer does not necessarily want to know what will happen next, but simply whether what s/he *wants* to happen will occur. Levy-Bruhl pointed out that this is the motive of diviners who try to solicit a good omen which, when received, negates all those that went before. The 'curious' state of mind behind this activity, Levy-Bruhl says, 'is not unlike that of gamblers [who also] solicit the verdict of dice or cards', and repeat the process until they get the outcome they want – '[putting their] fate to the touch once more' (Levy-Bruhl 1966, p. 229).

So, in the hope that the outcome will be different in another game, players simply repeat their questioning until the desired result is eventually achieved. The thoughts behind Rousseau's divinatory stone-throwing could be those of any gambler. The motivation for his actions was the uncertainty of his status: '"In what state am I in?" he asks himself, "If I were to die at this moment should I be damned? . . . Being always fearful, and now a prey to this cruel uncertainty, I resorted to the most ludicrous experiments to overcome it".' His tryst with the stones then began: '"I am going to throw this stone" he decided "at the tree facing me. If I hit it, it is a sign that I am saved; if I miss it I am damned".' Rousseau's quest for salvation was accompanied by all the physiological discord of the gambler – trembling hands and 'a terrible throbbing of the heart', until he hit the tree and was finally relieved of his anxiety (Rousseau 1967, p. 231).

When winning, however, gamblers are no better off, for they are dogged by perennial uncertainty, forever unsure as to whether their favour is permanent, for the end of a game signifies the end of favour. Illustrative of this tension between faith and uncertainty is Reik's case study of a compulsive card player. She would establish a set of criteria, telling herself that if she won, 'this or that for which I hope, will happen; if not . . . my wish will not be fulfilled'. However, the powers of destiny were regarded as particularly fickle, so that even when she won, she could never be certain that she would be completely successful in whatever project her game was prophetic of. If she asked, 'Will Franz [her husband] get a job within the next year?' and was assured, by winning, that he would, she would worry incessantly: 'But does that mean the present year? As measured by the calendar? Am I thinking of the Gregorian calendar? There's a Jewish calendar too. And what about the Russian calendar?' (Reik 1951, p. 170). And so, after every round, she felt obliged to begin the game again.

The foundation of the order induced by winning is tenuous, and collapses completely as soon as uncertainty begins to creep in. The dynamic between faith and uncertainty is in a constant state of flux. Despite their confidence in their special, favoured status, gamblers' relation with fate is ambivalent – how can they be sure preference has not been realigned and that they are still the favourite? Their insecurity leads to the repetition of a cycle of supplication, posing the same question over and over in a constant quest for reassurance. As Alesky lamented in *The Gambler*, what he *really* wanted, what compelled him to continue playing, was not the hope of financial gain, but simply to be 'above all these absurd turns of fate' (Dostoevsky 1992, p. 154); in other words, to be above uncertainty, and to know, unequivocally, his destiny.

This perennial uncertainty is the predicament of the gambler,[4] for the security offered by a single outcome is soon placed in doubt by the possibility of a different outcome in all *future* games: hence the endless repetition of play.

The motivation of gamblers is not then, as the psychoanalysts would have it, a masochistic compulsion to *lose*, but rather a compulsion to *question*. The uncertainty that it is based on can be regarded as a manifestation of the compulsion to repeat; a tendency which, for Freud, was more powerful than – and hence lay beyond – the pleasure principle. This basic and primal compulsion (which Freud also calls the 'compulsion of destiny') is derived from the search for security and urges the endless repetition of an act regardless of its outcome. Repetition is here justified as an end in itself, independent of result, and is responsible for the exercise of a degree of control over the act being repeated. Hence, Freud writes, 'the repetition of an activity or event . . . is pursued in order to facilitate a gradual mastery over a situation' (Freud 1984, pp. 275–338). Immersed in an environment of uncertainty and risk, gamblers derive a similar sensation of security and control out of the ritualised, repeated actions of the game being played.

In the repetition of these symbolic rituals then, we can see the creation of meaning and order out of the random operation of pure chance. When we consider magical and religious beliefs in forces such as luck, omens, fate and destiny in this context, as aspects of an entire worldview, the motives of players described as labouring under an 'illusion of control' and other so-called 'irrational cognitions' becomes clearer. Such beliefs can be regarded as an order of knowledge which works to make sense of the gambling environment in a way that the scientific explanation of probability theory does not. The latter does not really 'explain' the situation any more effectively – it cannot advise on what will happen next or how to act. The magical-religious worldview, on the other hand, empowers gamblers in a situation in which they have no real influence or control; providing a means of understanding the situation, as well as a rationale for acting while in it.

Within the rituals of gambling drama, the order of games of chance, and, what is more, of the world, becomes apparent. Wins and losses and the unpredictable unfolding of all previous games are now 'explained' – but not by probability theory. Now, the broad dispersal of the outcomes of individual games becomes emotionally meaningful as signs of favour and disapproval, and not as mathematical expressions of average distributions. In the magical-religious worldview then, order and harmony reign supreme: but this is an order and harmony of a *sacred*, not a 'rational' kind.

EPILOGUE

Chance has always been regarded as problematic. Throughout history, various societies have struggled to come to terms with its existence and feared its implications for social cohesion and moral order when they could not. As the deliberate courting of chance, gambling has assumed similar associations and so has been similarly feared, or at the very least, regarded as an activity which should be controlled and regulated. This is the reason for its lengthy historical condemnation, and also the source of its almost universal appeal. The widespread fascination with gambling is indicative of ambivalent human relationships with chance, with the changing status of the latter being reflected in the types of game played. As chance shifted from a religious to an epistemological and then to an ontological category, the games on which individuals gambled subtly altered, their every configuration reflecting wider socioeconomic processes in the world around them.

This dynamic relationship is exemplified in the modern world in the elevation of chance to ontological status and in the widespread commodification of gambling by western capitalist economies. Now, not only is the existence of chance accepted, it is actively bought and sold as just another type of commodity, its problematic status delegated to a handful of 'pathological' gamblers – a concern of the individual, to be dealt with by medicine.

For the first time in human history, chance has been stripped of religious and metaphysical meaning to emerge as a tool of scientific explanation and an intrinsic – even mundane – feature of the world. This ontological status gives it a central place in the universe, but it is a *secular* place, with no implications beyond those of scientific explanation. The repercussions of this are vast.

As chance became significant in its own right, metaphysical meaning retreated from the world around it and an era of ontological insecurity was ushered in. The elevation of one evacuated meaning from the other: it might be said that the genie was let out of the bottle and, once free to roam, it quickly established its own empire, secularising every area it touched. So, the corollary of ascribing ontological status to chance was the enforcement of ontological insecurity on the age which allowed it. And, at the start of the twenty-first century, life *does* seem to be increasingly insecure. Uncertainty and risk are endemic in social and economic life. In the 'dizzy land' of casino capitalism, financial markets fluctuate wildly, plunging global economies into turmoil and recession, then arbitrarily plucking them back into prosperity. In the post-Fordist restructuring of labour markets, job security is replaced by flexible specialisation, de-skilling, and the perennial insecurity of short-term contracts. Environmentalists warn of the constant threat of disaster – global warming, nuclear catastrophe and the devastation of natural resources – while postmodernist commentators advise us to give up the quest for 'truth' or meaning, to look instead to shifting relative values and to 'ironically' distance ourselves from the world around us.

In this secular, disenchanted universe, ontological insecurity creeps into every sphere: nothing is certain, everything is unpredictable.

Some of these insecurities are endemic to human life in general, but many more are new. As we enter the new millennium, it does sometimes seem as if the world has never been more chaotic and that, as Beck says, we are living on 'the volcano of civilisation'. Within it, individuals still have to find a way to reconcile the fundamental existence of chance and uncertainty with the equally fundamental desire for security.

Gambling has always existed as a conduit for chance: an arena in which the latter appears in an intensified and, more importantly, controlled form. As a sphere which is marked off from the everyday world, limited in time and space and removed from economic utility, gambling games act as a kind of theatre in which human relations with uncertainty are symbolically played out. These games have a dual nature, for as well as offering the possibility of plunging into chance and unpredictability, they also offer a means of resolving that unpredictability: at the same time, the possibility of both complete certainty and complete *un*certainty. The strict rules of games, their repetitive actions and their unequivocal outcomes are actually the converse of the random play of pure chance. So, in the face of apparently limitless freedom, gamblers paradoxically find themselves in a situation of constraint – a curtailment of that freedom. In this, gambling offers a microcosm of the uncertainty of the outside world, but it is a highly ritualised and structured arena of uncertainty which is sharply demarcated from its surroundings and which can be entered and left at will. In such an environment, chance can be controlled and made to offer up clear, unambiguous verdicts on games – and this in a world in which life itself is increasingly unclear and ambiguous. The appeal of gambling has often been obscured by the involvement of money, with explanations for the former (especially given its modern commercial-isation) concentrating heavily on the latter. This is misleading however, for the ancient and widespread popularity of the activity taps into more fundamental human concerns – not the desire to be rich, but the desire to be *secure*.

Since they exist as microcosms of social life, the outcomes of gambling games can be extrapolated to the wider world and interpreted as symbolic of the gambler's relations with chance in general. Under this interpretation, the concept of chance is sacralised, once more becoming a sign of metaphysical meaning through which gamblers can infer something of their status – not only in the game, but, through the dynamic interrelation of gambling and society, also in the wider world. This is significant for the understanding of the creation of meaning under more general conditions of insecurity. This issue is particularly pressing in an era in which the need for meaningful explanation is great, and is apparent in the rise of all kinds of 'alternative' beliefs: superstitions, cults, faith in a mythical past and fear of millennial reckoning in the future. In an Age of Chance, surrounded by a multitude of risks and existing precariously in a general climate of ontological insecurity, the actions of the gambler have implications for existence that extend far beyond the individual game being played.

If we recall Sartre's statement that humanity is a totality, revealing its basic nature in even the most insignificant activities, we can go on to interpret those activities as indicative, not of an idle pastime, but as a part of the 'bigger picture' of human reality. Gambling is one such activity, and in the actions of the gambler we can see in microcosm an image of more universal human concerns. Within these worlds of chance, the pursuit of play reveals a fundamental facet of human existence, for, along with the image of *homo ludens*, *homo faber* and *homo economicus*, the sphere of human activity also embraces *homo aleator*: man the gambler.

NOTES

INTRODUCTION

1 Some methodological problems with these models should be noted here. Firstly, many researchers conduct experiments using non-gamblers in non-gambling situations. Research carried out in laboratories and clinical settings loses the 'ecological validity' of genuine locations (Anderson and Brown 1984), while the use of students as subjects by some academics seriously compromises the findings of the research. Secondly, the criteria for pathology tend to be defined partly in terms of the percentage of gambling losses to income. The problem with such a definition is simply that some gamblers have more money than others and can literally buy their way out of the pathological label. As Dickerson points out, there are only *regular* gamblers, some of whom encounter financial difficulties. The status of pathology is only a function of their seeking help (Dickerson 1985).

2 Estimates range from 0.25 per cent of the adult population (Dickerson and Hinchy 1988), to 2.8 per cent (Volberg and Steadman 1988).

3 Although this is not meant to imply that *all* gambling is simply 'harmless fun': that there are casualties (although often overestimated by the 'pathological' psychologists) is a fact often wilfully overlooked by the vested interests which promote it.

1 THE IDEA OF CHANCE

1 See Plato's distinction between two main forms: *inductive* or artificial divination, and *intuitive* or natural divination. The former was based on the study of natural phenomena, such as clouds and birds, which were regarded as signs and omens, while the latter consisted of a kind of madness; a prophetic ecstasy of divine inspiration. See 'Phaedrus' (1987b, p. 123) and 'Ion' (1987c, p. 144) for his views on divination and divine madness.

2 References to such practices are also found in I Chronicles 24–26, when David distributed offices among the Levite princes by lot. Mathias was selected as an apostle in the same fashion in Acts I: 24–26, while in Leviticus 16:8, Aaron cast lots on two goats to decide which one would be for God and which a scapegoat.

3 In fact, he anticipates Darwin by two millennia when he draws attention to Empedocles' assertion that 'most of the parts of animals result from luck' (Aristotle 1990, p. 207).

4 See the protection of the apparently 'miraculous', in a deterministic universe, by the theory of metaphysical occasionalism developed by William of Ockham and the Israeli Mutakallinums (Courtenay 1984).

5 A throw in which each of four dice fell with a different number on its upper face.

6 The continued use of the lot can be seen as an illustration of this new orientation to chance. From being a hierophany of divine will, in the nineteenth century the outcome of the lot came to be regarded as efficacious precisely because it signified *nothing*. When viewed in a secular light, the arbitrary nature of the lot made it a suitably democratic tool for the resolution of dilemmas, one whose selection would guarantee, not an individual who was special or 'chosen' in any way, but on the contrary, one who was particularly *average*.

7 The formation of order – however complicated – in such models has been the subject of a number of recent studies exploring the possibility of overall coherence in the apparently haphazard and diverse. Lowry considers the consistent creation of 'structure, order and regularity' in multiplicity; and the production of 'predictable structures' whose principle is 'distinctly archetronic' out of theories of chaos and complexity (Lowry 1989, p. 8). In a similar vein, Harris looks to the larger picture in his quest for a new metaphysics for the new physics, outlining the order and coherence underlying apparent chaos and indeterminacy. Adopting a neo-Darwinian approach he argues for the widespread recognition of 'the possibility of seemingly teleological order coming into being by chance variation and natural selection' (Harris 1991, p. 4).

8 See Smith (1993) for an overview of changing sociological perspectives on chance, where the author describes how, until the undermining of the 'orthodox consensus' of structural-functionalism in the 1960s, a determinist paradigm excluded the consideration of chance. This useful summary is marred when Smith fails to notice that, in the general move towards the increasing status of indeterminism, his analysis of chance slides into a consideration of *risk*.

2 THE PURSUIT OF CHANCE

1 The parallel between games of chance and religious belief has been widely recognised (Culin 1896; Otto 1925; David 1969; Csikszentmihalyi and Bennett 1971) with Roberts *et al.* arguing that the former are 'exercises in relationships with the supernatural' (Roberts *et al.* 1959, p. 602). According to Martinez, the earliest games were not 'performed independently of a belief in some sort of spiritual power'. Dice and cards were 'important components of natural religious rituals, seeking to foretell the future' (Martinez 1976, p. 16). It is impossible to know the process by which religious ceremony becomes a 'mere' game. What is certain however, is that even when such activities have become pastimes, a relation to 'genuine divination' still exists (Csikzentmihalyi and Bennett 1971, p. 47).

2 The intense ceremonial activity which preceded divination ritual was often observed before engagement in gambling games. Fasting, sexual continence, incantations, exorcisms and the emphasis on dreams and other omens of good luck were as important to gamblers before a game as they were to shamen about to undertake divination. In some societies, divination itself could precede a game, and was carried out in order to determine the outcome of the latter.

3 Although in Chaucer we find a condemnation of gambling specifically among the higher ranks. In *The Canterbury Tales*, he criticised it for its squandering of time and money:

And now that I have spoken of glotonye,	
Now wol I yow deffenden hasardrye.	[forbid gambling]
Hasard is verry mooder of lesynges	[lies]
And of deceite, and cursed forswerynges,	[perjury]
Blaspheme of Crist, manslaughtre, and wast also	[blasphemy]
Of catel and of tyme.	[property]

Unusually in medieval thought, Chaucer believed the higher the station of the gambler, the greater the magnitude of the sin:

And ever the hyer he is of estaat,	[rank]
The moore is he yholden desolaat.	[considered abandoned]
(Chaucer 1966, pp. 351–352)	

4 The images on these *trionfi* have been the subject of mystical association since the eighteenth century when a tract by de Gebelin, fuelled by the centuries' revival of eastern mysticism, interpreted them in terms of occult Egyptian wisdom. The images are of Italian origin however, and represent the stages that make up the semi-religious pre-Lenten carnival processions in fourteenth-century Italy (Strayer 1982, p. 352). Nor is the fortune-telling function of the cards peculiarly 'eastern', but typical of the continued association of all cards with their divinatory origin.

5 Evidence that cards were popular among at least the nobility at this time comes from a letter by Margaret Paston to her husband in 1459. She wrote that the Christmas activities of a neighbouring noble household were 'none disguisings, nor harping, nor luting, nor singing, nor no loud disports, but playing at the tables and chess and cards' (Paston 1991, p. 54).

6 The French lottery was known as *Blanques*, from the Italian term *blanca carta* – white tickets – since all the losing tickets were considered blanks. Hence the derivation of the phrase 'to draw a blank' (Neville 1909, p. 296).

7 Similarly today, when people declare 'I bet you!' when establishing an opinion on some matter.

8 Furthermore, a Germanic form of the gift relationship – the *wadium* – displays a particularly clear affinity with gambling. The contractual bond of the *wadium* engages the honour, authority and *mana* of the individual who hands it over, and places recipients in an inferior position until they can respond in kind. Here, the words *wette* and *wetter*, translations of *wadium*, 'imply wager as much as pledge' (Mauss 1954, p. 61). Mauss' collaborator, Davy, makes the affinity of the potlach with gambling even clearer when he likens the communities that practise it to 'big gambling dens where, as a result of bets and challenges, reputations are made and whole fortunes exchange hands' (in Huizinga 1949, p. 61).

9 See Clapson (1992) and Chinn (1991) on the social history of this sport.

10 See Russell T. Barnhart's history of these gambling centres, as well as the illustrious figures who frequented them (Barnhart 1983).

11 The first being the dissemination of cards from the printing presses of the fifteenth century.

12 Both of these Acts were hugely unpopular, and largely unworkable. In particular, the 1906 legislation represented an attempt by anti-gambling lobbies (mainly the National Anti-Gambling League) to outlaw all forms of working-class gambling. In this, it has been described as 'a monstrous sample of class legislation' (Clapson 1992, p. 31), which ensured that gambling was to remain a political issue.

13 A similar view of gambling as theft was observed by Marco Polo to be held by the ruler Kubilai Khan, who told his subjects: 'I have acquired you by force of arms and all that you possess is mine. So, if you gamble, you are gambling with my property' (Polo 1958, p. 161).

14 Although, interestingly, some Protestant sects found them unproblematic, with, for example, John Wesley's Methodists utilising scriptural playing cards to reveal the will of God, and Zinzedorf's Pietists advocating the use of the lot for the same purpose (see Hargrave 1966, p. 324).

15 On this point, a description by Steinmetz of a congregation of the poor around a lottery drawing is instructive. His criticism (and Steinmetz writes as a dispassionate observer, not an ideologue) was excited not so much by the possibility that the crowd may have stolen money to enter the draw, but by their very *presence*, which meant that they were 'stealing from their masters' time' (Steinmetz 1870, p. 402).

16 Or the importance of leisure, for on top of all this, gambling also challenged notions of 'rational leisure': the idea that free time should be used to 'better' the individual, especially if that individual was working class and therefore, presumably, more in need of 'betterment'.

17 Similar criticisms were levelled against the opium habits of the industrial working classes; see Berridge and Edwards (1981).

3 PLAYGROUNDS – A MAP OF THE MODERN GAMBLING SITES

1 It is beyond the scope of this discussion to go into the mechanics of the relationship here, but see, for example, Abt *et al.* 1985; Caldwell *et al.* 1985; Eadington 1988, vols 1 and 2; McMillen 1996; Munting 1996.

2 This fantastic social upheaval was once reality when a sixteenth-century British lottery win brought with it, as well as a cash prize, immunity from arrest except for major crimes (Brenner and Brenner 1990, p. 10). In Borges' words, 'I stole bread and they did not behead me' (Borges 1985, p. 55).

3 Despite the various rates of different types of games, gamblers tend to act in a manner that shortens the rate of play. By placing their bets on any game at the last possible moment (Dickerson 1985, p. 141), gamblers actually homogenise rates of play, despite the different structural characteristics of individual games. This intensifies the tension of a game, an effect which will be further examined in Chapter 4.

4 See Griffiths (1995a, pp. 200–210) on the structural determinants of machines such as 'nudge' buttons and the 'near-miss' effect on the continuation of play.

5 Although this does not preclude the important *social* aspect of these games.

6 Although easy access creates a profile of the British slot-machine player as someone who is primarily young and male, limited access in, for example, America and

Australia where machines are confined to casinos creates an average player who is both adult and female (Walker 1992, p. 77; see also Dickerson 1996).

7 See also Scott's (1968) Goffman-esque study of race-track culture and etiquette.
8 This is not to imply that American casino policy is more straightforwardly permissive than British. It is certainly more inconsistent, with policies controlled by the state and not the federal government and frequently put to public referendum. Such an approach has resulted in the lack of a single, coherent policy on casino expansion and an uneven development of casinos across the US. In contrast to the British system, where casinos are legal throughout the country, at present American casinos are only legal in Nevada, New Jersey, on Indian reservations, and on riverboats in five states along the Mississippi. However, what gambling *does* go on within these legal areas is not subject to the same type of restrictive legislation that governs British casinos, and it is with these models that this discussion is concerned.
9 See Findlay (1986) on the forces behind the development of Nevada casinos.
10 Caillois was also impressed by the unique appeal of Las Vegas, describing it as a 'huge opium den', in which the time passed by its nomadic visitors 'is merely a set of parentheses in their ordinary lives' (Caillois 1962, p. 117).
11 See Scott and Venturi's (1972) description of the 'antiarchitectural' nature of time and light in casinos.
12 Although see e.g. Griffiths 1996, 1998; McMillen 1996.

4 THE EXPERIENCE OF PLAY

1 Nor should it be taken to imply that gambling has some kind of 'essential' nature: the heterogeneity of the typology outlined in Chapter 3 should have demonstrated that this is not the case.
2 See the work of phenomenologists and existentialists on this: e.g. Merleau-Ponty 1981; Straus 1966; Minkowski 1970; May *et al.* 1958; Ey 1978.
3 Exemplified, for example, in the radical sequestration of Herman Hesse's ultimate game of chance, *The Glass Bead Game* (1975).
4 Similar literary accounts of the alteration of consciousness under extreme conditions have been given by other writers. For example, Thomas Mann's *The Magic Mountain* (1962) describes the effects of long-term illness, while Jean Cocteau's *Opium* (1930), Thomas De Quincey's *Confessions of an English Opium Eater* (1821) and William Burroughs' *Junky* (1977) describe the experience of drug addiction.
5 Described by his translator as 'a wrenching of biography into fiction' (Wasiolek 1972, p. xxxviii).
6 See also e.g. Bjorgvinsson and Wilde (1996) on the effect of risk taking on the perception of the future.
7 Cheating is an exception. This is the pursuit of pure profit, a form of work which attempts to impose a rational order on chance. Its calculative attitude removes it from the sphere of play, and so cheating can be disregarded as gambling proper. Caillois (1962) discounted it as a 'perversion' of the spirit of chance, as did Baudrillard (1990), for whom it was a 'refusal of the vertigo of seduction'.
8 Such actions contradict Benjamin's assertion that games of chance exist as the counterpart to the drudgery of the machine labourer. If anything, as we have

already stated, it is the calculation and self-restraint involved in games of *skill* that represent such drudgery.

9 The manufacture of these magical discs from plastic is a particularly suitable combination, for plastic itself is 'the stuff of alchemy' (Barthes 1976, p. 97). In his essay on its metaphysical properties, Barthes wrote that plastic is a 'miraculous substance' which, like the chip as a temporary representative of value, has no real character of its own. It is a uniquely modern substance for it has no origins and is thus, according to Barthes, a 'universal equivalent' just as the chip is the universal equivalent of value in the casino.

10 A similar psychological effect can be found with the use of credit cards.

5   THE MAGICAL-RELIGIOUS WORLDVIEW

1 Although many gamblers do, however, try to do just that, and many gambling establishments encourage the fallacy, with casinos providing cards and pencils at their roulette tables for punters to note down the numbers that come up. These then frequently form the basis of complicated 'systems' (such as the Martingale system, the Trend system and the Cancellation system, to name but three) – attempts to pre-empt the random fluctuations of chance: all pursued with optimistic zeal, all vastly complex, and all completely useless.

2 A similar, hierarchical separation of chance, luck, fate and destiny in gambling is postulated by Rosenthal (1997). Whereas chance is blind and meaningless, luck can be influential, fate is immutable and destiny represents the goal of all striving: absolute control and mastery of the gambling situation.

3 Many writers in the psychoanalytic tradition have made much of the oracular origins of gambling, but have interpreted the idea of fate as a father figure at the centre of Oedipal conflicts, thus making the fundamental dynamic of play not religious but *sexual* (see Halliday and Fuller 1974).

4 And also, as Straus (1966) showed, of compulsives, who attempt to find security through the repetition of a single act.

REFERENCES

Abt, V. and Smith, J. (1986) 'Easy money: gambling in America', *Research Penn State*, vol. 7, no. 4.

Abt, V., Smith, J.F. and Christiansen, E.M. (1985) *The Business of Risk: Commercial Gambling in Mainstream America*, University Press of Kansas.

Allcock, C. (1985) 'Psychiatry and gambling', in G. Caldwell (ed.) *Gambling in Australia*, Sydney: Croom Helm.

Alvarez, A. (1991) *The Biggest Game in Town*, Herts: Oldcastle Books.

Anderson, G. and Brown, R.I.F. (1984) 'Some applications of reversal theory to the explanation of gambling and gambling addictions', *Journal of Gambling Behaviour*, 3, 179–189.

Anselm, Saint, Archbishop of Canterbury (1033–1109) *Opera Omnia*, ed. F.S. Schmitt, Edinburgh: Nelson (1946–1951).

Aristotle (1980) *Nichomachean Ethics*, trans. D. Ross, Oxford: Oxford University Press.

—— (1990) 'Physics', in S.M. Cahn (ed.) *Classics of Western Philosophy*, Indianapolis: Hacklett Publishing Company Inc.

Arnold, P. (1993) *The Book of Games*, London: Hamlyn Chancellor Press.

Arrow, K. (1970) *Essays in the Theory of Risk Bearing*, Amsterdam and Oxford: North Holland.

Ashton, J. (1898) *A History of Gambling in England*, London: Duckworth.

Auster, P. (1990) *The Music of Chance*, London and Boston: Faber and Faber.

Balzac, H. (1977) *The Wild Ass's Skin*, trans. H.J. Hunt, Harmondsworth: Penguin Classics.

—— (1984) *The Black Sheep*, trans. D. Adamson, Harmondsworth, Penguin Classics.

Barnhart, R.T. (1983) *Gamblers of Yesteryear*, Las Vegas: Gamblers Book Club Press.

Barthes, R. (1976) *Mythologies*, trans. A. Lavers, London: Paladin.

Bataille, G. (1985) *Visions of Excess*, trans. A. Stoekl, C.R. Lovitt and D.M. Leslie, Manchester: Manchester University Press.

—— (1988) *The Accursed Share*, vol. 1., trans. R. Hurley, New York: Zone Books.

—— (1992) *On Nietzsche*, trans. B. Boone, London: The Athlone Press.

Baudelaire, C. (1982) *Les Fleurs du Mal*, trans. R. Howard, Brighton: John Spiers/The Harvester Press.

Baudrillard, J. (1990) *Cool Memories 1980–1985*, London: Verso.

Beck, U. (1992) *Risk Society: Towards a New Modernity*, trans. M. Ritter, London: Sage.

Bellini, J. (1993) 'The biggest crap game in the world', *Business Life*, March, 57–60.

Benjamin, W. (1977) *Illuminations*, trans. M. Zohn, Glasgow: Fontana / Collins.

—— (1979) *One Way Street*, trans. E. Jephcott and K. Shorter, London: NLB.

—— (1985) 'Central Park', *New German Critique*, 34, winter, 32–58.

—— (1992) *Charles Baudelaire: A Lyric Poet in the Era of High Capitalism*, trans. H. Zohn, London: Verso.

Bergler, E. (1970) *The Psychology of Gambling*, New York: International Universities Press.

Bergson, H. (1910) *Time and Free Will*, trans. F.L. Pogson, New York and London: Macmillan.

—— (1911) *Matter and Memory*, trans. N.M. Paul and W.S. Palmer, New York and London: Macmillan.

Berridge, V. and Edwards, G. (1981) *Opium and the People: Opiate Use in Nineteenth Century England*, London: Allen Lane.

Birren, F. (1961) *Colour, Form and Space*, New York: Reinhold.

Bjorgvinsson, T. and Wilde, G.J.S. (1996) 'Risky health and safety habits related to perceived value of the future', *Safety Science*, 22, 1–3, 27–33.

Bloch, H. (1951) 'The sociology of gambling', *The American Journal of Sociology*, 57, 3, 215–221.

Boethius (1991) *On the Consolation of Philosophy*, trans. R.W. Sharples, Warminster: Aris and Phillips.

Bolen, D. (1976) 'Gambling: historical highlights and trends and their implications for contemporary society', in W.R. Eadington (ed.) *Gambling and Society*, Springfield, IL: Charles C. Thomas.

Borges, J. L. (1985) 'The lottery of Babylon', in D.A. Yates and J.E. Irby (eds), trans. J.M. Fein, *Labyrinths: Selected Stories and other Writings*, Harmondsworth: Penguin.

Boyd, D. (1976) 'Excitement: the gamblers' drug', in W.R Eadington (ed.) *Gambling and Society*, Springfield, IL: Charles C. Thomas.

Brenner, R. and Brenner, G. (1990) *Gambling and Speculation: A Theory, A History and a Future of Some Human Decisions*, Cambridge: Cambridge University Press.

Brown, R.I.F. (1987) 'Classical and operant paradigms in the management of compulsive gamblers', *Behavioral Psychotherapy*, 15, 111–122.

—— (1994) 'Dissociation phenomena among addicted gamblers', *Paper presented at the Ninth International Conference on Gambling and Risk-Taking Behaviour*, Las Vegas, June.

Bruce, A.C. and Johnson, J.E.V. (1992) 'Toward an explanation of betting as a leisure pursuit', *Leisure Studies*, 11, 201–218.

—— (1995) 'Costing excitement in leisure betting', *Leisure Studies*, 14, 48–63.

—— (1996) 'Gender based differences in leisure behaviour: performance, risk-taking and confidence in off-course betting', *Leisure Studies*, 15, 65–78.

Buck-Morss, S. (1990) *The Dialectics of Seeing: Walter Benjamin and the Arcades Project*, Cambridge, MA: MIT Press.

Burns, R. (1786) 'The twa dogs', in H.W. Meikle and W. Beattie (eds) *Burns*, 1987, Harmondsworth: The Penguin Poetry Library.

Burroughs, W. (1977) *Junky*, New York: Penguin.

Caillois, R. (1962) *Man, Play and Games*, trans. M. Barash, London: Thames and Hudson.

Caldwell, G., Haig, B., Dickerson, M. and Sylvan, L. (eds) (1985) *Gambling in Australia*, Sydney: Croom Helm.

Calvino, I. (1979) *Invisible Cities*, trans. W.Weaver, London: Pan Books.

Cardano, G. (1953) *Liber de Ludo Alea*, trans. S.H. Gould, Princeton, NJ: Princeton University Press.

Carlton, P. and Manowitzl, P. (1987) 'Psychological factors in determinants of pathological gambling', *Journal of Gambling Behaviour*, 3, 274–285.

Cassirer, E. (1944) *An Essay on Man: An Introduction to a Philosophy of Human Culture*, New Haven, CT: Yale University Press.

—— (1953) *The Philosophy of Symbolic Forms*, vol. 2, trans. R. Manheim, New Haven, CT: Oxford University Press.

Charmaz, K. (1992) *Good Days, Bad Days: The Self in Chronic Illness and Time*, New Brunswick, NJ: Rutgers University Press.

Chaucer, G. (1966) *The Canterbury Tales*, ed. A.C. Cawley, London: Dent and Sons.

Chinn, C. (1991) *Better Betting with a Decent Feller: Bookmakers, Betting and the British Working Class 1750–1990*, Hemel Hempstead, Herts: Harvester Wheatsheaf.

Cicero (1971) *De Divinatiore*, trans. W.A Falconer, London: Harvard University Press.

—— (1991) *On Fate*, trans. R.W. Sharples, Warminster: Aris and Phillips.

Clapson, M. (1992) *A Bit of a Flutter: Popular Gambling and English Society 1823–1961*, Manchester: Manchester University Press.

Clotfelter, C.T. and Cook, O.J. (1989) *Selling Hope: State Lotteries in America*, Cambridge, MA: Harvard University Press.

Cocteau, J. (1930 / 1966) *Opium*, trans. M. Crosland, London: Peter Owen.

Cohen, J. (1960) *Chance, Skill and Luck*, Baltimore, MD: Penguin.

—— (1972) *Psychological Probability, or, the Art of Doubt*, London: Allen and Unwin.

Cohen, S. and Taylor, L. (1972) *Psychological Survival: The Experience of Long-Term Imprisonment*, Harmondsworth: Penguin.

—— (1978) *Escape Attempts: the Theory and Practice of Resistance to Everyday Life*, Harmondsworth: Penguin.

Collins, A.F. (1996) 'The pathological gambler and the government of gambling', *History of the Human Sciences*, 9, 3, 69–100.

Comings, D.E., Rosenthal, R.J., Leiseur, H.R., Rugle, L.J., Muhleman, D., Chiu, C., Dietz, G. and Gade, R. (1994) 'The molecular genetics of pathological gambling: the DRD2 gene', *Paper presented at the Ninth International Conference on Gambling and Risk-Taking Behaviour*, Las Vegas, June.

Comstock, A. (1961) *Traps for the Young*, Cambridge: Belknap Press.

Costa, N. (1988) *Automatic Pleasures: The History of the Coin Machine*, London: The Bath Press.

Cotton, C. (1674) *The Compleat Gamester*, London: R. Cutler.

Courtenay, W.J. (1984) *Covenant and Causality in Medieval Thought*, London: Variorum Reprints.

Crombie, A.C. (1994) *Styles of Scientific Thinking in the European Tradition: The History of Argument and Explanation Especially in the Mathematical and Biomedical Sciences and Arts*, vol. 2, London: Duckworth.

Cryer, F. (1994) *Divination in Ancient Israel and its Near Eastern Environment*, Sheffield: J.S.O.T. Press.

Csikszentmihalyi, M. (1975) 'Play and intrinsic rewards', *Journal of Humanistic Psychology*, 15, 3, 41–63.

Csikszentmihalyi, M. and Bennett, S. (1971) 'An exploratory model of play', *American Anthropologist*, 73, 1, 45–58.

Culin, S. (1896) *Chess and Playing Cards*, New York: Arno Press.

Cunningham, H. (1980) *Leisure in the Industrial Revolution*, London: Croom Helm.

Custer, R. and Milt, H. (1984) *When Luck Runs Out*, New York: Facts on File.

Darwin, C. (1857) 'On natural selection', in R.C. Stauffer (ed.) (1987) *Charles Darwin's Natural Selection, being the Second Part of his Big Species Book Written From 1856 to 1858*, Cambridge: Cambridge University Press.

—— (1888) *The Origin of Species By Means of Natural Selection*, vol. 2, London: John Murray.

Daston, L. (1988) *Classical Probability in the Enlightenment*, Princeton, NJ: Princeton University Press.

David, F.N. (1969) *Games, Gods and Gambling*, London: Griffin.

de Jong, A. (1975) *Dostoevsky and the Age of Intensity*, London: Secker and Warburg.

De Quincey, T. (1821/1982) *Confessions of an English Opium Eater*, Harmondsworth: Penguin.

Debord, G. (1987) *Society of the Spectacle*, Exeter: Rebel Press, Aim Publications.

Deregulation Committee Ninth Report (1996) *Proposal for the Deregulation (Gaming Machines and Betting Office Facilities) Order 1996*, House of Commons Session 1995–1996, London: HMSO.

Descartes, R. (1985) *Discourse on Method and the Meditations*, trans. F.E. Sutcliffe, Harmondsworth: Penguin.

Devereaux, E. (1949) *Gambling and the Social Structure*, unpublished Ph.D. thesis, Harvard University.

Dickerson, M. (1985) 'The characteristics of the compulsive gambler: a rejection of a typology', in G. Caldwell, B. Haig, M. Dickerson and L. Sylvan (eds) *Gambling in Australia*, Sydney: Croom Helm.

—— (1996) 'Why "slots" equals "grind" in any language: the cross-cultural popularity of the slot machine', in J. McMillen (ed.) *Gambling Cultures: Studies in History and Interpretation*, London: Routledge.

Dickerson, M. and Hinchy, J. (1988) 'The prevalence of excessive and problem gambling in Australia', *Journal of Gambling Behaviour*, 4, 14–21.

Dixey, R. (1987) 'It's a great feeling when you win: women and bingo', *Leisure Studies*, 6, 199–214.

—— (1996) 'Bingo in Britain: an analysis of leisure and class', in J. McMillen (ed.) *Gambling Cultures: Studies in History and Interpretation*, London: Routledge.

Dixon, D. (1991) *From Prohibition to Regulation: Bookmaking, Anti-Gambling and the Law*, Oxford: Clarendon Press.

Dostoevsky, F. (1914) *Letters*, trans. E.C. Mayne, London: Chatto and Windus.

—— (1951) *Crime and Punishment*, trans. D. Magarshack, Harmondsworth: Penguin.

—— (1972) *The Gambler*, trans. V. Terras, ed. E. Wasiolek, Chicago and London: University of Chicago Press.

—— (1987) *Selected Letters of Fydor Dostoevsky*, trans. A.R. MacAndrew, ed. J. Frank and D. Goldstein, New Brunswick and London: Rutgers University Press.

—— (1992) *The Gambler*, trans. J. Kentish, Oxford: Oxford University Press.

Douglas, M. (1992) *Risk and Blame: Essays in Cultural Theory*, London: Routledge.

Downes, D.M., Davies, B.P., David, M.E. and Stone, P. (1976) *Gambling, Work and Leisure: A Study Across Three Areas*, London: Routledge and Kegan Paul.

Drake, S. and Clayton, H. (1967) '"Policy": poor man's roulette', in R. Herman (ed.) *Gambling*, London: Harper and Row.

Dream Script: Lotto Players Guide (1988) California: LA Press.

Dunkley, J. (1985) *Gambling: A Social and Moral Problem in France 1685–1792*, Oxford: The Voltaire Foundation.

Eadington, W.R. (ed.) (1976) *Gambling and Society*, Springfield, IL: Charles C. Thomas.

—— (1988) *Gambling Research: Proceedings of the Seventh International Conference on Gambling and Risk-Taking*, vol. 3, University of Nevada: Reno.

Eco, U. (1995) *Travels in Hyper-Reality*, London: Pan Books.

Ekeland, I. (1993) *The Broken Dice and Other Mathematical Tales of Chance*, trans. C. Volk, Chicago and London: University of Chicago Press.

Encyclopedia Britannica (1992) 15th edn, Chicago: Encyclopedia Britannica Inc.

Epicurus (1990) 'Letter to Menoceus', in *Classics of Western Philosophy*, ed. S.M. Cahn, Indianapolis: Hackett Publishing.

Evans-Pritchard, E.E. (1965) *Theories of Primitive Religion*, Oxford: Clarendon Press.

—— (1991) *Witchcraft, Magic and Oracles among the Azande*, Oxford: Clarendon Press.

Ey, H. (1978) *Consciousness*, trans. J.F. Floodstrom, Bloomington: Indiana University Press.

Feuerbach, L. (1957) *The Essence of Christianity*, trans. G. Eliot, New York: Harper and Row.

Filby, M.P. and Harvey, L. (1988) 'Recreational betting: everyday activity and strategies', *Leisure Studies*, 7, 159–172.

Findlay, J. (1986) *People of Chance: Gambling in American Society from Jamestown to Las Vegas*, Oxford: Oxford University Press.

Fisher, S. (1991) 'Governmental response to juvenile fruit machine gambling in the UK: where do we go from here?' *Journal of Gambling Studies*, 7, 217–247.

—— (1993) 'The pull of the fruit machine: a sociological typology of young players', *Sociological Review*, 41, 3, 446–474.

—— (1995) 'The amusement arcade as a social space for adolescents', *Journal of Adolescence*, 18, 71–86.

—— (1998) *Gambling and Problem Gambling among Young People in England and Wales*, London: Office of the National Lottery.

FitzHerbert, L., Giussani, C. and Hurd, H. (1996) *The National Lottery Yearbook*, London: The Directory of Social Change.

Flaceliere, R. (1965) *Greek Oracles*, trans. Douglas Garman, London: Elek.

Freestone, F. (1995) 'A socio-economic and political history of bingo, the licensed bingo industry and the growth of gaming in Britain', unpublished draft manuscript.

Freud, S. (1928) 'Dostoevsky and parricide', in J. Strachey (ed.) *Collected Papers*, vol. 5, London: Hogarth Press.

—— (1939) *The Psychopathology of Everyday Life*, trans. A. Brill, Harmondsworth: Penguin.

—— (1984) 'Beyond the pleasure principle', in *The Pelican Freud Library*, vol. 11, trans. J. Strachey, Harmondsworth: Penguin.

—— (1985) 'Totem and taboo', in *The Pelican Freud Library*, vol. 13, trans. J. Strachey, Harmondsworth: Penguin.

Fukuyama, F. (1992) *The End of History*, London: Hamilton.

Furnham, A. and Lewis, A. (1983) *The Economic Mind*, London: Harvester Press.

Gadamer, H. (1975) *Truth and Method*, trans. G. Barden and J. Cumming, London: Sheed and Ward.

Gadboury, A. and Ladouceur, R. (1988) 'Irrational thinking and gambling', in W. R. Eadington (ed.) *Gambling Research: Proceedings of the Seventh International Conference on Gambling and Risk-Taking*, vol. 3, University of Nevada: Reno.

Giddens, A. (1991) *Modernity and Self-Identity: Self and Society in the Late Modern Age*, Cambridge: Polity Press.

Gigerenzer, G., Swijinck, Z., Porter, T., Daston, L., Beatty, J. and Kruger, L. (1989) *The Empire of Chance*, Cambridge: Cambridge University Press.

Gilovich, T. (1983) 'Biased evaluation and persistence in gambling', *Journal of Personality and Social Psychology*, 44, 1110–1126.

Gilovich, T. and Douglas, C. (1986) 'Biased evaluations of randomly determined gambling outcomes', *Journal of Experimental Social Psychology*, 22, 228–241.

Goffman, E. (1961) *Encounters: Two Studies in the Sociology of Interaction*, Indianapolis: Bobbs-Merrill.

—— (1963) *Behaviour in Public Places: Notes on the Social Organisation of Gatherings*, Free Press of Glencoe: Collier Macmillan.

—— (1969) *Where the Action Is: Three Essays*, London: Allen Lane.

Gogol, N. (1926) 'The gamblers', in *The Government Inspector and Other Plays*, trans. C. Garnett, London: Chatto and Windus.

Goldstein, L. and Carlton, P. (1988) 'Hemispheric EEG correlates of compulsive behaviour: the case of pathological gamblers', *Research Communications in Psychology, Psychiatry and Behaviour*, 13 (1 and 2), 103–111.

Greenson, R. (1974) 'On gambling', in J. Halliday and P. Fuller (eds) *The Psychology of Gambling*, London: Allen Lane.

Greenwood, M. (1970) 'Medical statistics from Graunt to Farr', in E.S. Pearson and M.G. Kendall (eds) *Studies in the History of Statistics and Probability*, London: Griffin.

Griffiths, M.D. (1990) 'The acquisition, development and maintenance of fruit machine gambling in adolescents', *Journal of Gambling Studies*, 6, 193–204.

—— (1993) 'Fruit machine gambling: the importance of structural characteristics', *Journal of Gambling Studies*, 9, 387–399.

—— (1994) 'The role of cognitive bias and skill in fruit machine gambling', *British Journal of Psychology*, 85, 351–369.

—— (1995a) *Adolescent Gambling*, London: Routledge.

—— (1995b) 'Technological addictions', *Clinical Psychology Forum*, 76, 14–19.

—— (1996) 'Gambling on the Internet: a brief note', *Journal of Gambling Studies*, 12, 4, 471–473.

—— (1998) 'Gambling technologies: lessons from scholarly literature and prospects for pathological gambling', Paper Presented at the US National Academy of Sciences, Washington, DC, 2 September.

Guttman, A. (1978) *From Ritual to Record: The Nature of Modern Sports*, New York: Columbia University Press.

Hacking, I. (1975) *The Emergence of Probability*, London: Cambridge University Press.

—— (1990) *The Taming of Chance*, Cambridge: Cambridge University Press.

Halliday, J. and Fuller, P. (eds) (1974) *The Psychology of Gambling*, London: Allen Lane.

Hargrave, C. (1966) *A History of Playing Cards*, New York: Dover Publications, Inc.

Harris, E. (1991) *Cosmos and Anthropos*, London: Humanities Press International.

Harris, M. (1972) *Sport in Greece and Rome*, London: Thames and Hudson.

Henley Centre (1995) *Lottery Fallout*, The Henley Centre.

Henslin, J.M. (1967) 'Craps and magic', *American Journal of Sociology*, 73, 316–330.

Herman, R. (ed.) (1967) *Gambling*, London: Harper and Row.

—— (1976) *Gamblers and Gambling*, Lexington: Lexington Books.

Hesse, H. (1975) *The Glass Bead Game*, trans. R. and C. Winston, Harmondsworth: Penguin.

Hibbert, C. (1987) *The English*, London: Grafton Press.

Hoffman, E.T.A. (1963) *Gambler's Luck*, trans. M. Bullock, London: Fredertick Ungar Publishing.

Holtgraves, T.M. (1988) 'Gambling as self-presentation', *Journal of Gambling Behaviour*, 4, 2, 78–91.

Huizinga, J. (1949) *Homo Ludens*, London: Routledge and Kegan Paul.

Hunter, R. (1995) 'Lottery stress disorder', *British Medical Journal*, 6983 (310), 875.

Ide-Smith, S.G. and Lea, S.E.G. (1988) 'Gambling in young adolescents', *Journal of Gambling Behaviour*, 4, 2, 110–118.

Jacobs, D. (1988) 'Evidence for a common dissociative-like reaction among addicts', *Journal of Gambling Behaviour*, 1, 4, 27–37.

James, H. and Weisheipl, L. (1982) 'The interpretation of Aristotle's Physics and the science of motion', in N. Kretzmann, A. Kenny and J. Pinborg (eds) *The Cambridge History of Later Medieval Philosophy: From the Rediscovery of Aristotle to the Disintegration of Scholasticism 1100–1600*, Cambridge: Cambridge University Press.

James, W. (1982) *The Varieties of Religious Experience: A Study in Human Nature*, Harmondsworth: Penguin.

Jonson, S. (1987) *The Alchemist*, ed. P. Bennet, London and New York: Routledge.

Kahneman, D. and Tversky, A. (1982) 'The psychology of preferences', *Scientific American*, January, 136–142.

Kaplan, R. (1978) *Lottery Winners: How they Won and How Winning Changed their Lives*, New York: Harper and Row.

—— (1988) 'Gambling among lottery players: before and after the big win', *Journal of Gambling Behaviour*, 3, 4, 171–182.

Kavanagh, T.M. (1993) *Enlightenment and the Shadows of Chance: The Novel and the Culture of Gambling in Eighteenth-Century France*, Baltimore and London: The Johns Hopkins University Press.

Kendall, M.G. (1970) 'The beginnings of a probability calculus', in E.S. Pearson and M.G. Kendall (eds) *Studies in the History of Statistics and Probability*, London: Griffin.

Kierkegaard, S. (1983) *Repetition*, trans. H.V. Hong and E.H. Hong, Princeton, NJ: Princeton University Press.

Kirzner, I.M. (1985) *Discovery and the Capitalist Process*, Chicago and London: The University of Chicago Press.

Knight, F. (1921) *Risk, Uncertainty and Profit*, Cambridge: The Riverside Press.

Koteliansky, S.S. (ed.) (1923) *Dostoevsky: Letters and Reminiscences*, trans. S.S. Koteliansky, London: Chatto and Windus.

Kusyszyn, I. (1990) 'Existence, effectance, esteem: from gambling to a new theory of human motivation', *International Journal of the Addictions*, 25, 2, 159–177.

Langer, E. (1975) 'The illusion of control', *Journal of Personality and Social Psychology*, 32, 311–328.

REFERENCES

Laplace, P.S. (1830) *The System of the World*, vol. 2, trans. H.H. Harte, Dublin: Longman, Rees, Orme, Brown and Green.

—— (1951) *A Philosophical Essay on Probabilities*, with an introductory note by E.T. Bell, New York: Dover Publications.

Leibniz, G. (1990) 'Discourse on metaphysics', in S.M. Cahn, *Classics of Western Philosophy*, Indianapolis: Hacklett Publishing Company.

Leiseur, H. (1984) *The Chase: Career of the Compulsive Gambler*, Cambridge, MA: Schenkman Books.

Levy-Bruhl, L. (1936) *Primitives and the Supernatural*, trans. L.A. Clare, London: Allen and Unwin.

—— (1966) *Primitive Mentality*, trans. L.A. Clare, Boston, MA: Beacon Press.

Li, W. and Smith, M. (1976) 'The propensity to gamble: some structural determinants', in W. Eadington (ed.) *Gambling and Society*, Springfield, IL: Charles C. Thomas.

Lindner, R. (1974) 'The psychodynamics of gambling', in J. Halliday and P. Fuller (eds) *The Psychology of Gambling*, London: Allen Lane.

Lowry, R. (1989) *The Architecture of Chance*, New York: Oxford University Press.

Luhmann, N. (1993) *Risk: A Sociological Theory*, trans. R. Barnet, Berlin: Walter de Gruyter.

McGuigan, P.P. (1997) 'Stakes are high in battle to bar Internet gambling', *National Law Journal*, 3 November.

McKibbon, N. (1979) 'Working class gambling in Britain 1880–1937', *Past and Present*, 82, 147–178.

McMillen, J. (ed.) (1996) *Gambling Cultures: Studies in History and Interpretation*, London: Routledge.

The Mahabharata (1975) trans. J.A.B. von Buiten, Chicago, IL: University of Chicago Press.

Malinowski, B. (1935) *Coral Gardens and their Magic*, London: Allen and Unwin (2 vols) (1966).

—— (1948) *Magic, Science and Religion and other Essays*, Boston, MA: Beacon Press.

Mann, T. (1962) *The Magic Mountain*, trans. H.T. Lowe-Porter, London: Penguin.

Marenbon, J. (1983) *Early Medieval Philosophy*, London: Routledge and Kegan Paul.

Martinez, T. (1976) 'Compulsive gambling in the conscious mood perspective', in W. Eadington (ed.) *Gambling and Society*, Springfield, IL: Charles C. Thomas.

—— (1983) *The Gambling Scene*, Springfield, IL: Charles C. Thomas.

Mauss, M. (1954) *The Gift: Forms and Functions of Exchange in Archaic Societies*, trans. I. Cunnison, London: Cohen and West.

—— (1972) *A General Theory of Magic*, trans. R. Brain, London: Routledge and Kegan Paul.

May, R., Angel, E. and Ellenberger, H. (eds) (1958) *Existence: A New Dimension in Psychiatry*, Touchstone: Simon and Schuster.

Mellor, D. (1971) *The Matter of Chance*, London: Cambridge University Press.

Merleau-Ponty, M. (1981) *The Phenomenology of Perception*, trans. C. Smith, London: Routledge and Kegan Paul.

Minkowski, E. (1970) *Lived Time: Phenomenological and Psychopathological Studies*, Evanston: Northwestern University Press.

Mintel (1995) *Mintel International Report*, London: The Mintel Group.

Mitchell, R.J. and Leys, H.D.R. (1950) *A History of the English People*, London: Longmans Green.

Monod, J. (1971) *Chance and Necessity: An Essay on the Natural Philosophy of Modern Biology*, trans. A. Wainhouse, London: Fontana Books.

Montesquieu, C. (1977) *Persian Letters*, trans. C.J. Betts, Harmondsworth: Penguin.

Munting, R. (1996) *An Economic and Social History of Gambling in Britain and the USA*, Manchester and New York: Manchester University Press.

Neal, M. (1998) '"You lucky punters!" a study of gambling in betting shops', *Sociology*, 32, 3, 581–600.

Neville, M. (1909) *Light Come, Light Go*, London: Macmillan.

Newman, O. (1972) *Gambling: Hazard and Reward*, London: Athlone Press.

Nietzsche, F. (1968) 'Notes', in V. Kaufman (ed.) *The Portable Nietzsche*, New York: Viking Press.

—— (1969) *Thus Spoke Zarathustra*, trans. R.J. Hollingdale, Harmondsworth: Penguin.

—— (1982) *Daybreak*, trans. R.J. Hollingdale, Cambridge: Cambridge University Press.

Norris, F. (1985) *McTeague*, Harmondsworth: Penguin.

Northbrooke, J. (1843) *A Treatise Against Dicing, Dancing, Playes and Interludes*, London: The Shakespeare Society.

Nussbaum, M. (1986) *The Fragility of Goodness: Luck and Ethics in Greek Tragedy and Philosophy*, Cambridge: Cambridge University Press.

OFLOT (1998) *Office of the National Lottery Annual Report 1997–98*, London: The Stationery Office.

Oldman, D. (1974) 'Chance and skill: a study of roulette', *Sociology*, 8, 407–426.

Onians, R.B. (1988) *The Origins of European Thought*, Cambridge: Cambridge University Press.

Ore, O. (1953) *Cardano: The Gambling Scholar*, Princeton, NJ: Princeton University Press.

Orwell, G. (1984) *Nineteen Eighty-Four*, Harmondsworth: Penguin.

Otto, R. (1925) *The Idea of the Holy*, London: Oxford University Press.

Oxford English Dictionary (1989) Second edn, vols 3, 7 and 13. Prepared by J.A. Simpson and E.S.C. Weiner, Oxford: Clarendon Press.

Parlett, D. (1979) *The Penguin Book of Card Games*, Harmondsworth: Penguin.

—— (1991) *A History of Card Games*, Oxford and New York: Oxford University Press.

Pascal, B. (1987) *Pensées*, trans. A.J. Krailsheimer, Harmondsworth: Penguin.

Paston, M. (1991) *The Paston Letters*, ed. N. Davis, Oxford: Oxford University Press.

Pepys, S. (1976) *Diaries*, vol. 9, ed. R.C. Latham and W. Mathews, London: G. Bell and Sons.

Piaget, J. (1977) *The Child's Conception of the World*, trans. J. and A. Tomlinson, London: Paladin.

Plato (1934) *Laws*, trans. A.E. Taylor, London: J.M. Dent and Sons.

—— (1969) *Laws*, trans. A.E. Taylor, ed. E. Hamilton and M. Cairns, Bollingen Series, Princeton, NJ: Princeton University Press.

—— (1987a) 'Statesman', in *The Dialogues of Plato*, trans. B. Jowett, Oxford: Oxford University Press.

—— (1987b) 'Phaedrus', in *The Dialogues of Plato*, trans. B. Jowett, Oxford: Oxford University Press.

—— (1987c) 'Ion', in *The Dialogues of Plato*, trans. B. Jowett, Oxford: Oxford University Press.

Polo, M. (1958) *The Travels*, trans. R. Latham, Harmondsworth: Penguin.

Pope, A. (1963) 'An essay on Man', in J. Butt (ed.) *The Poems of Alexander Pope*, London: Methuen.

Pratt, M., Malzman, I., Hauprich, W. and Ziskind, E. (1982) 'Electrodermal activity of sociopaths and controls in the pressor test', *Psychophysiology*, 19, 342.

Proust, M. (1983) *Remembrance of Things Past*, vol. 3, trans. C.K. Scott-Moncrieff, T. Kilmartin and A. Mayor, Harmondsworth: Penguin.

Pushkin, A. (1962) *The Queen of Spades and Other Stories*, trans. R. Edmonds, Harmondsworth: Penguin.

—— (1983) *Eugene Onegin*, trans. C. Johnston, Harmondsworth: Penguin.

Puzo, M. (1977) *Inside Las Vegas*, Charter: New York.

Reeve, S. (1998) 'www. casino', *The European*, 14–20 September, 26–27.

Reik, T. (1951) *Dogma and Compulsion: Psychoanalytic Studies of Religion and Myths*, trans. B. Miall, New York: International Universities Press.

Reith, G. (1999) 'In search of lost time: recall, projection and the phenomenology of addiction', *Time and Society*, 8, 1, 101–118.

Report of the Gaming Board for Great Britain (1994–1995) House of Commons 11 July 1996, London: HMSO.

Rhinehart, L. (1972) *The Dice Man*, London: Collins, Grafton Press.

Richardson, J. (1980) *Memoir of a Gambler*, London: Jonathan Cape.

Roberts, S.J., Arth, M.J. and Bush, R.R. (1959) 'Games in culture', *American Anthropologist*, 61, 4, 597–605.

Rosecrance, J. (1985) *The Degenerates of Lake Tahoe: A Study in Persistence in the Social World of Horse Race Gambling*, New York: Peter Lang.

—— (1986) 'Why regular gamblers don't quit: a sociological perspective', *Sociological Perspectives*, 29, 3, 357–379.

—— (1988) 'Professional horse race gambling: working without a safety net', *Work and Occupations*, 15, 220–236.

Rosenthal, R. (1986) 'The pathological gambler's system for self-deception', *Journal of Gambling Behaviour*, 2, 2, 108–120.

—— (1997) '"The Gambler" as case history and literary twin: Dostoevsky's false beauty and the poetics of perversity', *Psychoanalytic Review*, 84, 4, 593–616.

Rousseau, J.J. (1967) *The Confessions*, trans. J.H. Cohen, Harmondsworth: Penguin.

Sartre, J.P. (1957) *Existentialism and Human Emotions*, trans. H.E. Barnes, New York: The Wisdom Library.

Saunders, D.M. and Turner, D.E. (1987) 'Gambling and leisure: the case of racing', *Journal of Leisure Studies*, 6, 281–299.

Scarne, J. (1974) *Scarne on Dice*, Harrisburg, PA: Stackpole Books.

Schiller, F. (1845) *Philosophical and Aesthetic Letters and Essays*, trans. J. Weiss, London: Chapman.

Schimmel, A. (1993) *The Mystery of Numbers*, New York and Oxford: Oxford University Press.

Schopenhauer, A. (1970) *Essays and Aphorisms*, trans. R.J. Hollingdale, Harmondsworth: Penguin.

Scolarios, D. and Brown, R.I.F. (1988) 'A classification of gambling superstitions', unpublished manuscript, University of Glasgow.

Scott, D. and Venturi, R. (1972) *Learning from Las Vegas*, Cambridge, MA: MIT Press.

Scott, M. (1968) *The Racing Game*, Chicago, IL: Aldine.

Seneca (1986) *The Apocolocyntosis of the Divine Claudius*, trans. J.P. Sullivan, Harmondsworth: Penguin.

Sharples, R.W. (1983) *Alexander of Aphrodisias on Fate*, London: Duckworth.

Sifakis, C. (1990) *The Encyclopedia of Gambling*, New York: Facts on File.

Simmel, G. (1971a) 'The miser and the spendthrift', in D.N. Levine (ed.) *On Individuality and Social Forms*, Chicago, IL: University of Chicago Press.

—— (1971b) 'The adventurer', in D.N. Levine (ed.) *On Individuality and Social Forms*, Chicago, IL: University of Chicago Press.

—— (1971c) 'The metropolis and mental life', in D.N. Levine (ed.) *On Individuality and Social Forms*, Chicago, IL: University of Chicago Press.

Smith, M. (1993) 'Changing sociological perspectives on chance', *Sociology*, 27, 3, 513–531.

Spanier, D. (1992) *All Right, O.K., You Win: Inside Las Vegas*, London: Mandarin.

Spencer, L. (1985) 'Allegory in the world in the commodity', *The New German Critique*, 34, winter, 59–77.

Spinoza, B. (1990) 'Ethics', in S.M. Cahn (ed.) *Classics of Western Philosophy*, Indianapolis: Hacklett Publishing.

Steinmetz, A. (1870) *The Gaming Table*, vol. 2, London: Tinsley Brothers.

Stone, L. (1967) *The Crisis of the Aristocracy 1558–1641*, London: Oxford University Press.

Strange, S. (1986) *Casino Capitalism*, Oxford: Blackwell.

Straus, E. (1966) *Phenomenological Psychology*, trans. E. Eng, London: Tavistock.

Strauss, A. (1968) *Time for Dying*, Chicago, IL: Aldine Press.

Strayer, J.R. (1982) *A Dictionary of the Middle Ages*, New York: Scribner.

Strickland, L., Lewicki, R.J. and Katz, A. (1966) 'Temporal orientations and perceived control as determinants of risk-taking', *Journal of Experimental and Social Psychology*, 2, 143–151.

Suetonius (1958) *The Twelve Caesars*, trans. R. Graves, Harmondsworth: Penguin.

Sullivan, G. (1972) *By Chance a Winner*, New York: Dodd, Mead.

Tacitus, C. (1982) 'The Germania', in M. Mattingly (trans. and ed.) *The Agricola and The Germania*, Harmondsworth: Penguin.

Taylor, E.S. (1865) *The History of Playing Cards, with Anecdotes of their use in Ancient and Modern Games, Conjuring, Fortune-Telling and Card Sharping*, London: John Camden Hotten, Piccadilly.

Tec, N. (1967) *Gambling in Sweden*, New Jersey: The Bedminster Press.

Traill, H.D. (ed.) (1893) *Social England: A Record of the Progress of the People from Earliest Times to the Present Day*, London: 1893–1897.

Tsukahara, T. and Brumm, H. (1976) 'Economic rationality, psychology and decision making under uncertainty', in W.R. Eadington (ed.) *Gambling and Society*, Springfield, IL: Charles C. Thomas.

Turner, L. and Ash, J. (1975) *The Golden Hordes: International Tourism and the Pleasure Periphery*, London: Constable.

Tylor, E.B. (1871) *Primitive Culture: Researches into the Development of Mythology, Philosophy, Religion, Language, Art and Custom*, London: John Murray (2 vols).

REFERENCES

—— (1913) *Primitive Culture*, vol. 1, London: J. Murray.

University of Salford (1996) *The UK Gambling Industry*, Centre for the Study of Gambling and Commercial Gaming, The University of Salford.

van der Leeuw, G. (1967) *Religion in Essence and Manifestation*, trans. J.R Turner, Gloucester: P. Smith.

van Rensselaer, J.K. (1893) *The Devil's Picture Books: A History of Playing Cards*, New York: Dodd, Mead and Co.

Veblen, T. (1925) *The Theory of the Leisure Class: An Economic Study of Institutions*, London: Allen and Unwin.

Vinson, B. (1988) *Las Vegas Behind the Tables*, Michigan, OH: Gollehon.

Volberg, R. and Steadman, H. (1988) 'Refining prevalence estimates of pathological gambling', *American Journal of Psychiatry*, 145, 502–505.

Voltaire (1990) 'Zadig', in R. Pearson (trans.) *Candide and other Stories*, Oxford and New York: Oxford University Press.

von Hagen, V. (1962) *The Ancient Sun Kingdoms of the Americas*, London: Thames and Hudson.

von Mises, L. (1949) *Human Action*, New Haven, CT: Yale University Press.

von Neumann, J. and Morgenstern, O. (1953) *Theory of Games and Economic Behaviour*, London: Hurst and Blackett.

Wagenaar, W. (1988) *Paradoxes of Gambling Behaviour*, London: Erlbaum.

Waldrop, M. (1992) *Complexity*, London: Viking Penguin.

Walker, M.B. (1992) *The Psychology of Gambling*, Oxford: Pergamon Press.

Wasiolek, E. (1972) 'Introduction' to F. Dostoevsky, *The Gambler*, Chicago and London: University of Chicago Press.

Weber, M. (1990) *The Protestant Ethic and the Spirit of Capitalism*, trans. T. Parsons, London: Unwin Hyman.

Wolfe, T. (1981) *The Kandy-Kolored Tangerine Flake Streamline Baby*, London: Picador.

Zohar, D. and Marshall, I. (1993) *The Quantum Society*, London: Bloomsbury.

Zola, I. (1967) 'Observations on gambling in a lower class setting', in R. Herman (ed.) *Gambling*, London: Harper and Row.

Zurcher, L.A. (1970) 'The friendly poker player: a study of an ephemeral role', *Social Forces*, 49, 173–185.

Websites

http://www.casinoland.com/
http://www.ccasino.com/
http://www.internet-magazine.com.news.oct.02a.htm
http://www.virtualvegas.com

NAME INDEX

SUBJECT INDEX